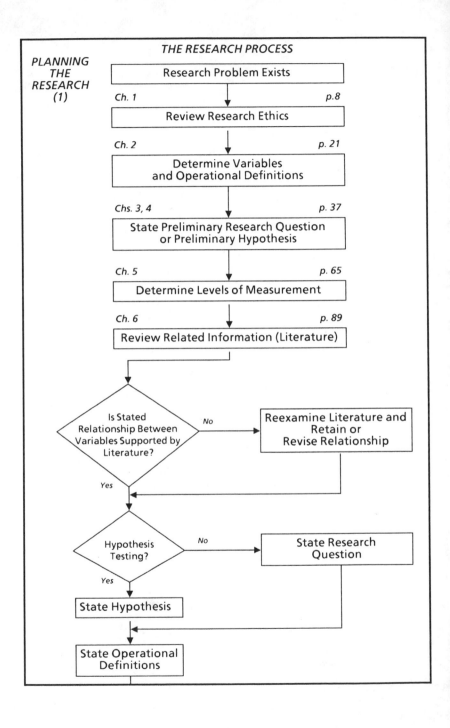

THE RESEARCH PROCESS

PLANNING
THE
RESEARCH
(1)

Research Problem Exists

Ch. 1   *p.8*

Review Research Ethics

Ch. 2   *p. 21*

Determine Variables
and Operational Definitions

Chs. 3, 4   *p. 37*

State Preliminary Research Question
or Preliminary Hypothesis

Ch. 5   *p. 65*

Determine Levels of Measurement

Ch. 6   *p. 89*

Review Related Information (Literature)

Is Stated
Relationship Between
Variables Supported by
Literature?   *No* →   Reexamine Literature and
Retain or
Revise Relationship

Yes

Hypothesis
Testing?   *No* →   State Research
Question

Yes

State Hypothesis

State Operational
Definitions

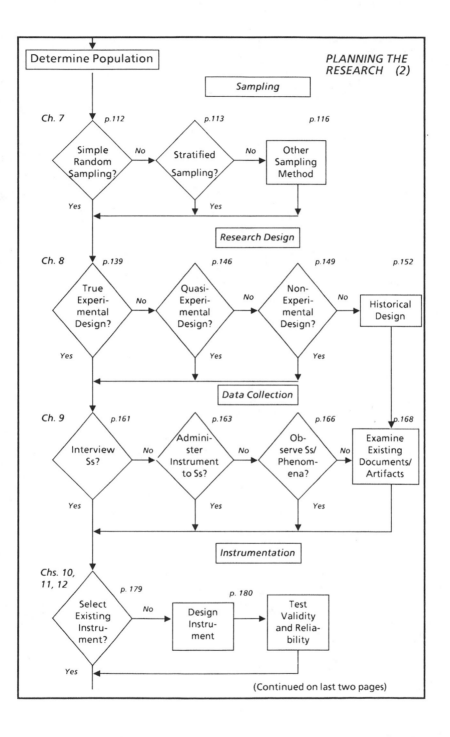

Determine Population

PLANNING THE
RESEARCH   (2)

Sampling

Ch. 7   p.112

Simple Random Sampling?   — No → p.113 Stratified Sampling?   — No → p.116 Other Sampling Method

Yes

Yes

Research Design

Ch. 8   p.139

True Experimental Design?   — No → p.146 Quasi-Experimental Design?   — No → p.149 Non-Experimental Design?   — No → p.152 Historical Design

Yes

Yes

Yes

Data Collection

Ch. 9   p.161

Interview Ss?   — No → p.163 Administer Instrument to Ss?   — No → p.166 Observe Ss/Phenomena?   — No → p.168 Examine Existing Documents/Artifacts

Yes

Yes

Yes

Instrumentation

Chs. 10, 11, 12

Select Existing Instrument?   — No → p.179 Design Instrument → p.180 Test Validity and Reliability

Yes

(Continued on last two pages)

HANDBOOK OF RESEARCH METHODS:

a guide for practitioners and students in the social sciences

NATALIE L. SPROULL

The Scarecrow Press, Inc.
Metuchen, N.J., & London
1988

Library of Congress Cataloging-in-Publication Data

Sproull, Natalie L., 1928-
    Handbook of research methods : a guide for practitioners and
students in the social sciences / by Natalie L. Sproull.
        p.   cm.
    Bibliography: p.
    Includes index.
    ISBN 0-8108-2116-8
    1. Research--Methodology--Handbooks, manuals, etc. I. Title.
Q180.55.M4S67 1988
001.4'2--dc19   88-3036

To my mother, Thelma:

An exemplary model

of lifelong learning.

CONTENTS

TO THE READER

This book was designed for three groups of people; practitioners of research, managers and administrators who must make research-based decisions and students of research. For managers and research practitioners, the book can be used as a reference handbook as it provides easily accessible basic information presented in a concise format which includes reminders and checklists of frequently forgotten material. Students are provided with aids for helping them understand not only the what-to-do and how-to-do-it of research but also to answer the often neglected question of WHY it is done.

Research can be a fascinating occupation. It incorporates many elements of a mystery novel; the heroes and heroines (researchers), the crimes (societal or theoretical problems), villains (unexpected crises, frustrating computer software and occasionally even recalcitrant subjects), deductions and inductions (hypotheses and theories), the investigation (systematic and objective examination and analysis of data) and of course, suspense (waiting for the resolution). On rare occasions there might even be a surprise ending when, in addition to answering the major question or hypothesis, some unanticipated finding occurs.

Unfortunately, many research consumers and students do not view the research process as fascinating because they perceive research as an esoteric and arduous field with inexplicable procedures and unfathomable references. One of the goals of this book was to overcome these perceptions by presenting basic information about the research process, in relatively simple words, to answer the who, what, where, when, why and how questions.

Thus, every major concept is accompanied by its definition and purpose, the advantages and disadvantages of its use, the process involved and an example. The many exhibits condense much information so that related information can appear in one place in a concise form.

Flow charts are used to help your decision making during the research process by presenting alternatives from which you select the appropriate choice for your project. A glossary of definitions is provided so you can easily find meanings of the various concepts. The steps to take at each phase of the research process are given at the beginning of each chapter. All of these features are easily accessible aids for understanding the research process and conducting research.

I would like to acknowledge the many people who influenced the content of this book. My first debt is to the authors whose writings have become classics in research methodology. Of particular importance to me were the works of D.T. Campbell and J.C. Stanley, Sidney Siegel, F. N. Kerlinger and Sir Ronald Fisher, all of whom made major contributions to the field.

Several colleagues and friends helped with different aspects of the book. I especially want to express my appreciation to the following people.

Dr. Lawrence Aleamoni, Director of Instructional Research and Development at the University of Arizona and nationally recognized expert in research methodology, critiqued the entire first draft and suggested several modifications which greatly improved the methodology sections.

R. I. Wilson, Las Vegas author, business consultant, and expert in managing a variety of businesses, critiqued the first draft from a manager's viewpoint and made several important suggestions which improved the clarity and usefulness of the material for managers who must make research-based decisions.

Dr. Michael Pledge, Professor of Economics at Western Illinois University and recipient of many awards for excellence in teaching, critiqued the entire second draft and contributed many very helpful suggestions which improved the presentation for students.

From Western Illinois University, **Drs. Ed Knod** and **Steve Axley**, Professors of Management, critiqued portions of the manuscript and contributed helpful and humorous comments. **Dr. Hugh Shane**, Chairman, **Carmen Baker** and **Sharon Shepard**, all of the Management Department helped greatly with their support in various aspects of the process. **Dr. Richard Hattwick**, Director of the Center for Business and Economic Research, very kindly provided copies of the manuscript for students' reactions. **Dr. Eric Ward**, Professor of Psychology, graciously critiqued the measurement, statistics, and research design sections of the final draft.

Finally, I would like to thank **Barbara Ritchey,** who steadfastly continued through the typing of a manuscript full of flow charts, diagrams and statistical symbols and still maintained her sense of humor throughout the entire process.

Natalie L. Sproull
September, 1987

1

PRELIMINARIES

TERMS DEFINED IN CHAPTER ONE

CHAPTER ONE

PRELIMINARIES

STEPS TO TAKE AFTER READING THIS CHAPTER

1. Review how to use this book for use throughout your project.

2. Review planning and control for use throughout your project.

3. Review the steps in the research process.

4. Review ethical practices for later use.

5. Review writing the proposal for use throughout your project.

HOW TO USE THIS BOOK

Planning, decision making and control of the research process are emphasized throughout this book. The major focus is that research is a process which requires decision making and control factors during the extensive planning stage and "how to do it" information and control during the actual conduct of the research.

The purpose of the book is to guide the researcher by pointing out: (1) the decision points by the use of flow charts, (2) the possible alternatives available at the decision points, (3) the advantages and disadvantages which help in choosing these alternatives, (4) factors which help in the control process and (5) step-by-step procedures to complete the various processes.

This book is designed for easy and quick access to information so that you do not have to read through irrelevant material to find what you want.

To access information use any of the following features.

1. FLOW CHARTS. A flow chart of the entire research process appears on the front and back covers for instant access. Flow charts for specific procedures appear at the beginning of some chapters. In the flow charts the diamond shapes indicate points at which a decision must be made and rectangular shapes indicate instructions.

2. TOPICS appear at the top of the page.

3

3. DEFINITIONS appear with the discussion of each major concept and in the glossary and are listed in front of each chapter.

4. RELATED DEFINITIONS occasionally appear to help understand the major concepts.

5. SYNONYMS are given to alert the reader to different terms.

6. PURPOSE tells you why the concepts are used.

7. ADVANTAGES AND DISADVANTAGES are presented to help in your decision making.

8. CAUTIONS warn the reader of possible problems.

9. RECOMMENDATIONS are based on accepted research practice.

10. RATINGS are based on a consensus of experts' opinions.

11. PROCESSES OR STEPS are step-by-step action guides which can also be used as CHECKLISTS.

12. EXAMPLES illustrate concepts and processes.

13. RECOMMENDED REFERENCES are suggested for further information.

14. COMMENTS provide additional information about the concepts.

15. STEPS TO TAKE AFTER READING EACH CHAPTER are given at the beginning of each chapter.

16. WHERE YOU ARE NOW appears at the end of each chapter.

17. APPENDICES provide much related information for reference.

Please note the use of "Ss" throughout the book to indicate subjects, often people, studied in the research. Subjects (Ss) might be chief executive officers, bank customers, legal clients, robots or even animals or microbes. A list of other commonly used symbols and abbreviations appears in the appendices.

The chapters coincide, for the most part, with the steps in the flow chart depicting the research process. The order of these steps was carefully considered. However, research is really not a straight line process as the flow chart might indicate. Many steps can be done simultaneously and for some projects it may be better to change the order of the steps.

THE IMPACT OF RESEARCH

Research has had a direct effect on the clothes you are wearing, the food you ate today and the automobile, bus, train or airplane in which you traveled. Computer microchips, robots, "test tube" babies, lunar modules, satellites and video recorders all came about from decisions based on research results. There are few areas in modern life which have not been touched by research.

Major decisions which affect our lives are based on research results from research projects conducted in both the private and public sectors. These decisions range from the type of education our children receive to the type of weaponry available to protect nations.

Most products and processes used in retail and wholesale stores, banking institutions, steel, chemical, genetics, transportation, health and telecommunication industries, government facilities and educational institutions are research based.

Billions of dollars are spent on research not only in the United States but in other countries. Large firms have their own Research & Development departments and governments rely heavily on their own and sponsored research to answer questions ranging from the efficiency of nuclear weapons to the effects of food stamps.

Smaller organizations also conduct research which can have major impacts on them. For example, a bank in the Midwest with total deposits between 50 and 100 million dollars recently conducted a survey of customers to assess their preferences for bank services. The results of the survey indicated that customers desired some new services which the bank subsequently initiated. A few months after initiating the new services the bank had increased its deposits by 11 million dollars; a substantial increase for a bank that size. The board of directors attributed the increase directly to the results and recommendations of the research study. They also considered their investment in the project, a few thousand dollars, well worth the return they received.

CAUTION: Despite the products surrounding us and the billions spent on research, a mystique has grown up about research. Many people view it with loathing, fear, distaste or even contempt, or consider it difficult, too theoretical or too action oriented, time-consuming and costly. This often makes the researcher's job more difficult and the researcher should be aware of such attitudes and be prepared to deal with them.

PLANNING AND CONTROL

More businesses than ever before in history are conducting research, either in-house or by hiring consultants. Since research costs money and is time consuming, these organizations expect to get a return on their investment. The better the planning and control of the research process, the more likely it is that the research results will be valuable for decision making.

The basics of "good" research, like those of "good" management, are planning and control. However, in research, control has an important meaning in addition to that of monitoring; control means using a variety of procedures to try and rule out various factors which might affect the research process and consequently the research results.

The amount of control is decided during the planning process and is carried out through techniques such as random selection or assignment, selecting the appropriate research design, ruling out various factors by statistical techniques and hypothesis testing.

Definition: *Research Controls*: Procedures which rule out potential extraneous causes of research results by defining and restricting the research conditions.

Purpose: To maximize the confidence in the results of the study and to minimize the possibility of alternative explanations.

EXHIBIT 1.1   EXAMPLES OF CONTROL TECHNIQUES

1. Random selection of subjects.

2. Random selection of documents/events/time periods where appropriate.

3. Random assignment of subjects to experimental/control groups where appropriate.

4. Hypothesis testing.

5. Giving all subjects the same questionnaire items.

6. Statistical methods which eliminate or isolate the effects of factors extraneous to the research.

Comment: Don't worry if you do not understand at this point how these control techniques work. Explanations appear later.

Recommended Reference: Kerlinger [37, pp. 110-116].

Planning consumes a large share of the time allotted to research. Note that over 70% of the steps in the research process involve planning. Planning should be done so thoroughly that the actual conduct of the research takes comparatively little time as the researcher follows the prespecified steps.

Planning is necessary to ensure that the research design and methodology will result in the appropriate information to answer your research problem adequately, to minimize unanticipated events occurring which might affect the research results and to keep the research project within the budget and time constraints allotted. Control is necessary for each of the above plus to increase the degree of confidence you have in the research results.

Both planning and control cost money and time. You cannot do without the planning but you can cut down on the amount of control. However, THE LOWER THE AMOUNT OF CONTROL, THE LESS CONFIDENCE YOU WILL HAVE IN THE RESULTS. With insufficient control you will always sacrifice confidence. How do you decide how many control techniques to use? The degree of control is a function of the criticality of the decisions to be made based on research results and the feasibility (resources, availability of subjects, etc.) of using the controls.

CRITICALITY OF DECISIONS

If the decisions to be made after the research results are obtained are critical for survival, the research sponsor should insist that the researcher use the maximum amount of control appropriate to the specific research. Less critical decisions might be based on fewer control techniques, always remembering that the more controls you have the more confidence you can have in the results but also that more resources are usually required.

BUDGET AND TIME CONSTRAINTS

Using control techniques usually -- but not always -- costs more. For example, random sampling not only requires a pool of subjects but also requires more time to select them than selecting a convenient sample. The researcher and sponsor together must decide if those controls which enhance the confidence in the results are worth the additional cost and time.

Recommendation: Use the maximum number of control techniques feasible for any type of research project. For example, if using a survey, determine if it is feasible to do random sampling; if conducting historical research, determine if it is feasible to randomly sample from the known existing data.

The major aim is to have the research results be as valuable as possible for the intended purpose of aiding in decision making. The more appropriate the various aspects of the research process are, the higher the probability is that the research results will be considered valid and the more likely it is that productive actions will follow from the research. Research processes which are inadequately conceived and structured are costly and will be of little value to anyone.

THE RESEARCH PROCESS

Definition: *Applied Research*: Research conducted for the purpose of practical application, usually in response to a specific problem and the need for decision making.

Definition: *Basic Research*: Research conducted for the purpose of adding to general knowledge, usually not prompted by a specific problem.

The research PROCESS is the same whether the results are used for immediate, practical application (applied research) or for the purpose of adding to general knowledge (basic research). However, the methods within the process, such as the research design, the sampling or the data collection methods, change; usually according to how much control is feasible for a specific project.

The literature is replete with discussions about the similarities and differences between applied and basic research [31, 44, 55]. For example, Tull & Hawkins [68] see major differences between the hypothesis testing mode of basic research and the steps of decisional research, while Emory [27] recommends that business research use the scientific method for applied research.

Much research is practice and action oriented [5, 61], with the results usually used to aid decision making. However, as the amount of research increases there appears to be a concommitant increase in the use of more sophisticated and scientific methodology and techniques. Among these is the use of hypothesis testing.

The outcome of hypothesis testing is a determination of the probability that something will or will not occur or that a relationship will or will not exist between variables. One of the major strengths of hypothesis testing is that the researcher or client, or both together, decide before the research is conducted what that probability should be. By doing this, the researchers are also specifying the amount of risk they wish to take that their conclusions might be wrong. This a priori researcher-selected decision rule is made during the planning stage so that the excitement and results of the data collection and analysis do not affect that decision.

Thus, hypothesis testing is another control process. This does not mean that all research should include hypothesis testing, as you will see later. It does mean that hypothesis testing should be used more frequently than is currently done.

Definition: *Research Process*: Specific planned and controlled steps for empirically investigating a problem.

Purpose: To provide findings, conclusions or products in which a high degree of confidence can be placed which in turn improves the productivity and effectiveness of the decision making which follows the research.

The flow chart on the front and back covers of this book gives the various steps of the research process and notes at what points the researcher will have to make major decisions. These steps are repeated in Exhibit 1.2. MOST OF THE STEPS OF THE RESEARCH PROCESS ARE THE SAME FOR ANY RESEARCH PROJECT. THE METHODS WITHIN THE PROCESS CHANGE.

RESEARCH ETHICS

Before starting any research project the researcher should become familiar with or review the factors and practices involved with research ethics.

Definition: *Ethical Research Practices*: Those practices and procedures which lead to: (1) protection of human and non-human subjects, (2) appropriate methodology, (3) inferences, conclusions and

---

EXHIBIT 1.2   STEPS IN THE RESEARCH PROCESS

PLAN AND PREPARE
1. Review research ethics.
2. Determine variables.
3. State preliminary research question/hypothesis.
4. Review related information/literature.
5. State final research question/hypothesis.
6. State operational definitions.
7. Determine levels of measurement.
8. Define the population.
9. Select the sampling method.
10. Select the design.
11. Select the data collection method.
12. Select or design the instruments.
13. Determine validity & reliability of instrument.
14. Determine statistical purpose.
15. Select the statistical tests.
16. Design and conduct a pilot study, if needed.
17. Write proposal; submit to sponsor, if needed.

CONDUCT
18. Select sample.
19. Conduct experiment, if needed.
20. Collect data.
21. Analyze data.
22. Test hypothesis or answer research question.

REPORT
23. Write research report.
24. Submit report to sponsor.

---

recommendations based on the actual findings and (4) complete and accurate research reports.

Purpose: To protect Ss from physical and psychological harm and to see that their rights are not violated. To assure that the research results are based on sufficiently adequate and appropriate methodology to warrant the findings, conclusions and recommendations presented.

CAUTION: Grants funded by federal and state governments and some private organizations usually require clearance on ethical considerations before the research is conducted. Universities have "Protection of Human Subjects" committees which review all proposals dealing with human Ss to ensure that human rights are not violated. There are also guidelines on animal research.

Advantages:

1. The research sponsor is not misled.

2. Private or public money for needed research is more easily obtained if ethical research procedures are used.

3. The research will meet organizational guidelines for ethical practices.

4. The researcher's reputation will be enhanced.

Disadvantages:

1. It takes time to obtain Ss consent and to complete the appropriate forms.

2. Occasionally Ss object to signing consent forms and refuse to participate in the project.

ETHICAL PRACTICES

Seven of the most violated ethical practices are: (1) obtaining free consent and (2) informed consent; (3) assuring and maintaining confidentiality, (4) privacy and (5) anonymity; (6) using appropriate methodology and (7) reporting the research appropriately and completely.

Recommended References: U.S. Department of Health and Human Services [69]. American Psychological Association [2].

THE RIGHT TO FREE CONSENT

Definition: *The Right to Free Consent*: The potential research participant has the right not to be pressured in any way to participate in the research project.

Comment: As with any ethical consideration it is sometimes difficult to determine what is or is not pressure. For example, often pens, pencils and sometimes coins are enclosed with questionnaires to enhance the probability of the recipient responding. Is that pressure? Most people would say not, but these practices could be interpreted as pressure tactics. What about giving prisoners, service personnel, employees or students time off for participating in research projects? Many people would consider time off a pressure tactic. If you have questions in this area, refer to published guidelines available from such agencies as the U.S. Department of Health and Human Services [69] and the American Psychological Association [2].

THE RIGHT TO INFORMED CONSENT

Definition: *The Right to Informed Consent*: The potential research participants must be given sufficient information to make knowledgeable decisions about participation or nonparticipation.

Comment: While informed consent is obligatory it is difficult for the potential participant to consent knowledgeably because few people have sufficient knowledge of the research process to make an "informed" decision whether participation will be psychologically harmful. Very few researchers would conduct research which might be physically harmful without giving maximum amounts of information about potential consequences of the research, going through some sort of ethical checks by professionals and ensuring there were sufficient safeguards.

For certain research projects, informing the potential participants of the nature of the research would compromise the results. In such cases, the researcher is obligated to tell the person as much as possible without compromising the data and to offer the potential participants a report of the research upon completion of the project.

CAUTION: Consent is usually obtained directly from the persons who will participate in the research. Use written consent forms signed by parents or guardians for ALL research involving children or incapacitated adults. It is wise to obtain signed consent forms for any project in which the Ss will be physically or psychologically manipulated.

THE RIGHT TO CONFIDENTIALITY

Definition: *The Right to Confidentiality*: The research participant has the right to expect the researcher to limit access to and maintain the security of information obtained from or about the participant.

Comment: Research participants, particularly members of business firms, are usually concerned -- as they should be -- with confidentiality of data. Who will be handling and reading the information? Will tight security measures be maintained for identifiable information until it can be discarded, returned or shredded? Will copies be made?

Recommendation: Keep to a minimum the number of people who have access to identifiable information. Maintain security on information and return or discard it safely when it is no longer necessary.

THE RIGHT TO PRIVACY

Definition: *The Right to Privacy*: Research participants have the right to withhold information about which they feel uncomfortable.

Comment: Examples of information which is often considered private to some people include income, sexual activities or preferences and religious beliefs.

Recommendation: Inform the potential participant of the type of information requested. Do not use sensitive items unless it is absolutely necessary and pertinent to the specific research project. These two steps will help in avoiding invasion of privacy and possible loss of participants.

THE RIGHT TO ANONYMITY

Definition: *The Right to Anonymity*: The research participant has the right to expect the researcher not to identify specific data with a specific individual.

EXHIBIT 1.3   CHECKLIST TO AVOID UNETHICAL PRACTICES

TO AVOID VIOLATION OF FREE AND INFORMED CONSENT

1. Obtain free and informed consent. Have consent forms signed by participants or parents/guardians of children.

TO AVOID VIOLATION OF CONFIDENTIALITY, PRIVACY AND ANONYMITY

2. Assure potential research participants of confidentiality, privacy and anonymity in writing.

3. Maintain security on identifiable information with locked files or other arrangements.

4. Return information to the participant or discard it safely when it is no longer necessary.

5. Limit the number of people who have access to information on a "need to know" basis.

TO AVOID THE MISUSE OF STATISTICS

6. Determine the appropriate level of measurement for each variable and use corresponding statistical techniques.

7. Check the assumptions and requirements of statistical tests and have a knowledgeable person examine the analysis.

8. Don't use complex, sophisticated analyses if simple ones will do.

9. Don't be overprecise on imprecise data.

TO AVOID OMISSION OF METHODOLOGY AND NEGATIVE FINDINGS

10. Report thoroughly every aspect of the research including sampling and data collection methods and instrumentation.

11. Report all findings, even those which might be considered negative.

TO AVOID MISLEADING FINDINGS AND CONCLUSIONS

12. Never twist findings or conclusions to make them appear more positive or negative, larger or smaller, than warranted by the data.

Comment: Anonymity is relatively easy to ensure because most research projects report information about groups rather than on an individual basis.

Recommendation: Identify Ss by numbers rather than names to further ensure anonymity.

APPROPRIATE METHODOLOGY

All researchers have the obligation to conduct their research systematically and objectively using as many controls as feasible (considering cost versus value) and acceptable research procedures appropriate for the specific project.

Definition: *Systematic Research*: Research which uses specific pre-planned procedures in the research process.

Definition: *Objective Research*: Research in which the procedures and findings are not influenced or changed by the researcher's feelings, values or beliefs after the research has begun.

APPROPRIATE RESEARCH REPORTING

All researchers have the obligation to report their research methodology, findings and conclusions in a complete and unbiased manner. This includes reporting negative findings and any errors in the procedures and a complete description of the research questions or hypotheses, research design, sampling methods, data collection methods, instruments used with their validities and reliabilities, and the statistical methods and probability levels. The report should be complete but as concise as possible. Report only that which is necessary for the research consumer to understand exactly what was done, how it was done and what was found. Sufficient information should be given for any reader to replicate the study.

Recommendation: Report the probability levels, not just if a statistical test was significant or not. The research sponsors can make better decisions if they know there is a 90% chance of X occurring AND that the test was significant at the .10 level.

THE RESEARCH PROPOSAL

A research proposal should be prepared before any research is actually conducted. Often a proposal is REQUIRED prior to funding of the project by management or outside public or private funding agencies. Although some researchers try to avoid this step, the research proposal should be viewed as the plan of action which no good administrator, including research project directors, should omit.

Research proposals are so widely used and are of such importance for planning and funding that you need to begin considering your proposal even if, at this point, you know little about the research process. The

EXHIBIT 1.4   SUGGESTIONS FOR WRITING A RESEARCH PROPOSAL

1. **Title Page:** The first page which includes the title of the project, name of the researcher(s) or organization proposing the research and date of transmittal. The researcher's address, telephone number and title are often included. The title should be brief but descriptive of the proposed project.
2. **Abstract:** A summary of each of the other sections to alert the reader who is too busy to read the whole proposal to the most important information. Sometimes the abstract is placed in a Letter of Transmittal which includes why the research is needed and accompanies the proposal. Since many people will look only at the abstract and the budget (and some will only read the budget) it is usually helpful to point out the value of the research results.
3. **Problem:** A description of what the specific problem was that initiated the research. Perhaps sales have fallen dramatically or the production department wants a new process. Provide sufficient background in language that a stranger to the problem can understand. People who recommend funding, including managers, do not always understand the technicalities. For proposals to be submitted to funding agencies, a review of the literature is usually included in this section.
4. **Purpose:** A specific statement of the purpose of the research in the form of hypotheses, research questions or objectives.
5. **Research Procedures:** Detailed descriptions of the operational definitions, the population, the sampling methods, the research design, data collection methods, instruments and data analyses. Charts and graphs are useful but may be placed in the appendices to keep the proposal brief.
6. **Results of the Pilot Study:** A brief description of the outcomes of the pilot study and changes, if any, as a result of the pilot study.
7. **Expected Product of the Research:** The form in which the outcomes of the research will be presented to the sponsor. Examples include written reports, products and oral reports.
8. **Time Schedule:** A realistic estimate of the time required to complete the project. A PERT chart combined with the Critical Path Method is useful for estimating the time and is illustrated below.
9. **Budget:** A detailed listing of costs of the project. This should include costs for personnel, equipment, supplies and travel, where appropriate. For many projects overhead and/or indirect costs are included. The budget is the fiscal plan of the project and costs should coincide with the selected research procedures. It is helpful to ask the aid of a person experienced with research budgets. The PERT chart is also useful in estimating budgets as each activity and time is listed.
10. **References:** A listing of authors and information about their publications to which you referred in the body of the proposal. Include author's name, the title of the reference and date and place of publication. Page numbers are given in some instances. Examine publications of the sponsor to determine the specific reference style desired.
11. **Appendices:** Charts, graphs and other information which may interfere with the flow of the proposal or lengthen it may be placed in the appendices.
12. **Researcher's Resumé:** A listing of the qualifications of the researcher. This should include any similar projects the researcher has completed and the researcher's unique qualifications for the project. Business and educational backgrounds are usually included.

proposal writing task is easier if you start writing the proposal as soon as you begin planning, adding to it as you complete each of the planning stages.

Definition: *Research Proposal:* A plan stating the problem which prompted the research and the research objectives, procedures and budget proposed to answer the questions or solve the problem.

Purpose: To force the researcher to: (1) carefully delineate the research problem and objectives, (2) select the most appropriate and feasible research procedures, (3) specify costs and (4) follow a specific, carefully considered plan of action.

To provide the research sponsor control by: (1) assurance that the researcher understands the research problem and the outcomes will be in the form desired, (2) evaluation of the research procedures and budget and (3) comparison of proposals from various researchers before awarding a contract. Often the proposal itself serves as the contract.

It can be seen from the various purposes that proposals serve important and beneficial functions. WHETHER YOU RECEIVE FUNDING OR NOT OFTEN DEPENDS ON HOW WELL WRITTEN THE PROPOSAL IS.

RESEARCH PROPOSAL FORMATS

There is a wide variety of research proposal formats because there are differing requirements for proposals from the organizations which request them. Proposals are requested from sources either internal or external to the organization.

External proposals often are a response to a company or government agency sending out a Request for Proposal (RFP). RFP's usually list: (1) the topic of the desired research, (2) the desired output, such as a report and/or product, expected and (3) time deadlines. Expected costs are not usually included since one of the purposes of requesting proposals is to compare cost figures from various researchers or organizations.

Some of the proposals requested from external sources, especially those requested by government agencies, tend to be quite complex and lengthy. Some RFP's request a brief overview of the proposed research prior to submission of a full proposal.

CAUTION: Request for Bid (RFB) and Request for Quote (RFQ) are often used as synonyms for Request for Proposal. However, the terms do not mean the same thing to all organizations.

Internal proposals, those funded by your own organization, also vary considerably in format. Generally the proposals tend to be much shorter and often the budgets are not as comprehensive as for external proposals because of working in-house.

HOW TO WRITE THE PROPOSAL

The proposal should combine that rare form of writing which includes all pertinent information and specificity with brevity and clarity. While research proposals vary widely depending on the source of the funding, the sections usually included are given in Exhibit 1.4.

Recommended Reference: See Krathwohl [42] for additional information on how to write research proposals.

PERT/CPM

Definition: *PERT Chart:* A flow chart which indicates the planned sequencing, scheduling and estimated times of activities of a project or program. PERT is an acronym for Program Evaluation and Review Technique.

EXHIBIT 1.5 HOW TO CONSTRUCT A PERT/CPM CHART

1. Identify and define each activity in the project.

2. List which activities are dependent on the completion of other activities and which are not.

3. Chart the dependent activities in time sequence.

4. Chart the independent activities in appropriate concurrent times as illustrated on the following chart.

5. Connect the activities with lines as illustrated below.

6. Assign time estimates for each activity and place on chart.

   6.1   Most likely time = usual time for the activity.

   6.2   Optimistic time = minimum time.

   6.3   Pessimistic time = maximum time.

   6.4   Combination = weighted average of the 3 estimates.

       The most commonly used weighting [68] is:

       [4 (most likely time) + 1 (optimistic) + 1 (pessimistic)] ÷ 6

7. Sum the time estimates for each path in the network.

8. Select the path with the longest total time as the critical path. If any activity in this path is delayed, the project will be delayed.

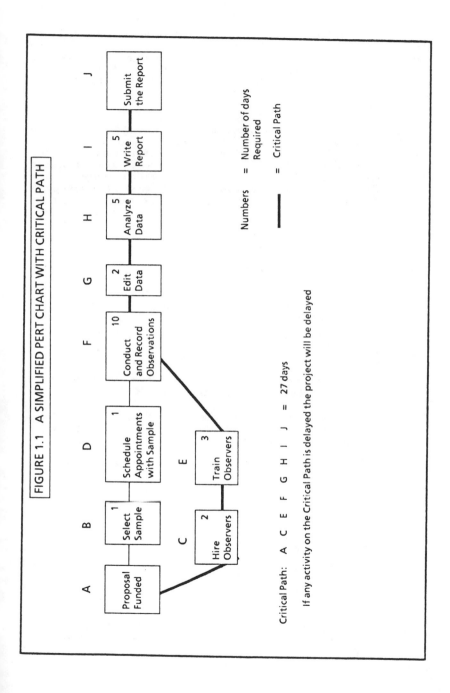

FIGURE 1.1   A SIMPLIFIED PERT CHART WITH CRITICAL PATH

Critical Path: A   C   E   F   G   H   I   J   = 27 days

If any activity on the Critical Path is delayed the project will be delayed

Definition: *Critical Path Method*: A procedure in which the estimated times for activities in a PERT chart are summed for each path in the network. The critical path is the sequence of activities which take the longest total time to complete. A delay in the critical path will create a delay in the project. A delay in the noncritical path is called slack time.

Abbreviation: *CPM*

Both PERT and CPM were developed during the 1950's. Since then common usage has led to their being intertwined and most PERT charts now include the critical path method whether they are called PERT charts or the critical path method. Both were developed to avoid critical delays in defense industries. The assumptions are that project activities are completed either simultaneously or in time sequence and that managers can keep a project on the best time and cost basis if they monitor the critical path.

Slack time for any noncritical path can be computed by subtracting the noncritical path time from the critical path time.

TIME ESTIMATES FOR A PERT CHART

Time estimates are important to both the sponsor and the researcher. The sponsor expects the project to be completed within the time estimates and most researchers try to bring in their projects on time. Thus, many researchers use either the most likely time or combination time estimates. An example of computing a combination time estimate appears in Exhibit 1.6.

EXHIBIT 1.6   EXAMPLE OF COMPUTING TIME ESTIMATES

1. Examine Figure 1.1. The most likely time given for training observers is 3 days. Assume that optimistic time is 2 days and pessimistic time is 10 days.

2. Compute the combination time estimate using the formula in Exhibit 1.5.

   Most likely time = 3 days

   Optimistic time = 2 days

   Pessimistic time = 10 days

   $$\frac{4(3) + 1(2) + 1(10)}{6} = 4 \text{ days}$$

3. Combination time estimate for training observers is 4 days.

CAUTION: Be as realistic as possible about time estimates. You may not receive funding if the estimated time is not agreeable to the sponsor. Yet you must have sufficient time to bring the project in by the deadline. Time estimates are often negotiable between client and researcher. If the client wishes to shorten the time considerably, you may have to also negotiate some modifications of the proposed research.

WHERE YOU ARE NOW

At this point you should recognize:

1. How to use this book,

2. The importance of planning and control in research,

3. The steps in the research process,

4. Ethical practices,

5. How to write the proposal and,

6. How to construct a PERT chart.

2

DETERMINE THE VARIABLES AND OPERATIONAL DEFINITIONS

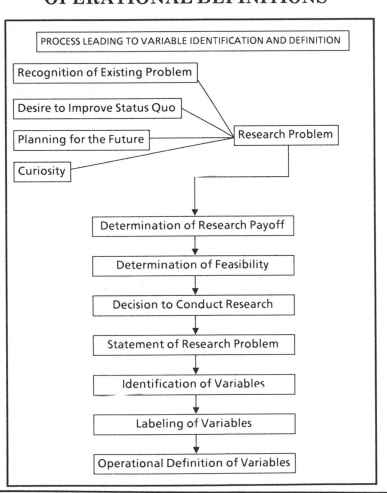

PROCESS LEADING TO VARIABLE IDENTIFICATION AND DEFINITION

Recognition of Existing Problem

Desire to Improve Status Quo

Planning for the Future

Curiosity

Research Problem

Determination of Research Payoff

Determination of Feasibility

Decision to Conduct Research

Statement of Research Problem

Identification of Variables

Labeling of Variables

Operational Definition of Variables

TERMS DEFINED IN CHAPTER TWO

CHAPTER TWO

DETERMINE THE VARIABLES AND OPERATIONAL DEFINITIONS

STEPS TO TAKE AFTER READING THIS CHAPTER

1. Clarify the research problem with sponsor, if needed.

2. Determine the variables to be studied.

3. State the variables specifically.

4. State operational definitions for each variable.

5. Review the types of variables for possible later use.

HOW RESEARCH PROBLEMS ORIGINATE

The decision to conduct research begins with discussion of issues which require more information prior to decision making. Research problems originate from a variety of sources and events. The most common events which prompt research problems occur when people: (1) recognize an existing problem, (2) desire to improve the status quo, (3) plan for the future or (4) are curious about some phenomenon.

RECOGNITION OF EXISTING PROBLEMS

Often a research problem is prompted by recognition of some existing problem for which insufficient information is available. For example, "Why did gross sales decrease 10% last year?", "what are the effects of toxic waste?" or "why is the turnover in the marketing department higher?"

Comment: Recognition of existing problems is probably the most frequent source of research problems. Unfortunately the research often occurs too late. It might have been much wiser to conduct the research before the problem occurred.

DESIRE TO IMPROVE THE STATUS QUO

Research problems can also stem from the desire to improve the status quo. An organization may be without major problems and still conduct research for the purpose of improvement. Such questions as "would a different keyboard configuration on our computer make it faster to use?" or "would the use of fiber optics improve our telecommunication capabilities?" might fall in this category.

Comment: If more research problems were generated from a desire to improve the status quo, there would be fewer research problems generated from recognition of existing problems.

PLANNING FOR THE FUTURE

Some research problems originate from the process of short and long range planning for the future. Most major organizations conduct planning activities. Many of these organizations use a planning technique called environmental scanning.

Definition: *Environmental Scanning:* A process in which specific indicators critical to an organization's survival are recorded and monitored for changes. Indicators from both the internal and external environment are included. For example, an oil company might monitor gross sales (internal) and competitors' actions (external). A clothing manufacturer might monitor cotton prices (external) and their absenteeism rate (internal).

Synonym: *Environmental Monitoring*

Purpose: To have current information and projections for use in planning. To monitor high impact and worst case events in order to prepare alternative contingency plans.

Often information from the environmental scanning process prompts a research problem. This is because the information consists of current, specific data and expert opinion on what will probably happen in the future. Because scanning always includes those indicators critical to organizational survival, the process can serve as an early warning system to indicate the areas in which research is needed.

Comment: There is little doubt that some companies have not conducted adequate environmental scanning. The introduction of the hand held calculator left several companies reeling in dismay as they viewed their inventory of "old fashioned" calculators. In the early 1980's several computer manufacturers declared bankruptcy because they overestimated the personal computer market.

In such cases adequate environmental scanning may have led to research and consequently, different decisions and actions might have occurred.

Environmental scanning often operates in conjunction with Management Information Systems (MIS). Information from the MIS often prompts research problems.

Definition: *Management Information System:* Methods of organizing, classifying and relating information, using computers, to provide managers with appropriate information to aid decision making.

CURIOSITY/DISCOVERY

Some research problems originate from people who become curious about how a certain phenomenon operates or simply have a great desire to discover more than is currently known about a phenomenon. Some major organizations have Research and Development Laboratories or departments where such researchers are permitted considerable freedom to pursue their activities. However, research costs and organizational goals prohibit widespread use of curiosity as a source of research problems.

Comment: Note from the sources of research problems listed that although the word "problem" is used, the decision to conduct research is not always prompted in reaction to current or anticipated problems. That is, the term "research problem" means the question the research is trying to answer.

THE DECISION TO CONDUCT RESEARCH

Although a research problem is brought to the attention of a manager, it does not necessarily follow that research will be conducted on the problem. Many factors weigh in the decision to conduct research. Two of the most important factors are determining the: (1) payoff of the research results and (2) feasibility of conducting the research.

THE PAYOFF OF RESEARCH

As all organizations have budgetary constraints, managers and research sponsors usually must select from a number of research problems those they wish to fund. This decision is often heavily weighted by the expected payoff of the research results, whether the payoff is monetary or in the form of societal benefits.

These decision makers often make a list of the cost/benefit of conducting research on each of the research problems and then make a priority list. While computational techniques, such as a payoff matrix, are sometimes used to assess the value of the research [22] [68], their accuracy depends on someone's ability to estimate such items as the probability of successful research outcomes. In other words, these computational techniques for assessing the cost/benefit of research are highly subjective and the accuracy of the results depends on the expertise of the person doing the estimating.

Recommended References: For computational formulas assessing the value of conducting a specific research project see Tull and Hawkins [68, pp. 71-88] or Davis and Cosenza [22, pp. 51-58].

FEASIBILITY OF CONDUCTING THE RESEARCH

A second area incorporated in the decision to fund or not fund research is the feasibility of conducting the research. Research problems can be impractical for a number of reasons including the availability of: (1) subjects, (2) materials, (3) time and (4) competent researchers.

For example, studying the long term effects of brand advertising might require following up the same group of people over a 5 or 10 year period; a difficult task with the current high mobility rate. Research requiring subjects such as trained experts in specialty fields, for example, international terrorism, may have to be postponed because the experts are scarce or unavailable.

Research requiring scarce materials, such as uranium, may not be feasible. Time is an important factor when determining the feasibility of a research project. Often the appropriate research cannot be carried out in time for decision making deadlines.

Finding competent researchers sometimes affects the feasibility of conducting a research project. For example, finding researchers who are experts in a specialty field and also experts in conducting research is difficult at times. One common way to overcome this problem is to hire a competent researcher and use specialty experts as consultants.

CAUTION: Using specialty experts as consultants works out well only when the researchers and the experts can communicate with each other. If you are in this situation you may need to spend time developing and improving the communication required when these two groups work together.

When the payoff and feasibility of the research are determined, a decision is made to initiate the research or not. If the decision is to conduct research, the research problem is stated.

RESEARCH PROBLEMS

Definition: *Research Problem*: An inquiry which asks to what degree or how two or more phenomena are related, usually stated in question form.

Purpose: To direct the inquiry to the major area of concern.

Comment: Note that a minimum of two variables and a potential relationship are specified. Thus the question "what was the unemployment rate last year?" would be considered an information gathering question not a research problem while the question "what was the unemployment rate last year by geographical area?" would be considered a research problem because it asks the relationship between the variable "unemployment rate" and the variable "geographical area."

EXHIBIT 2.1   EXAMPLES OF RESEARCH PROBLEMS

1. What are the effects on production of offering a "cafeteria" list of benefits?

2. Does forced compliance with safety regulations lower the number of accidents?

3. Will a satellite communication system be as cost-effective as our current system?

4. Does color of computer make a difference in the number sold?

5. Does use of electric shavers vary by social class?

6. Will genetic manipulation produce stronger stalks of corn?

7. How long can people remain in space stations without severe anxiety symptoms?

8. Would market share increase if the product packaging is changed?

9. Will increased lighting in common areas of the apartment complex make the tenants feel more secure?

CAUTION: A major concern is that managers often misstate the research problem and consequently the research results may not be useful. Also, researchers do not always understand the research problem. Thus, it is helpful for the researcher and sponsor to meet and clarify the research problem so that they have a common interpretation. This should be done prior to beginning the research.

IDENTIFY AND LABEL THE VARIABLES

It is important to think in terms of variables as early as possible. The sooner you identify and label those variables you wish to use in the research, the faster the research process will be.

Definition: *Variable:* A factor, phenomenon or characteristic which has more than one value or category, either quantitative or qualitative. (If a characteristic has only one value, it is a constant, not a variable).

Example: Type of compliance with safety regulations is a variable which could have two categories, forced and not forced. Number of accidents is a variable with values ranging from zero to infinity.

IDENTIFYING VARIABLES

Note in Exhibit 2.1 that each of the research problems listed includes the variables to be examined in the research. For example, in research problem #4 the variables are computer color and number of computers sold.

Unfortunately not all research problems are stated so that the researcher can identify the variables so easily. For some problems you may have to work with the sponsor to discover the variables which should be studied to provide useful information.

LABELING VARIABLES

As soon as the variables are identified they should be labeled specifically. For example, in research problem #5 the variables appear as "use of electric shavers" and "social class." What is meant by "use of electric shavers"? Does that mean frequency of use or if a person has ever used an electric shaver?

Examine research problem #9. Does "increased lighting" mean an increase in the brilliance (wattage) of the existing lights or an increase in the number of lights or perhaps different placement of lights?

Early identification and labeling of variables will move the research process along more quickly.

Selected variables which are frequently used are listed in Exhibit 2.2. There are many thousands of variables used in research and the few listed cannot possibly indicate the full range of potential variables. Thus Exhibit 2.2 should be viewed as a very small sample of variables.

TYPES OF VARIABLES

Research consists of exploring the relationship of at least two variables. In experimental research (research in which an intervention of some kind is done) the major variables are named DEPENDENT and INDEPENDENT while in nonexperimental research they are simply called variables. Additional variables which may or may not be included in the research are named MODERATOR, CONTROL and INTERVENING variables.

DEPENDENT VARIABLES

Definition: *Dependent Variable*: The phenomenon or characteristic hypothesized to be the OUTCOME, EFFECT, CONSEQUENT or OUTPUT of some input variable. Its occurrence depends on some other variable which (usually) has preceded it in time.

Purpose: To identify the output or presumed effect of one or more independent variables.

Example: In the hypothesis "y depends on x," y is the dependent variable or presumed effect of x. Y's value is dependent on the value of the independent variable x. In the hypothesis "If the frequency of sales calls increases, the dollar amount of monthly sales will increase," dollar amount of monthly sales is the dependent variable. Dollar amount of monthly sales depends on frequency of sales calls.

EXHIBIT 2.2   SELECTED EXAMPLES OF FREQUENTLY USED
VARIABLES

LEVEL OF PRODUCTIVITY	DEGREE OF JOB SATISFACTION
DEGREE OF WORKER DISCONTENT	DEGREE OF JOB INTEREST
PERCENT OF WORKER RETENTION	PERCENT OF REJECTS
ATTITUDE TOWARD CHANGE	DEGREE OF LOYALTY
TYPE OF WORK CONDITIONS	TYPE OF EMPLOYMENT SITE
AMOUNT OF NET WORTH	AMOUNT OF CAPITAL
AMOUNT OF NON-CASH ASSETS	AMOUNT OF DEBT
COST OF CAPITAL	INTEREST RATE
CURRENT PAYMENT/INCOME RATIO	RATE OF UNEMPLOYMENT
COST OF ACQUISITIONS	BANK SIZE
BRAND ADVERTISING RECALL	BRAND AWARENESS
PREDISPOSITION TO BUY BRAND	BRAND PREFERENCE
AMOUNT OF FRANCHISE EXPERIENCE	SIZE OF SALESFORCE
LOCATION OF STORE	SIZE OF STORE
PERCENT OF MARKET GROWTH	AMOUNT OF PROFIT
AMOUNT OF NET SALES	AMOUNT OF GROSS SALES
SELLING EXPENSE	COST OF WAGES
TOTAL ASSETS	INVENTORY TURNOVER
CHANGE IN DAILY STOCK RETURNS	CLIENT SIZE
CHANGE IN SHAREHOLDER WEALTH	AMOUNT OF TOTAL ASSETS
AMOUNT OF FEDFRAL PURCHASES	AMOUNT OF HOUSEHOLD INCOME
TERM TO MATURITY OF BONDS	NUMBER OF SHARES OUTSTANDING
LEVEL OF EDUCATION	SEX OF RESPONDENT
MARITAL STATUS OF RESPONDENT	AGE OF RESPONDENT

EXHIBIT 2.3 TYPES AND PURPOSES OF VARIABLES

Name of Variable	Purpose
Dependent	Idenfity the output/presumed effect
Independent	Identify the input/presumed cause
Moderator	Study the effects of a variable which may modify the relationship between the dependent and independent variables.
Control	Rule out the effects of a variable by minimizing it, eliminating it or holding it constant.
Intervening	Explain what probably happens between the occurrence of the independent variable and the dependent variable.

Comment: The research problem often comes about by considering dependent variables. Why did gross sales (dependent variable) decline? Why did the number of accidents (dependent variable) increase?

INDEPENDENT VARIABLES

Definition: *Independent Variable:* The phenomenon or characteristic hypothesized to be the INPUT or ANTECEDENT variable. It is presumed to CAUSE the dependent variable and is manipulated, measured or selected prior to measuring the outcome or dependent variable.

Purpose: To identify the input or presumed cause of the dependent variable.

Example: In the hypothesis "There will be a higher number of tire blowouts for people driving at a speed over 75 miles an hour," driving speed is the independent variable. In the hypothesis "If air conditioning is installed and used then the number of units produced per hour will increase," installation and use of air conditioning is the independent variable or cause.

Comment: Businesses would make fewer mistakes if they began their research at the independent variable point. That is, if they started from a basis of "if we change this what will happen" rather than "why did that happen."

Recommendation: If you have difficulty distinguishing between the independent and dependent variables, begin by phrasing the hypothesis "y depends on x" using your variables in place of y and x. If y depends on x it is the dependent variable. You can rephrase the hypothesis later. An alternative suggested by Kerlinger [37, p. 34] is to use if-then statements, such as "if x then y." The "if" variable is independent and the "then" variable is dependent.

CAUTION: The terms independent and dependent variables are usually reserved for experimental research only, because they imply cause and effect and with true experimental designs cause and effect can be inferred. However, it is helpful to start your research by thinking in terms of independent and dependent variables. What caused those defective products (dependent variable)? Was it worker carelessness (independent variable)? Then if you decide to use a nonexperimental research design, avoid using the terms independent and dependent variables. Their use can mislead research consumers to think that one variable caused the other and that cannot be demonstrated in nonexperimental research.

MODERATOR VARIABLES

Definition: *Moderator Variable*: Another independent variable which is hypothesized to modify the relationship between the dependent and independent variable.

Purpose: To identify and study the impact of variables which might change (moderate) the major relationship between the independent and dependent variable.

Example:

Hypothesis 1:   Male employee turnover rates will be lower for employees working on flextime than for those not working on flextime, with less turnover for older workers on flextime than for younger workers on flextime who hold the same job position.

Dependent Variable: Employee turnover rate

Independent Variable: Type of work schedule (flextime/other)

Moderator Variable: Age of employee

Comment: Since the moderator variable is an independent variable also it is up to the researcher to determine which is the independent and which is the moderator variable.

Recommendation: If you are using moderator variables, consider all variables which might affect the relationship between the independent and dependent variables. Then select the one (or two) which could have the largest impact on the relationship for study as the moderator variable. It becomes very difficult to study more than two moderator variables.

CONTROL VARIABLES

Definition: *Control Variable*: A variable which may affect the relationship between the independent and dependent variables which is "controlled" (effects canceled out) by eliminating the variable, holding the variable constant or using statistical methods.

Purpose: To minimize or eliminate the potential effects of some of the many variables which might affect the research results.

Example:

Hypothesis 1:   Male employee turnover rate will be lower for employees working on flextime than for those not working on flextime, with less turnover for older workers on flextime than for younger workers on flextime who hold the same job position.

Dependent Variable: Employee turnover rate

Independent Variable: Type of workschedule (flextime/other)

Moderator Variable: Age of employee

Control Variable: Job position

Control Variable: Sex of employee

Comment: The difference between a control and a moderator variable is that the effects of the control variable are minimized, eliminated or held constant while the effects of the moderator variable are studied. Note that all subjects studied will be male and hold the same job positions, thus sex of employee and job position are held constant (are the same) and should not affect the relationship between type of workschedule and employee turnover rate.

Since both control and moderator variables are considered independent variables, it is up to the researcher to determine which are the independent, moderator and control variables.

INTERVENING VARIABLES

Definition: *Intervening Variable*: A variable which is hypothesized to exist but cannot be observed and is presumed to occur to explain the relationship between the independent and dependent variables.

Purpose: To explain the relationship between the independent and dependent variables.

Example:

Hypothesis 1:   Male employee turnover rate will be lower for employees working on flextime than for those not working on flextime, with less turnover for older workers on flextime than for younger workers on flextime who hold the same job position.

Dependent Variable: Employee turnover rate

Independent Variable: Type of workschedule (flextime/other)

Moderator Variable: Age of employee

Control Variable: Job position

Control Variable: Sex of employee

Intervening Variable: Motivation

Comment: Note that motivation is assumed to occur but cannot be directly observed. It is used here as an explanatory factor for the relationship between type of work schedule and employee turnover rate.

CAUTION: Note that a variable can be a dependent variable for one study and an independent, moderator or control variable for another study. For example, employee turnover rate and type of work schedule were the dependent and independent variables in Figure 2.1 but could be different types of variables in other studies.

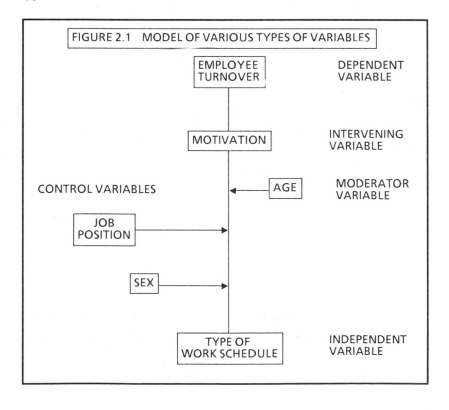

FIGURE 2.1   MODEL OF VARIOUS TYPES OF VARIABLES

DETERMINE AND STATE THE OPERATIONAL DEFINITIONS

After the variables are determined an operational definition of each variable is generated.

Definition: *Operational Definition:* A statement which defines a variable by specifying the operations used to measure or manipulate it.

Purpose: To limit the definition of the variable to only the exact way the researcher used to measure it in the specific study so that the research consumer knows not only what measures and manipulations were used but that other ways to measure the variable were not used.

Comment: People are most familiar with dictionary definitions which are certainly useful but not the same as operational definitions. It may be helpful to think of definitions as two types: operational and conceptual. Conceptual definitions describe the concept in words while operational definitions describe a variable with the measures used. For example, work overload might be conceptually described as "an amount of work which a person cannot complete in the work time period" and operationally defined as "having appointments scheduled every half hour between 8:00 a.m. and 6:00 p.m. for two weeks."

Recommendation: Define the variables so precisely that anyone reading the operational definition could measure the variables in exactly the same way you measured them. For example, a conceptual definition of self concept might be "how people feel about themselves," which is not measureable in the way it is stated. An operational definition of self concept might be "an individual's score on the XYZ Self Concept instrument." Anyone reading this operational definition will know how self concept was measured and could measure self concept exactly the same way if desired.

CAUTION: Variables may have different operational definitions in different studies. A dozen studies may use a dozen different operational definitions for the same variable. It is important that you define the variables in ways which will provide the most information for the research problem.

Exhibit 2.4 lists possible alternative operational definitions for selected variables. Remember there could be many other appropriate definitions for the same variables.

Note how the process of moving from a research problem to identifying and labeling variables to stating operational definitions is moving from the general information to very specific information. For example, in Exhibit 2.1 research problem #8 asks if market share would increase if the product packaging is changed. Packaging could be changed in a variety of ways including different colors, different labeling, different sizes or different shapes. Narrowing down the variable "product packaging" might result in the following.

Variable in the research problem:	Product packaging
Labeling the variable:	Size of product package
Operational Definition:	Size of product package will be defined as either the 9" x 12" size or the 6" x 18" size

---

EXHIBIT 2.4 ALTERNATIVE OPERATIONAL DEFINITIONS FOR
SELECTED VARIABLES

VARIABLE: ACTIVE CLIENT

1. Any client who has held an office apointment from June 1st through Dec. 30th.

OR

2. Any person who has been billed for services from Jan. 1st through Dec. 30th.

VARIABLE: AUTOCRATIC LEADER

1. A person whose title is Foreman, Department Head or Manager who scores above the median on the XYZ Autocracy Scale.

OR

2. A person who is assigned responsibility for at least one subordinate and is designated "Autocratic" by the supervisor when the supervisor is asked "does this person demonstrate autocratic or democratic leadership?"

VARIABLE: GROSS SALES

1. All total sales rung on the cash registers between 9 A.M. and 5 P.M. for 15 consecutive workdays.

OR

2. Sales figures posted in the income ledger as gross sales from May 1st through June 30th.

WHERE YOU ARE NOW

You should now have:

1. Clarified the research problem with the sponsor, if needed,

2. Determined, labeled and operationally defined the variables,

and recognized that:

3. There are several sources of research problems,

4. The decision to conduct research is largely based on the anticipated payoff of the results and the feasibility of conducting the research,

5. Variables are appropriately labeled dependent and independent only in experimental research, and

6. Other variables are named moderator, control and intervening and each has a specific purpose.

3

DETERMINE THE RESEARCH QUESTIONS OR HYPOTHESES

TERMS DEFINED IN CHAPTER THREE

Term   **Page**

CHAPTER THREE

DETERMINE THE RESEARCH QUESTIONS OR HYPOTHESES

STEPS TO TAKE AFTER READING THIS CHAPTER

1. State the relationship between or among the variables

2. Decide whether to state hypotheses or ask research questions.

3. State a preliminary hypothesis or research question which you may or may not revise later.

STATE THE EXPECTED RELATIONSHIP BETWEEN VARIABLES

You have already determined and operationally defined the variables which you wish to use. To form hypotheses or research questions you need to add a relationship. Do you expect that one variable caused another? Do you expect that the two variables are correlated in some way? Do you think that one group of people will perform better than a second group?

Research can be generally categorized as examining causal relationships or assessing associations. Each of these two types examines the relationship between or among variables. Exhibit 3.1 indicates some ways of stating these relationships.

Comment: Whether you are dealing with causality or association depends on whether you use experimental design or not. Cause and effect can only be assessed with one of the experimental research designs. At this point you have not selected your design and may not know what experimental design is but it is helpful to understand this concept before you go further.

To illustrate this concept, assume you hypothesize that the percent of rejects will be lower for employees on 7 hour shifts than for those on 8 hour shifts. You will compare percent of rejects of two groups, 7 and 8 hour shift employees. If you use experimental design you can conclude that the percent of rejects is or is not a function of (depends on, is a result of) the number of shift hours. If you do not use an experimental design you can conclude that the percent of rejects is or is not associated with the number of shift hours.

EXHIBIT 3.1   EXAMPLES OF POSSIBLE WAYS TO STATE
               RELATIONSHIPS

Causal Relationships	Association
1. X causes Y	1. As X increases, Y will increase
2. X produces Y	2. As X increases, Y will decrease
3. If X then Y	3. X is positively related to Y
4. Y is a function of X	4. X is negatively related to Y
5. Y depends on X	5. X is correlated with Y
6. Y is a consequence of X	6. X is associated with Y

If you feel you need more information at this time on experimental design, see Chapter 8.

CAUTION: Causal relationships (cause and effect) can be assessed only with experimental research designs. Other research designs will assess the association or relationship of the variables to each other.

Exhibit 3.2 indicates several ways relationships might be stated in hypotheses and research questions.

MULTIVARIATE RESEARCH

The previous discussions have centered on research problems with two variables. However, much of the research conducted today uses more than two variables; that is, a multivariate approach.

Instead of stating that A causes B, a multivariate hypothesis might state that A causes B, given conditions C and D. For example, "establishing daycare centers at the workplace will decrease the absenteeism rate of female employees, if the centers are open from 7:00 A.M. to 6:00 P.M.; but male absenteeism rate will not change."

This hypothesis is saying that establishment of daycare centers at the workplace (A) will cause a decrease in absenteeism (B) given the conditions of female employee (C) and daycare availability from 7:00 A.M. to 6:00 P.M. (D).

Comment: Multivariate research can involve two or more dependent variables, two or more independent variables or combinations of both. Multivariate research takes many forms including predicting relationships using several variables as predictors and reducing hundreds

---

EXHIBIT 3.2　　EXAMPLES OF RELATIONSHIPS BETWEEN TWO
VARIABLES

1. Degree of job satisfaction is NEGATIVELY CORRELATED with the amount of supervision received.

2. Food stores located near banks WILL SHOW HIGHER PROFITS than food stores distant from banks.

3. Is the level of female participation in the workforce CORRELATED WITH the number of children they have who are under 6 years old?

4. The number of new customers DEPENDS ON product price.

5. Is promotion potential POSITIVELY ASSOCIATED with goal acceptance?

6. Salespeople who receive positive reinforcement from their manager WILL PRODUCE A HIGHER NUMBER of sales.

---

of variables into a smaller number of factors. The associated statistical techniques, called Multivariate Analyses or Methods, are generally quite complex.

SOURCES OF HYPOTHESES AND RESEARCH QUESTIONS

Perhaps you have insufficient information to predict a relationship. Information is the key word. A search for related information is carried out to discover variables related to the "what if" or "why" questions and a research question or hypothesis is structured.

Hypotheses usually come from: (1) past experience, (2) theory or (3) review of related information (literature). To find out plausible relationships among variables, review information related to your variables. Chapter 6 will help if you are unsure how to proceed.

DECIDE WHETHER TO USE HYPOTHESIS TESTING OR RESEARCH QUESTIONS

Do all research projects require hypothesis testing? Definitely not. In fact, many research projects do not use the hypothesis testing format.

The decision to use hypotheses or research questions depends on whether or not the researcher chooses to use hypothesis testing procedures. Hypotheses state predicted relationships between variables while research questions ask if a relationship exists. The forms of each are much the same except the research question is interrogative and the hypothesis is a statement. The research process is similar in almost all respects and most steps are identical.

If the researcher chooses not to use hypothesis testing, then the more appropriate form for specification of the research problem is to ask a research question. Stating hypotheses implies that the researcher will be conducting hypothesis testing.

Comment: Research projects can include both hypotheses and research questions.

HYPOTHESIS TESTING

Comment: Do not worry if you do not understand the concept of significance levels in the following discussion. Significance levels are discussed in Chapter 4.

Definition: *Hypothesis Testing:* The process of making statistical inferences about population characteristics by using data obtained from samples of that population.

Synonym: *Significance Testing.*

Purpose: To gather information and make decisions about population characteristics without the expense or time required if the total population were examined and to statistically assess the probability of the sample characteristics' similarity to the population characteristics.

Advantages:

1. Sampling saves resources (money and time).

2. The a priori (prespecified) selection of the significance level provides an objective researcher-selected decision rule about the probability level at which the hypothesis will be considered supported by the data.

3. Hypothesis testing is the recognized and accepted form for research using the "scientific method," often a strong advantage.

Disadvantages:

1. Some researchers feel restricted by prespecifying the significance level, e.g., if the preselected significance level is .01 and the research analysis results in a probability of .012 the researcher's hypothesis would be rejected (and the null hypothesis accepted). An obtained probability of .009 would result in the researcher's hypothesis being supported (and the null hypothesis rejected). However, remember that the researcher has preselected the probability level at which the hypothesis will be either rejected or supported.

Comment: This concern can be somewhat alleviated and it is more informative to also report the probability of the observed results occurring which is 1.00 minus the significance level (1.00 - .012 = .988), in addition to the significance level. Thus the research consumer reads that the researcher's hypothesis was rejected at a probability level of .012 which means that the same results have a .988 probability of occurring again.

This gives the reader more complete information on which to base decisions.

2. Random sampling or random assignment may not be worth the cost. If the research is not critical but rather exploratory, then nonrandom sampling methods might be used. However, the conclusions from nonrandom procedures cannot be held with the same degree of confidence that random procedures yield.

Comment: If random sampling is not feasible, perhaps random assignment of subjects can be used to meet the requirement of random procedures.

Process: The process of conducting hypothesis testing is given in Chapter 4. The major differences between hypothesis testing and using research questions is that with hypothesis testing the significance level is selected prior to conducting the research and if the analysis yields nonsignificant results, the hypothesis is not supported. With research questions the results of the analysis are simply reported and decisions are NOT based on a prespecified significance level.

Comment: Although the hypothesis testing process differs slightly from the process used for research questions, the rest of the research processes are the same whether you choose to use hypotheses or research questions. Refer to the flow chart on the inside covers of the book (or the steps listed in chapter one) and you will see that the steps of the research process will be much the same. In either case you will determine the variables, use operational definitions, select the design, data collection methods and instrumentation, collect and analyze the data and make a decision about either the hypothesis or research question.

IF YOU USE A POPULATION

If you are using the population instead of a sample of the population, you will NOT be using hypothesis testing. By definition hypothesis testing is used for the purpose of making inferences about populations from samples. When comparing characteristics of populations, any differences are considered real differences rather than a sample estimate requiring a probability level.

Example: Using a Population

A manager wishes to determine if the 80 people on the night shift produce as many parts per person as the 120 people on the day shift produce. The variables (number of parts per person and type of shift) and operational definitions are determined, and related information is gathered. It is decided to use the total population of the 200 day and night shift workers rather than to sample. Because they are using the entire population, hypothesis testing will not be used and a research question will be formulated. This could take several forms, e.g., "will day shift workers produce more parts per person than night shift workers?", "will day shift workers produce less parts per person than night shift workers?" or "will day or night shift workers produce more parts per person?"

After data collection and analysis it is found that day shift workers produced 8.7 parts per hour per person while night shift workers produced 6.9. Since the data was gathered from the entire population the difference between 8.7 and 6.9 is considered a "real" difference, not an estimate provided by a sample. There would be no sampling error involved since there is no sampling done. (There still could be measurement error.)

Now assume that another organization wants to conduct the same study but because they have a total of 6,000 day and night shift workers they decide to sample rather than spend the money and time to gather information about the total population of 6,000. Because they are sampling, they will use hypothesis testing procedures. After reviewing related information they hypothesize that "day shift workers will produce more parts per person per hour than will night shift workers."

After data collection and analysis it was found that the sample of day shift workers produced 10.2 parts per person per hour while the sample of night shift workers produced 9.7. Because these figures are based on samples, not populations, the difference cannot be considered a "real" difference. Thus, if after computations a significance level is reported as "The results were significant at the .05 level," it means that there is a 95% chance that the observed difference between the sample of day workers and the sample of night workers would also occur in the population.

STATE THE PRELIMINARY HYPOTHESIS OR RESEARCH QUESTION

After it has been decided whether to use a research question or hypothesis, a preliminary research question or hypothesis is stated. The reason for the word preliminary is that you cannot usually state the final hypothesis or research question until related information (literature) is reviewed to assess previous findings and information about the variables and their relationship. It appears to speed the research process to state a preliminary hypothesis or research question and revise later, if necessary.

HYPOTHESES

Definition: *Hypothesis*: A declarative statement indicating a conjectured relationship between two or more variables which can be tested.

Purpose: To keep the researcher's beliefs, values and biases out of the research process itself. Once the hypothesis is stated it is there for anyone to see and test to find out if it is probably correct or incorrect [37, p. 35].

Comment: The researcher's biases may have affected the formulation of the hypothesis but it is open to testing.

Advantages:

1. Provides objectivity in the research because of the freedom from beliefs and biases in the testing.

2. Can be viewed and tested by others.

EXHIBIT 3.3　　CHOOSING HYPOTHESIS TESTING OR RESEARCH QUESTIONS

USE HYPOTHESIS TESTING IF:

1. Sufficient information about the variables and their relationship can be found in the review of related information to formulate an hypothesis.

2. Samples, not populations, are used.

3. You are willing to select a probability level prior to data collection.

4. You wish to use hypothesis testing procedures.

USE RESEARCH QUESTIONS IF:

*1. There is insufficient information available to formulate hypotheses.

2. Populations, not samples, are used.

*3. You are not willing to prespecify a probability level at which the hypothesis will be considered supported.

4. You do not wish to use hypothesis testing procedures.

*These conditions often lead to what is called exploratory research.

RESEARCH QUESTIONS

Definition: *Research Question*: An interrogative statement asking about a conjectured relationship between two or more variables.

Purpose: To specify the variables and their conjectured relationship when not conducting hypothesis testing.

Advantages:

1. Specifies the variables of interest.

2. Specifies a possible relationship between the variables.

3. Directs the research to the exploration of 1 and 2 above.

Comment: Note that a research question is similar to a research problem. The difference lies in the degree of specificity. A research problem is usually more general while in the research question the variables have been labeled more specifically.

FORMS OF HYPOTHESES OR RESEARCH QUESTIONS

Hypotheses and research questions can take many forms in the way that the relationships are stated. Remember from the previous discussion that implying causal relationships is not appropriate unless you use an experimental design. If you are unsure at this point whether to state a relationship implying causation or association, play it safe and use a form which implies association.

Examples of alternative forms of hypotheses are given in Exhibit 3.4. To change the hypotheses to research questions, simply change the form from declarative to interrogative.

EXHIBIT 3.4   EXAMPLES OF ALTERNATIVE FORMS OF
                HYPOTHESES

1.1   Employee retention will improve if employees' identification with the organization increases.
                          OR
1.2   Employee retention is a function of degree of identification with the organization.
                          OR
1.3   The more that employees identify with the organization, the higher the retention rate will be.

2.1   Consumers who have children living with them will have a higher degree of brand awareness than will consumers who do not have children living with them.
                          OR
2.2   Degree of brand awareness is associated with family structure.

3.1   The more frequently bonuses are awarded to employees, the higher monthly sales will be.
                          OR
3.2   Monthly sales will be higher if bonuses are awarded more frequently to employees.
                          OR
3.3   Monthly sales are positively associated with frequency of bonuses.

Examples of changing these hypotheses to research questions are:

1.1   Will employee retention improve if employees' identification with the organization increases?

2.2   Is brand awareness associated with family structure?

3.3   Are monthly sales positively associated with frequency of bonuses?

WHERE YOU ARE NOW

At this point you should have:

1. Stated the expected relationship between variables,

2. Stated a preliminary hypothesis or research question,

and recognized:

3. The difference between causal and associational relationships,

4. Much research deals with many variables (multivariate research) in addition to research studies using two variables,

5. The difference between using hypothesis testing and research questions,

6. Advantages and disadvantages of using hypothesis testing and research questions,

7. When to choose hypothesis testing or research questions,

8. If a population is used, hypothesis testing is not used (unless information about subgroups from samples of the population is desired), and

9. Hypotheses and research questions can be stated in several different forms.

4

HYPOTHESIS TESTING

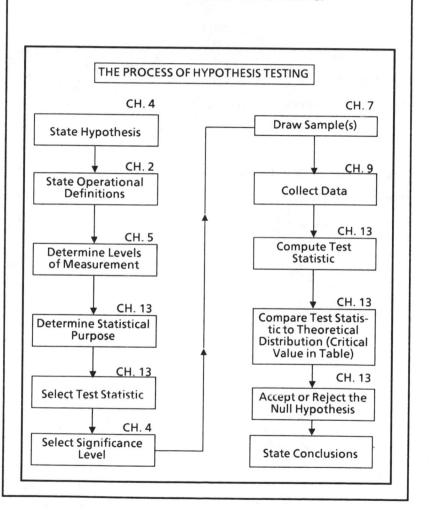

THE PROCESS OF HYPOTHESIS TESTING

CH. 4
State Hypothesis

CH. 2
State Operational Definitions

CH. 5
Determine Levels of Measurement

CH. 13
Determine Statistical Purpose

CH. 13
Select Test Statistic

CH. 4
Select Significance Level

CH. 7
Draw Sample(s)

CH. 9
Collect Data

CH. 13
Compute Test Statistic

CH. 13
Compare Test Statistic to Theoretical Distribution (Critical Value in Table)

CH. 13
Accept or Reject the Null Hypothesis

State Conclusions

TERMS DEFINED IN CHAPTER FOUR

Terms   **Page**

CHAPTER FOUR

HYPOTHESIS TESTING

STEPS TO TAKE AFTER READING THIS CHAPTER

1. Determine whether to state a directional or nondirectional hypothesis.

2. State the research hypothesis.

3. Select the significance level.

4. Review the flow chart at the beginning of the chapter for later use.

5. Review statistical and practical signficance for later use.

The process of hypothesis testing is given in the flow chart at the beginning of this chapter. If you are using hypothesis testing you will be referring to this flow chart throughout the research project. Note there are several steps to the hypothesis testing process, some of which you may not be familiar with at this time. This is because the process is really not linear (step after step) but is a process which requires integration of several concepts.

Two steps of the hypothesis testing process are discussed in this chapter: stating the hypothesis and selecting the significance level. The other steps are discussed in the chapters noted on the flow chart.

Remember from the previous chapter that hypothesis testing is for the purpose of estimating population characteristics from examining and testing sample characteristics.

RESEARCH HYPOTHESES

Definition: *Research Hypothesis*: A declarative sentence indicating a conjectured relationship between variables which can be tested and which the researcher believes will be demonstrated after hypothesis testing.

Synonyms: *Working hypothesis, alternate hypothesis, motivated hypothesis.*

Purpose: To keep the researcher's biases from affecting the research process by statement of the expected relationship among variables. The researcher expects this relationship to occur based on experience and/or review of related information.

Symbol: H_a, H_m, H_1, or the letter H with any alphabetical or numerical subscript except the letter "O" which is used only to indicate null hypotheses.

Comment: The research hypothesis is not the hypothesis which is tested. Instead another hypothesis called the null hypothesis is the one that is statistically tested.

NULL HYPOTHESES

Because it is almost impossible to test hypotheses under the many and various possible conditions, researchers attempt to find support for the research hypothesis by rejecting the negation of it, which is called the null hypothesis. If the null hypothesis is rejected, that is, there are sufficiently large statistical differences to reject the idea of the research results occurring by chance, the research hypothesis is supported.

EXHIBIT 4.1   EXAMPLES OF POSSIBLE RESEARCH HYPOTHESES
                 AND THEIR NULL HYPOTHESES

1. H_1:   Empathetic managers are more productive than non-empathetic managers. $H_1: \mu_E > \mu_N$

   Ho: Empathetic managers are less or equally productive to non-empathetic managers. $Ho: \mu_E \leq \mu_N$

2. H_1:   Nonempathetic managers are more productive than empathetic managers. $H_1: \mu_N > \mu_E$

   Ho: Nonempathetic managers are less or equally productive to empathetic managers. $Ho: \mu_N \leq \mu_E$

3. H_1:   Productivity levels will differ for empathetic and non-empathetic managers. $H_1: \mu_E \neq \mu_N$

   Ho: Productivity levels will not differ for empathetic and non-empathetic managers. $Ho: \mu_E = \mu_N$

                              OR

   Ho: Empathetic and nonempathetic managers are equally productive. $Ho: \mu_E = \mu_N$

Note that all the null hypotheses have equal signs.

Definition: *Null Hypothesis*: A declarative statement indicating that the relationship specified in the research hypothesis will NOT exist. To indicate this the symbolic form includes an equal sign. For example, Ho: μ_a = μ_b or Ho: $\mu_a \geq \mu_b$ or Ho: $\mu_a \leq \mu_b$.

Note: The null hypothesis is sometimes called the no-difference hypothesis.

Purpose: To provide a statement which can be statistically tested in order to provide evidence that the research hypothesis is either supported or not supported.

Symbol: Ho (The symbol is ALWAYS Ho for the null hypothesis).

Recommendation: State the research hypothesis, not the null hypothesis (despite what you may have learned in a statistics class). Experienced readers know that THE NULL HYPOTHESIS IS ALWAYS THE ONE WHICH IS STATISTICALLY TESTED and will consider it amateurish if you state the null. Inexperienced readers are usually very confused if null hypotheses are stated. THE RESEARCH HYPOTHESIS IS THE ONE IN WHICH YOU ARE INTERESTED.

It is important for the reader to be quite clear about the research hypothesis because it is the hypothesis the researcher actually believes will be supported. If it is a directional hypothesis, the direction of the research hypothesis should be clearly understood.

DIRECTIONAL AND NONDIRECTIONAL HYPOTHESES

Hypotheses can be directional or nondirectional: that is, they either predict the direction of research outcomes or they predict inequality.

DIRECTIONAL HYPOTHESES

Definition: *Directional Hypothesis*: An hypothesis in which the direction of the outcome is predicted rather than predicting inequality only. Examples: A will be better than B, X will be less than Y, A will be positively related to B.

Comment: Sometimes rather inaccurately called a one-tailed hypothesis (because a one-tailed statistical test is used with a directional hypothesis).

Purpose: To specify an hypothesis when the direction of the outcome is anticipated. A directional (one-tailed) statistical test rather than a non-directional (two-tailed) statistical test is then used. A directional hypothesis should be justified by support in the literature and related information that the specified outcome should occur.

NONDIRECTIONAL HYPOTHESES

Definition: *Nondirectional Hypothesis*: An hypothesis in which the direction of the outcome is not predicted and the stated relationship between the variables is one of inequality. Examples: A will be unequal to B, A will be related to B.

Comment: Sometimes rather inaccurately called a two-tailed hypothesis.

Purpose: To specify an hypothesis when there is insufficient evidence to specify the direction of the outcome.

EXHIBIT 4.2   EXAMPLES OF DIRECTIONAL AND
                NONDIRECTIONAL HYPOTHESES

DIRECTIONAL HYPOTHESES

H_1:   Female executives' annual compensation will be lower than
          male executives' annual compensation. $H_1: \mu_f < \mu_m$

H_2:   Female executives' annual compensation will be higher than
          male executives' annual compensation. $H_1: \mu_f > \mu_m$

NONDIRECTIONAL HYPOTHESIS

H_3:   Female and male executives' annual compensation will
          differ.
          $H_3: \mu_f \neq \mu_m$

Note that hypothesis 3 is nondirectional because it does not predict
which sex will have the higher compensation.

DECIDE WHETHER TO STATE DIRECTIONAL OR NONDIRECTIONAL HYPOTHESES

To determine whether to state directional or nondirectional hypotheses the researcher searches related information and literature. If evidence or theory is found which indicates that male executives tend to have higher compensation than females, hypothesis one would be selected. If the search yields information that female executives tend to have higher compensation, then hypothesis two would be selected. If there was insufficient or contradictory evidence, then nondirectional hypothesis three would be selected.

Recommendation: State a directional hypothesis if it can be justified by a review of literature and related information. A directional hypothesis leads to a one-tailed statistical test. Statistically significant results are always obtained more easily with a one-tailed statistical test because the critical value is less than for a two-tailed test. (Don't worry if you don't understand this now -- you will later.)

After you have stated the final hypothesis (remember a preliminary hypothesis is stated prior to review of the literature and the final hypothesis after the review of the literature), you continue the hypothesis testing process using the steps demonstrated in other chapters. That is, you will state operational definitions, determine the levels of measurement, determine the statistical purpose and select the test statistic. At that point you select the significance level at which you are willing to accept or reject the hypothesis.

SELECT THE SIGNIFICANCE LEVEL

It is easier to understand significance levels if you review the concept of probability.

Definition: *Probability*: the relative frequency of an event occurring, usually reported as a percentage or fraction.

Symbol: p

Examples: The probability of rolling a 5 on a die is 1/6 because there are six possible outcomes. The probability of drawing an Ace of Hearts from a 52 card deck is 1/52 or .019.

Probabilities range from 0 to 1 with 0 indicating no chance of occurrence and 1 indicating 100% probability or certainty that an event will occur. A probability of .05 means that an event should occur 5 times out of every 100 times the same situation takes place.

Comment: We deal with probability in our daily lives since few events are 100% certain to occur. One way researchers use probability is to specify the risk (probability) of coming to the wrong conclusions in hypothesis testing. They specify a probability of being wrong such as .05 or .01 which means they want to draw the correct conclusions 95 or 99 times out of 100. The following discussion on the rationale for selecting a significance level clarifies this.

THE RATIONALE FOR SELECTING SIGNIFICANCE LEVELS

When using a sampling method there is always the possibility of sampling error -- that the sample drawn does not represent the population. This means that the data obtained from a sample may be very different from the population data the sample is supposed to represent.

For example, assume that the following study was conducted.

Sample: Sample of janitors and sample of elevator operators.

H_a: Number of accidents will differ for janitors and elevator operators.

H_o: Number of accidents will be equal for janitors and elevator operators.

Significance Level Specified by Researcher: .05. This means that the researcher is willing to take a 5% risk of being wrong.

Average Number of Accidents: Janitors = 12.5
                                                      Elevator Operators = 15.3

Statistical Test Indicates: Significant differences between the number of accidents of the two groups, janitors and elevator operators, at a probability level of .05. This is determined by comparing the numerical result of the statistical test with a table of values which indicates the probability levels for a variety of possible results.

Decision about the Hypothesis: The null hypothesis of no differences between the two groups is rejected (because the statistical test was significant at the prespecified probability level).

Conclusion: The population of janitors has a lower number of accidents than the population of elevator operators. The probability of this conclusion being wrong is 5 percent (.05). The probability of this conclusion being correct is 95 percent.

There is no way of knowing if the difference in number of accidents found in the SAMPLE of janitors and the SAMPLE of elevator operators reflects actual differences in the number of accidents of the POPULATION of janitors and the POPULATION of elevator operators. The figures used in this study could be a result of sampling error and the actual number of accidents in the two populations might be 14.6 and 14.2 or some other figures.

Comment: The only way to discover actual population figures is to study the whole population. If you use populations you do not use hypothesis testing, since hypothesis testing is used to make inferences about populations by using samples.

Thus, when a null hypothesis is rejected it may be a correct decision or it may be an erroneous decision. Recognizing this, researchers specify the amount of risk of being wrong they wish to take.

The researchers studying the number of accidents for janitors and elevator operators specified that they were willing to be wrong 5 times out of 100 IN THE DECISION TO REJECT THE NULL HYPOTHESIS.

BECAUSE NO ONE IS EVER CERTAIN THAT THE SAMPLE INFORMATION ACCURATELY REPRESENTS THE POPULATION INFORMATION, RESEARCHERS SPECIFY THE RISK OF REJECTING THE NULL HYPOTHESIS WHEN IT IS CORRECT. THIS RISK, EXPRESSED IN PROBABILITY TERMS, IS CALLED THE SIGNIFICANCE LEVEL.

Definition: *Significance Level*: The probability, expressed in a percentage, of rejecting the null hypothesis when it is true and should not have been rejected.

Synonyms: *Alpha Level. Type I Error. Alpha Error*

Symbol: α

Purpose: to provide an objective researcher-selected decision rule for accepting or rejecting the null hypothesis.

TYPE I AND TYPE II ERRORS

The possibility of making two types of errors exists when accepting or rejecting a null hypothesis, because there is no way of knowing if the sample conditions accurately represent the population conditions. The first type of possible error is rejecting the null hypothesis when it is correct, which was discussed above. The second type of possible error is accepting the null hypothesis when it is incorrect. These are called Type I and Type II errors.

TYPE I ERROR = REJECTING THE Ho WHEN IT IS TRUE
TYPE II ERROR = ACCEPTING THE Ho WHEN IT IS FALSE

The definition of a Type I error has already been given, as a Type I error is a synonym for significance level or alpha level.

Definition: *Type II Error*: The probability, expressed in a percentage, of NOT rejecting the null hypothesis when it is false and should have been rejected.

Synonyms: *Beta. Beta Level. Beta Error*

Symbol: β

Purpose: To provide information on the likelihood of the null hypothesis being incorrectly accepted.

Comment: If a significance level (Alpha) and sample size are determined, then the Type II error (Beta) is already determined [58].

In choosing your significance level you should consider both types of errors. For example, assume the following study was planned. The example is exaggerated to illustrate Type I and Type II errors.

Need for the Study:

The cost of rejects in the Texas and Maine plants has been so great that the Vice President has decided to conduct a study to discover if the difference in reject rates is statistically significant or just a chance difference. Furthermore, the Vice President has decided if there is a significant difference the plant with the largest reject rate will be closed. If the difference in reject rates is not statistically significant both plants will remain in operation.

H_1:   The percent of rejects will be different for the Maine plant than for the Texas plant.

H_0:   The percent of rejects will be equal for the Maine and Texas plants.

Now look at the possible outcomes and consequences of testing the null hypothesis.

Possible Outcomes	Consequences
1. Ho is rejected.	Plant is closed, city suffers unemployment & economic deprivation.
Either Maine or Texas plant has significantly higher percent of rejects.	

If There Is A Type I Error (Ho Rejected When It Is True)

People will be unemployed and a city will suffer because of a Type I error of rejecting the Ho when it was true.

2. Ho is not rejected	Both plants remain in operation.
Maine and Texas plants have about the same percent of rejects.	

If There Is A Type II Error (Ho Accepted When It Is False)

The plant which should have been closed remains open because of a Type II error of failing to reject the Ho when it was false. Costly to the company.

Thus it should be determined by a decision maker which type of error has the most severe consequences.

Comment: Given the consequences of being wrong via either a Type I or Type II error, ideally the company would like to have a small probability of each error occurring. However that is not feasible because, generally, the smaller the researcher sets a Type I error, the larger the Type II error will be [58].

If both Types I and II errors (Alpha and Beta) are determined, the sample size would also be determined. In practice, many researchers determine the probability for a Type I error (the significance level), determine the sample size and ignore the Type II error. However if the consequences of being wrong via a Type II error are severe, two actions you can take to lower the risk of a Type II error are:

1. Increase the sample size (remember this will cost more)

2. Increase the significance level (if you do this you are increasing the risk of a Type I error).

There is also a relationship between a Type II error and the power of whatever statistical test you use to reject the Ho when you should. The lower the Type II error is, the greater will be the power of a statistical test to reject the Ho when it is false.

Definition: *Power:* The probability, expressed in a percentage, of rejecting the null hypothesis when it is false and should have been rejected; a correct decision.

Comment: Power is computed as 1.00-Beta (Type II error).

Purpose: To provide information on the likelihood of the null hypothesis being correctly rejected.

To summarize these concepts, there are four possible outcomes of hypothesis testing. These are given in Exhibit 4.3.

EXHIBIT 4.3	POSSIBLE RESULTS OF HYPOTHESIS TESTING	
	ACCEPT Ho	REJECT Ho
Ho IS TRUE	CORRECT DECISION (Prob. of accepting Ho when it is true = 1-Alpha)	TYPE I ERROR (Prob. of rejecting Ho when it is true = Alpha)
Ho IS FALSE	TYPE II ERROR (Prob. of accepting Ho when it is false = Beta)	CORRECT DECISION (Prob. of rejecting Ho when it is false = Power = 1-Beta)

Exhibit 4.4 summarizes information about Type I and Type II errors.

Comment: These concepts are usually somewhat puzzling to beginning researchers and may require a second reading.

Recommended References: The relationships among Alpha, Beta, Power and sample size are covered in statistical texts should you desire additional information. See Siegel [58, pp. 8-11].

WAYS TO SELECT A SIGNIFICANCE LEVEL

The choice of a significance level depends primarily on how much error the researcher is willing to tolerate and secondarily on what has become established practice.

EXHIBIT 4.4   SUMMARY OF TYPE I AND TYPE II ERRORS

1. The significance level, Alpha (α) is set by the researcher and indicates the probability of making a Type I error; incorrectly rejecting the Ho when it is true.

2. The probability of accepting the Ho when it is true is 1-Alpha. This is a correct decision.

3. Beta (β) is already determined if the significance level has been set and the sample size determined. Beta indicates the probability of making a Type II error; incorrectly accepting the Ho when it is false.

4. The power of a statistical test is 1-Beta. Power indicates the probability of rejecting the Ho when it is false; a correct decision.

5. The probability of making a Type II error (Beta) can be decreased by increasing the significance level or increasing the sample size.

6. If the significance level (Alpha) is increased the probability of a Type I error is increased.

7. If sample size is increased, the cost of the project is increased.

When selecting a significance level you are specifying the degree of risk of being wrong you are willing to take. The size of that risk depends on the consequences of being wrong. In social science research the most commonly used significance level is .05 or taking the risk of being wrong 5 times out of 100. In medical research it is not uncommon to select more stringent significance levels of .0001, .00001 or even .0000001 as the consequences of being wrong become more severe.

What if the building you are in was constructed with a 5% risk of error? Would you be willing to remain in it? Imagine 5 of every 100 buildings constructed by the same contractor have a possibility of collapsing because the contractor was willing to take a 5% risk of being wrong. Now assume that this same contractor built 1,000 buildings with a 5% risk of error and 50 buildings are in danger of collapsing.

This example is exaggerated to clearly indicate to you that the significance level selected depends largely on the consequences of being wrong. Although the .05 and .01 levels are commonly selected for social science research, these levels are considered enormous to people in other fields where tolerances must be very minute.

Comment: Because of this customary and established practice of selecting an alpha of .05 or smaller a researcher who selects any alpha level larger than .05 usually defends the choice. An alpha of .10 is common for exploratory research. An alpha larger than .10 probably indicates that a Type I error is not as important as a Type II error and this is usually pointed out in the written report.

A PRIORI SELECTION OF THE SIGNIFICANCE LEVEL

The researcher selects the significance level BEFORE DATA COLLECTION according to the dictates of the research and conventional practice.

WHICH SIGNIFICANCE LEVEL IS PRESELECTED MAKES A DIFFERENCE IN THE CONCLUSIONS. Once a significance level has been selected it does not change. It was selected by the researcher on the basis of the amount of risk warranted by the problem. This means that a study can have results which differ very little from the selected significance level and the conclusion would be that the results were nonsignificant.

For example, assume that two identical research studies are carried out. The data are identical also and statistical analysis yields a probability of .015 for each of the studies.

Researcher Smith had selected a significance level of .01, indicating a willingness to be wrong only 1 time out of 100 times the same research would be conducted. Since the probability obtained from the data was .015 it exceeded the preselected significance level of .01. Thus, researcher Smith accepted the Ho and the results of this study are considered nonsignificant.

Researcher Jones had selected a significance level of .02, indicating a willingness to be wrong 2 times out of 100. As the probability obtained from the data was .015, it was less than the preselected significance level of .02. Thus, researcher Jones rejected the Ho and the results of this study are considered significant.

The example illustrates that there could be two identical research studies with identical data yielding identical results. Yet in one study the Ho would be accepted and in the other study the Ho would be rejected simply because two different significance levels were selected.

Thus, it is important that you select the significance level carefully, based on the amount of risk you wish to tolerate. Bear in mind that while you may not be willing to accept a larger risk someone else might be willing to do so.

CAUTION: In hypothesis testing the results are either significant or not significant, according to the results of the statistical tests. Statements such as "the results approached significance" or "were close to significance" are inappropriate. It is helpful to the reader to report the probability of the same situation occurring along with the probability of error which the significance level indicates. For the above example such a statement might be "the probability of error yielded by the data was .015, indicating that the probability of this same situation occurring is .985."

THE NEXT STEPS

After selection of the significance level, you continue with the hypothesis testing process with the steps demonstrated in other chapters. That is, draw the sample, collect data, compute the test statistic, compare the test statistic to the tabled critical value, accept or reject the null hypothesis and state conclusions. Throughout the hypothesis testing procedure keep in mind the difference between statistical and practical significance.

STATISTICAL AND PRACTICAL SIGNIFICANCE

DECISION MAKING

Hypothesis testing leads to the reporting of a probability level and the interpretation of that probability level. This does NOT automatically mean that a decision will be made according to the direction of the results and the probability level. Decision making still relies on human judgment -- not on statistical significance but practical significance. What the hypothesis testing does is to help the manager make the decision by providing information about the degree to which results of the study can be attributed to the variables under study rather than to chance.

For example, if, after one month of training in data processing, a group's output is higher than that of a second group who did not receive the training and these results were obtained at the.05 significance level, the odds are 95 to 5 that the output of the first group was higher because of the training (assuming the study was conducted appropriately).

Now the manager is faced with a decision about incorporating training. This decision involves many variables including training time, willingness of employees, cost versus value of the additional output and the current economic climate of the organization. No statistical test makes that decision for a manager.

There will be situations when managers are willing to take a greater risk than 5% of being wrong; perhaps willing to take odds of 90 to 10 or even 80 to 20. In such cases the significance level should be set at these decision points.

WHEN THE NULL HYPOTHESIS IS ACCEPTED

When the statistical analysis fails to reject the null hypothesis, it does not mean literally there are no differences but simply that there are not enough differences to matter much, given the preselected significance level. In the above example, the researcher selected the .05 significance level. If the results had indicated an average output score of the trained group of 73 and average output of the untrained group of 68, and an obtained significance level of .20, the null hypothesis would be accepted because the results did not meet the preselected significance level of .05. This does not mean that 68 and 73 become the same score. It means that the difference between the two scores, 73 and 68, is simply not statistically significant UNDER THE PRESELECTED SIGNIFICANCE LEVEL.

STATISTICAL BUT NOT MEANINGFUL SIGNIFICANCE

The researcher should be reminded that some statistical tests result in what is called "statistical but not meaningful significance." For example, correlations can range from 0 to ±1.00. With a sufficiently large number of Ss a correlation of .09 can be statistically significant. Even with very little familiarity with statistics, most people understand that a correlation that small indicates very little relationship between variables. However, in some literature such correlations are reported as being statistically significant (which they are) but it should also be pointed out in the report that when the magnitude (size) of the correlations is that small, the significance is a function of the number of Ss and such correlations are virtually "meaningless."

WHERE YOU ARE NOW

At this point you have:

1. Determined whether to state a directional or nondirectional hypothesis, if you are using hypothesis testing,

2. Stated the research hypothesis,

3. Selected a significance level,

and recognized that:

4. The Ho is the hypothesis tested statistically,

5. Significance levels are reported in probability terms,

6. The possibility exists of making two types of errors, Type I and Type II,

7. In practice, many researchers select a significance level (Type I error) and a sample size and ignore the Type II error,

8. The significance level chosen depends on the consequences of being wrong and what has become established practice,

9. Given two identical research studies with identical results one set of results could be declared significant and the other declared nonsignificant because of different significance levels selected by the researchers and

10. Statistical significance does not always indicate meaningful significance.

5

LEVELS OF MEASUREMENT, VALIDITY AND RELIABILITY

TERMS DEFINED IN CHAPTER FIVE

CHAPTER FIVE

LEVELS OF MEASUREMENT, VALIDITY AND RELIABILITY

STEPS TO TAKE AFTER READING THIS CHAPTER

1. Determine the level of measurement for each variable.

2. Decide if the level of measurement could be changed to a higher level, and if this would improve the research.

3. Review validity and reliability in order to critique the literature and for later use at the instrumentation stage.

Measurement is used in every research project. No matter what type of research is being conducted, the variables need to be measured in some way and the validity and reliability of these measures need to be considered. It is helpful to understand levels of measurement, validity and reliability before reviewing the related information in order to critique the processes used in the literature.

THE LEVEL OF MEASUREMENT FOR EACH VARIABLE DETERMINES WHICH TYPES OF STATISTICAL ANALYSIS MAY BE USED. Thus, it is important to understand measurement before going too far in the research process.

Definition: *Measurement*: Assigning numbers to objects or events according to rules [60].

Purpose: To have information in a form in which variables can be related to each other.

Comment: Assigning numbers does not make an observation, instrument or test any better or worse than it was originally. That is, if the observation was poor in the first place it will still be poor and if it was good originally it will still be good.

LEVELS OF MEASUREMENT

Stevens [60] pointed out that there are four different levels of measurement and each of these levels has different rules for assigning numbers. Exhibit 5.1 indicates characteristics of these four levels of measurement.

EXHIBIT 5.1   THE FOUR LEVELS OF MEASUREMENT

LEVEL	NUMBERS ARE USED TO:	EXAMPLE OF ASSIGNING NUMBERS	NUMBERS INDICATE:	PERMISSIBLE ARITHMETIC OPERATIONS	TYPICAL STATISTICS USED
Nominal	• Classify (people, events, objects, etc.)	Stocks = 1 Bonds = 2	• Difference (stocks are different from bonds)	• Counting (e.g., there are 24 ones-stocks and 10 twos-bonds.)	Mode, Chi square or other Non-parametric tests
Ordinal	• Classify • Rank	High School Class = 1 Middle Social Class = 2 Low Social Class = 3	• Difference • Greater or Less than	• Counting • Ranking	Median, Sign test or other Nonparametric test.
Interval	• Classify • Rank • Indicate Equal Units • Indicate Arbitrary Zero Point	Scores on Math ability test e.g., Applicant A 82 Applicant B 51 Applicant C 41 Applicant D 00	• Difference • Greater or Less than • Equal Distance Between Numbers • Zero does not indicate absence of the variable	• Counting • Ranking • Addition • Subtraction	Mean, t-test or other Parametric tests.
Ratio	• Classify • Rank • Indicate Equal Units • Indicate Absolute Zero	Income e.g., $30,000.00 $15,000.00 $ 3,000.00 $ 0.00	• Difference • Greater or Less than • Equal Distance Between Numbers • Zero indicates absence of the variable	• Counting • Ranking • Addition • Subtraction • Multiplication • Division	Mean, Geometric Mean, t-tests or other Parametric tests.

Note that as the Levels are in a hierarchy from Nominal (the lowest) to Ratio (the highest) each level has all the properties of the previous level plus some property of its own. With higher levels of measurement more precise statistical tests are permissible.

NOMINAL LEVEL OF MEASUREMENT

Definition: *Nominal Level of Measurement*: Numbers assigned to objects or events which can be placed into mutually exclusive and exhaustive categories.

Synonym: *Nominal Scale.*

Related Definition: *Mutually Exclusive Categories*: Events which cannot occur at the same time. Thus a customer can be classified as having 12 or more years of education but cannot be classified as having less than 12 years of education at the same time.

Related Definition: *Exhaustive Categories*: Sufficient categories so that every event can be classified in one of the categories. For example, categories of more than 12 years of education and less than 12 years of education would not have a place to classify people with 12 years of education.

Nominal is the lowest level of measurement because numbers are assigned to variables only to classify or categorize them (the word nominal means "to name"). Some experts do not even consider it a level of measurement [67].

Examples

The variable "sex of respondent" currently is dichotomous (has two values). In a research study each male might be assigned the number one and each female be assigned the number two. Because the numbers are used only to place objects into mutually exclusive categories they cannot be used to indicate ordering of objects. That is, the number one assigned to males simply indicates a category, not that males are greater or less than females but that females are different from males. Thus, it makes no difference what numbers are used. The number 10 could be assigned to the category "female" and a 47 to males.

Social science research includes many nominal variables, particularly in marketing research. Examples include, sex of respondent, city of residence and color of products. A typical question with responses at the nominal level of measurement is:

At which food store do you shop most frequently?

□1. Kroger
□2. Safeway
□3. Smith's Supermarket
□4. Other (please specify) _____

CAUTION: Since numbers assigned at the nominal level have no meaning other than to classify objects or events, they cannot be used for mathematical computations such as addition or subtraction. Counting is permissible; there might be 200 number ones (males) and 75 number twos (females). With the nominal level of measurement statistical analyses appropriate for nominal data MUST be used.

ORDINAL LEVEL OF MEASUREMENT

Definition: *Ordinal Level of Measurement*: Numbers assigned to objects or events which can be placed into mutually exclusive categories and be ordered into a greater or less than scale.

Synonym: *Ordinal Scale.*

Related Definition: *Transitivity*: A greater than or less than relationship assigned to objects or events representing variables.

At the ordinal level of measurement numbers are assigned to objects or events not only to categorize them but to indicate a greater than or less than relationship. This is called a transitive relationship. With an ordinal scale transitivity of the variable exists but the scale has no absolute zero point and there are unequal distances between scale values. Numbers assigned at the ordinal level provide more information than at the nominal level because they also establish an ordering of the objects or events. The ordinal level of measurement provides more information than the nominal and is a higher level of measurement.

Examples

In a horse race win, place and show are also called 1st, 2nd, and 3rd places. The horse which comes in first is faster than the second and third horses. The 2nd horse is faster than the third horse. Not only do these numbers categorize first, second and third place, they also indicate in what order the horses came in. Note that even though the 2nd place winner is faster than the third place winner, we have no idea from the numbers how much faster #2 was, since the numbers do NOT indicate equal distances among the scale values.

A typical example of a question with responses at the ordinal level of measurement is:

Please rank the following television programs according to how much you enjoy viewing them. Rank the program you enjoy viewing the most as number 1 and the one you enjoy viewing the least as number 5.

Program	Rank
Dallas	_____
Dynasty	_____
Falcon Crest	_____
Knight Rider	_____
Miami Vice	_____

CAUTION: The numbers assigned at the ordinal level must maintain order in the numbering system: e.g., you could not use 6,9,5 because the numbers are not in order. Addition and subtraction are not permissible operations. You cannot add ranks 1,3, and 8 and have a meaningful figure. Counting and ranking are the only permissible operations. With the ordinal level of measurement, statistical analyses appropriate for nominal or ordinal data must be used.

INTERVAL LEVEL OF MEASUREMENT

Definition: *Interval Level of Measurement:* Numbers assigned to objects or events which can be categorized, ordered and assumed to have an equal distance between scale values. The zero point is set arbitrarily.

Synonym: *Interval Scale. Equal Interval Scale.*

Related Definition: *Arbitrary Zero Point:* A zero point which is set for convenience and does not mean absence of the variable.

At the interval level of measurement numbers are assigned to objects or events to categorize, order and indicate equal distance between scale values but there is an arbitrary zero point. An arbitrary zero point means one which is set for convenience when establishing the scale. Thus, a score of zero would not indicate absence of the variable. For example, a person who received a zero on an intelligence test would not be considered as having no intelligence.

The numbers assigned at the interval level of measurement give more information than do the numbers assigned at the ordinal or nominal levels because they also indicate equal distances. Thus interval scales are a higher level of measurement.

CAUTION: It has become quite common to ASSUME interval level of measurement for variables which are probably more accurately measured at the ordinal level. It is the researcher's responsibility to defend the choice of an interval scale if there is a question of equal distances between scale points. Remember you are measuring a variable. For example, many people analyze responses of "very important," "somewhat important," and "not very important" using statistical tests appropriate for interval data -- which assume an interval scale or equal distances between each of the three responses. That the distance between very and somewhat important is equal to the distance between somewhat and not very important is questionable and many researchers would consider this to be an ordinal scale.

Examples

With a Fahrenheit temperature scale, 72 degrees is one degree higher than 71 degrees, just as 40 degrees is one degree higher than 39. A distance of 10 degrees is the same distance at any 10 point difference in the scale. However, the zero point on this scale is arbitrarily set and zero does not mean absence of heat.

Many measurements at the interval level in business research occur in the use of personnel evaluation and tests, such as typing or mathematics ability tests. For example, scores on a mathematics ability test were:

Scott	50
Kelly	45
Shannan	25
Shawn	0

Although Shawn received a 0 on the test, it does not mean that he has no (zero) mathematical ability -- remember the zero point was set arbitrarily. Addition and subtraction are permissible operations, but, because of the arbitrary zero, multiplication and division are not permissible. This means that you can add up all the scores (and compute an average if you wish) but you cannot divide Scott's score of 50 by Shannan's score of 25 to obtain a ratio. Thus, you can say that Scott has more mathematical ability than Kelly, Shannan or Shawn (subtraction) but you cannot state that Scott has twice as much mathematical ability as Shannan (division).

RATIO LEVEL OF MEASUREMENT

Definition: *Ratio Level of Measurement:* Numbers assigned to objects or events which can be categorized, ordered, assumed to have equal intervals between scale points and have a real (nonarbitrary) zero point.

Synonym: *Ratio Scale.*

Related Definition: *Nonarbitrary Zero Point:* A zero point which is not set arbitrarily but is a real part of the numbering system indicating absence of the variable being measured.

Synonyms: *Absolute Zero. Real Zero. Meaningful Zero. True Zero.*

Comment: It is only at the ratio level of measurement that proportional statements, that something is twice as much or three fourths smaller, can be made. Permissible operations include addition, subtraction, multiplication and division. Statistical procedures appropriate for nominal, ordinal, interval or ratio data are permissible.

At the ratio level of measurement numbers are assigned to objects or events which can be categorized, ordered, assumed to have equal intervals and where the zero point is real and means absence of the variable.

Because of the real zero point, ratio level measurement has the additional characteristic of interpretation using proportional statements (or what is sometimes called the ratio factor). Thus, ratio scales offer the most information of any of the levels of measurement and are the highest level of measurement.

Examples

The number of cases of cola purchased per week is a ratio level variable because the zero is meaningful and indicates that no cola was purchased (absence of the variable). Because of the real zero point, it can be stated that store A purchased 10 times more cases of cola than store B and that store C purchased half as much as store D.

Business research probably includes more ratio level variables than any of the other social science research fields. Income, sales, profits and number of employees are all ratio level variables. Typical questions with responses at the ratio level of measurement are:

What was your gross income last year?
How many employees were retrained in 1985?
What was the price/earnings ratio?
What is the equity/debt ratio?

CHANGING LEVELS OF MEASUREMENT

How information is gathered often affects the level of measurement. For example, income is considered a ratio variable because it has a real zero point, but it is often changed to an ordinal variable by the way responses to questions are worded.

A. Example of Ratio Level Question

What was your income last year? _____

B. Example of Changing Ratio Level to Ordinal Level

In which category was your income last year?

☐1. Above $50,000
☐2. $30,000 to $50,000
☐3. Below $30,000

Because a ratio level of measurement was changed to ordinal, only statistical procedures for ordinal or nominal data may be used.

Recommendation: Examine the instruments you plan to use in the research process to see if you have changed variables which are normally at the higher levels of measurement to lower levels. Decide if you wish to change these to obtain a higher level of measurement in order to use more precise statistical procedures.

Recommended References: Stevens [60]. Coombs [19].

VALIDITY AND RELIABILITY

Prior to using any measure the validity and reliability of that measure should be assessed to estimate its accuracy and consistency. If the researcher is using existing instruments, there should be a pamphlet indicating the validity and reliability estimates based on several studies. If the researcher has designed the instrument, validity and reliability estimates should be generated prior to use.

Definition: *Validity:* Accuracy of measurement. The degree to which an instrument measures that which is supposed to be measured.

Purpose: To ascertain to what degree the measure is accurate for a specific purpose.

Related Definition: *Validity Coefficient:* An estimate of the validity of a measure in the form of a correlation coefficient.

Definition: *Reliability*: Consistency of measurement. The degree to which an instrument measures the same way each time it is used under the same conditions with the same subjects.

Purpose: To assess an instrument's ability to measure the same way in each administration to the same reliability sample.

Related Definition: *Reliability Coefficient*: An estimate of the reliability of a measure usually in the form of a correlation coefficient.

When examining an instrument for validity and reliability remember that three types of conditions may exist. An instrument might show evidence of being:

1. both valid and reliable or
2. reliable but not valid or
3. neither valid nor reliable.

Figure 5.1 depicts these three conditions with the typically used example of targets to illustrate the concepts.

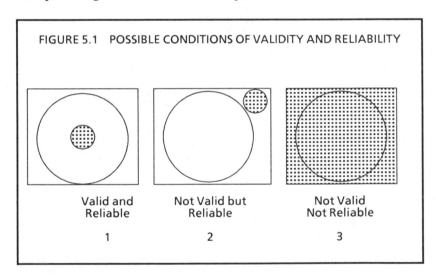

FIGURE 5.1   POSSIBLE CONDITIONS OF VALIDITY AND RELIABILITY

Valid and Reliable	Not Valid but Reliable	Not Valid Not Reliable
1	2	3

Note that in target number 1 the bullseye is hit both accurately (validity) and consistently (reliability). Target number 2 indicates high consistency in hits but the hits are inaccurate and miss the bullseye. In the third target the hits are neither accurate nor consistent.

Comment: Note that there is no fourth condition for a valid but not reliable measure. That is because an instrument which is valid will also have some degree of reliability [64].

EXHIBIT 5.2   INFORMATION ABOUT VALIDITY AND RELIABILITY

1. Validity is an extremely important, and perhaps the most important, aspect of a measure. If an instrument does not measure accurately what it is supposed to measure, there is no reason to use it, even if it does measure consistently.

2. Of validity and reliability, validity is far more important than reliability for the reason given in #1.

3. It is questionable practice to use measures for which: (1) there is no evidence of validity or (2) there is evidence of validity but the validity estimates are low.

4. Validity is specific. An instrument or measure can be valid for a specific criterion but not for other criteria, for a specific group of people but not other groups.

5. There are several types of validity and reliability estimates. Because of the confusion in using different names and meanings for the various types of estimates, standard labels and standard definitions for the various types of both validity and reliability estimates have been determined. These can be found in STANDARDS for EDUCATIONAL AND PSYCHOLOGICAL TESTS [3].

6. A single instrument may have several types of validity and reliability estimates.

7. Each type of validity and reliability estimate has a different purpose.

8. Validity and reliability are always estimated, not proven.

9. The statistical symbol for a validity coefficient is r_{xy} indicating correlation of two different measures. The statistical symbol for a reliability coefficient is r_{xx}, indicating two measures of the same variable.

10. A typical validity coefficient would be approximately .45 or higher. Higher would be better. However, validity coefficients rarely exceed .60 and many are in the range of .30 to .40 [21].

11. A typical reliability coefficient for a researcher designed instrument is approximately .70 or higher. For an instrument designed by a testing service one would expect a .90 or higher.

12. If the researcher designs an instrument, validity and reliability estimates should be made by the researcher. If an instrument is purchased, the company from which it is purchased should provide validity and reliability information which the researcher examines prior to purchase.

CAUTION: Validity and reliability are usually estimated by using correlation coefficients. These statistics estimate the degree of validity or reliability. Thus, it is not a question of an instrument having or not having validity or reliability; it is a question of to what degree is an instrument valid for a specific purpose and to what degree does the instrument evidence specific types of reliability.

There are several types of validity estimates, each with a different purpose. There are also several types of reliability estimates, each with a different purpose. The researcher needs to assess the research situation to determine which types of validity and reliability are appropriate for the specific research situation.

Comment: The terms internal and external validity are associated with experimental design and appear in Chapter 8. For an interesting discussion on validity see Cook and Campbell [18].

Recommended References: For acceptable definitions and interpretation of validity and reliability estimates see STANDARDS for EDUCATIONAL AND PSYCHOLOGICAL TESTS [3]. For additional information regarding validity and reliability see Cronbach [21].

VALIDITY ESTIMATES

The major types of validity estimates are: (1) content, (2) criterion related which includes both concurrent and predictive, and (3) construct. Each of these types of validity estimates serves a different purpose.

CONTENT VALIDITY

Definition: *Content Validity:* The representativeness of the content of the instrument to the objectives of using the instrument.

Purpose: To assess the degree to which the items or tasks used in a measure are a representative sample of all possible items or tasks which the variable being measured is supposed to include.

When assessing content validity, the major question is to what degree does the content of the instrument measure the objectives of the instrument. It is a logical process of comparing the frequency and types of items included in the instrument to the types and frequency of tasks or skills or other characteristics involved in the variable of interest. Usually more items are included to assess those skills which are considered crucial and those skills which are used frequently. Thus the number of items measuring each skill should also be representative of the variable.

It is especially important to assess the content validity of instruments which measure skills or achievement such as typing or mathematics preemployment tests.

EXHIBIT 5.3	PURPOSE AND PROCESS FOR VALIDITY ESTIMATES	
TYPE	PURPOSE	USUAL PROCESS
Content	Valid according to representativeness?	1. Examine objectives. 2. Compare objectives to content of instrument
Predictive*	Valid prediction of specific criterion?	1. Assess validation sample on predictor. 2. Assess validation sample on criterion at later time. 3. Correlate scores.
Concurrent*	Valid according to already validated measure of same variable?	1. Assess validation sample on new measure. 2. Assess validation sample on already validated measure of same variable at about same time. 3. Correlate scores.
Construct	Valid according to support of theory by assessment of various relationships to major variable?	1. Assess validation sample on major variable. 2. Assess validation sample on several hypothetically related variables. 3. Analyze to see if major variable differentiates Ss on the related variables.

*Predictive and concurrent validity are both also called Criterion-related validity

Example

The personnel department wished to assess the skills of applicants for secretarial positions. A list of tasks and skills required for the job was made and each task and skill was given a rating for criticality and frequency of occurrence.

EXHIBIT 5.4   THE PROCESS FOR ESTIMATING CONTENT VALIDITY

1. Examine the variables of interest and list the tasks or skills or other characteristics involved.

2. Add to the list the importance (criticality) and frequency of occurrence of each of the tasks or skills.

3. Reexamine the list and make sure that all skills or tasks which are crucial to the variable are included even if they occur infrequently. Add any which may have been omitted.

4. Compare each of the tasks or skills on the list to the items of the measure to ensure that each crucial and frequently occurring task or skill is measured by at least one item. Usually more items are included to assess those skills which are more important and those which occur frequently, an additional aspect of the representativeness of the measure to the variable being measured.

5. Examine each item of the measure to ensure that the difficulty level is appropriate for the variable being measured. For example, if algebra ability is being assessed, a series of items requiring calculus would indicate poor content validity. If the ability to follow simple directions is being assessed, items which require college level reading ability would indicate poor content validity.

NOTE: Content validity is rarely represented by a numerical figure because it is a logical process of comparing the components of a variable to items of a measure.

A search was made for an existing instrument which measured the tasks and skills required and several were found. Upon examination three of the instruments were discarded: one because it did not include items measuring numerical skills, a frequently occurring required skill; the second was discarded because it had too few items measuring typing skills which were both crucial and frequently occurring in the job; and the third was discarded because the items measuring vocabulary did not include a sufficient number of commonly used complex words. The fourth instrument examined was selected because it met the criteria of measuring the crucial and frequently occurring tasks and skills at the appropriate difficulty level for that job. In other words, the instrument included measures of the skills required for the job; they were representative measures of the job skills.

PREDICTIVE VALIDITY

Definition: *Predictive Validity*: The degree to which a measure predicts a second future measure.

Related Definition: *Predictor Variable*: The variable used to predict.

Related Definition: *Criterion Variable*: The variable which is predicted (or, in some situations, used as a standard).

Comment: A predictor variable predicts only one criterion variable at a time, illustrating the specific nature of validity. Thus, when an instrument supposedly has evidence of predictive validity you must check to see: (1) what variable it predicts, (2) what type of subjects were given the instrument for the validity assessment and (3) how well does it predict the criterion (how large is the validity coefficient). Often an instrument will predict more than one variable but for each of these criteria there will be a separate validity coefficient.

EXHIBIT 5.5   THE PROCESS FOR ESTIMATING PREDICTIVE VALIDITY

1. Gather scores on the predictor variable from a group of subjects (the validity sample) for whom the instrument is appropriate.

2. Gather scores on the criterion variable from the SAME sample AT A LATER TIME.

3. Compute a correlation coefficient between the two sets of scores. (See Chapter 13 for computation of correlation coefficients.)

Example

To aid with budgeting, a manager wanted to be able to predict the rate of employee retention. She felt that level of job satisfaction might be a good predictor of employee retention. She administered a job satisfaction questionnaire to employees and recorded their scores. Six months later she recorded the retention information for each employee and correlated the two sets of figures. The correlation coefficient was .59. She concluded that job satisfaction was a valid predictor of employee retention. She would gather job satisfaction information the following year and use it to help predict employee retention.

CONCURRENT VALIDITY

Definition: *Concurrent Validity*: The degree to which a measure correlates with another measure of the same variable which has already been validated.

Purpose: To demonstrate validity without going through the time and expense of assessing either predictive or construct validity.

EXHIBIT 5.6   THE PROCESS OF ESTIMATING CONCURRENT VALIDITY

1. Gather scores from the nonvalidated instrument administered to a validity sample.

2. Gather scores from a previously validated instrument which purports to measure the same variable and which is administered to THE SAME SAMPLE at APPROXIMATELY THE SAME TIME.

3. Compute a correlation coefficient between the two sets of scores.

Example

John Q. Smyth generated a new method of detecting rejects for the plastic parts his company produced which cost less than the current and already validated method in use. To test the validity of his method he used both his method and the current method on several batches of parts and recorded the number of correct decisions (parts which should have been rejected and were plus parts which should not have been rejected and were not). He then computed a correlation coefficient between the two sets of scores and obtained a value of .89. He had demonstrated that his method was correlated with the old method and thus could be said to have concurrent validity.

CONSTRUCT VALIDITY

Definition: *Construct Validity*: The degree to which a measure relates to expectations formed from theory for hypothetical constructs.

Purpose: To ascertain if the measure of the variable of interest (which is not directly observable) can be assumed to be an accepted measure.

Related Definition: *Hypothetical Construct*: A variable which is not directly observable but is inferred from other behaviors. Anxiety, self-concept and intelligence are hypothetical constructs because they cannot be observed directly but are inferred from other behaviors. Addition and subtraction ability, gross sales and net worth are observable variables.

Validity is assessed for hypothetical constructs by hypothesizing that if the theory is correct, certain behaviors should occur. Thus, construct validation usually includes several assessments of validity, using several of these expected behaviors as criteria. (Predictive and concurrent validity estimates usually involve only one criterion during the validity testing period.)

EXHIBIT 5.7   THE PROCESS OF ESTIMATING CONSTRUCT VALIDITY

1. Examine the theory associated with the variable of interest.

2. Select several behaviors which the theory indicates would differentiate subjects with differing amounts of the variable. For example, self-concept theory indicates that employees with high self-concept would achieve at a higher level, be promoted more often and be more open in interpersonal relationships than would low self-concept employees.

3. Administer the instrument measuring the variable of interest to the validity sample and record the scores.

4. Gather scores for the validity sample on each of the behaviors selected in step #2.

5. Analyze the data using appropriate statistical tests to ascertain if subjects scoring high on the major variable and those scoring low are statistically differentiated on each of the selected criterion variable.

6. Accept evidence of construct validity if each of the statistical tests indicates a significant difference or a significant relationship between high and low scorers on the major variable and the criterion variables. If even one of the hypothesized relationships is not supported statistically, then the instrument cannot be said to evidence construct validity.

7. Examine reasons if construct validity is not supported. Possible reasons include: (1) the theory is incorrect, (2) the instrument was not a valid measure of the variable of interest, or (3) there may have been errors in the administration of the instrument, scoring or analysis of the data.

Example

A microchip manufacturer notices that production errors have increased considerably. He feels that psychological aspects, and particularly anxiety of employees, are affecting production and tells the production manager to conduct a study exploring the relationship between anxiety and production.

The production manager searches for an existing instrument which measures anxiety and is appropriate for the employees but cannot find one so designs an instrument. Because anxiety is a hypothetical construct, construct validation of the new instrument is necessary.

The production manager examines anxiety theory and decides that employees with high anxiety scores should have more health insurance claims, more absenteeism and less attendance at company social functions than employees with low anxiety scores.

A group of employees is selected as a validity sample (these people will not be used in the later study). The new anxiety instrument is administered to them and data is collected on number of insurance claims, number of days absent and number of company social functions attended. Statistical analyses (using t tests) are conducted and in each of the 3 analyses significant differences were found between high and low scorers on the anxiety instrument. Thus, the production manager feels that the anxiety instrument has sufficient support for construct validity and sufficient support to be used in the study to follow.

RELIABILITY ESTIMATES

After determining the validity of an instrument, it is necessary to assess the reliability (consistency) of the instrument.

If you place a bag of sugar on a scale and it weighs 40# today, 40# tomorrow and 40# each day for the next year, you would consider the scale to be a reliable instrument. However, an instrument should be both valid and reliable. What if that same bag of sugar really weighed 50#?

A MEASURE CAN BE RELIABLE BUT TOTALLY LACK VALIDITY. This is why it is necessary to examine validity first. Unless the instrument has some degree of validity there is no point in using it. Interestingly, if a measure has statistical evidence of validity, it will also have some degree of statistical reliability. (See Thorndike and Hagen [64] if you desire additional information on this concept.)

There are several types of reliability estimates, each serving a different purpose. The major types are: (1) test-retest, (2) equivalent forms, (3) split-half, (4) Kuder-Richardson, (5) Coefficient Alpha and (6) interrater reliability.

TEST-RETEST RELIABILITY

Definition: *Test-Retest Reliability*: A reliability estimate, usually indicated by a correlation coefficient, computed from scores on an instrument administered at one time and scores on the same instrument administered at a later time to the same sample.

Purpose: To assess the stability (consistency) of the measure over a period of time.

EXHIBIT 5.8   THE PROCESS FOR ESTIMATING TEST-RETEST
                RELIABILITY

NOTE: One form and two administrations of the instrument are
required.

1. Administer the instrument to the reliability sample at Time 1.

2. Wait a period of time (e.g., 2-4 weeks).

3. Administer copies of the same instrument to the same sample at
   Time 2.

4. Correlate the scores from Time 1 and Time 2.

Comment: Test-retest reliability is particularly important for those variables which theoretically should remain stable over time, such as intelligence.

EQUIVALENT FORMS RELIABILITY

Definition: *Equivalent Forms Reliability*: A reliability estimate, usually indicated by a correlation, computed between scores from one form of an instrument and scores from a second form of the instrument administered to the same sample at approximately the same time.

Synonyms: *Alternate Forms* or *Parallel Forms Reliability*

Purpose: To estimate the equivalence of two different but equal forms of an instrument.

Comment: Equivalent forms reliability is necessary whenever two or more forms of a single instrument are used.

CAUTION: It is time consuming and expensive to generate equivalent forms of an instrument because they should: (1) measure the same content, and have (2) the same number of items, (3) approximately the same size mean (or other measure of central tendency) and (4) approximately the same size standard error and standard deviation. It requires a considerable amount of work to meet these specifications.

Sometimes equivalent forms and test-retest procedures are combined. In such a case the results estimate both the stability over time of the variable and the equivalence of the two forms.

EXHIBIT 5.9   SUMMARY OF TYPES AND PURPOSES OF RELIABILITY ESTIMATES

Type of Reliability Estimate	Used to Assess	Number of Forms	Number of Administrations	Usual Statistic
1. Test-Retest	Stability over time	1	2	Correlation
2. Equivalent Forms Parallel Forms Alternate Forms	Equivalence of Forms	2	2	Correlation
3. Split-Half	Equivalence of two halves	1	1	Correlation plus Spearman-Brown Prophecy Formula
4. Kuder-Richardson Formula 20	Internal Consistency When Responses are Dichotomous	1	1	KR Formula 20
5. Coefficient Alpha	Internal Consistency When Responses are not Dichotomous	1	1	Coefficient Alpha Formula

---

EXHIBIT 5.10   THE PROCESS FOR ESTIMATING EQUIVALENT FORMS
RELIABILITY

NOTE: Two forms and two administrations of the instrument are
required.

1. Administer Form A of the instrument to the reliability sample.

2. Break the sample for a short rest period (10-20 minutes).

3. Administer Form B of the instrument to the same reliability
sample.

4. Correlate the scores from Form A and Form B.

SPLIT-HALF RELIABILITY

Definition: *Split-Half Reliability*: A reliability estimate indicated by
a correlation of scores from one half of an instrument with scores from the
second half of the instrument.

Comment: Split-half reliability is often called internal consistency
reliability since it is one of several measures which estimate the internal
consistency of an instrument.

Purpose: To assess the equivalence of one half of an instrument to the
other half. Thus split half reliability estimates are very similar to
equivalent forms estimates, but require only one form and one
administration.

Comment: The split-half reliability process is less expensive and less
time consuming than the equivalent forms process because of one form and
one administration. However, the same care should be taken in generating
an instrument for which split-half reliability will be estimated as the care
taken in generating equivalent forms of an instrument.

KUDER-RICHARDSON RELIABILITY

Definition: *Kuder-Richardson Reliability*: A reliability estimate
computed by using one of several formulas which measure the internal
consistency of an instrument which is administered one time.

Purpose: To assess the degree to which the individual items of an
instrument measure the same variable (homogeneity of items or internal
consistency).

There are several Kuder-Richardson formulas. The most commonly
used one is called KR-20 which is equivalent to computing the average of
all possible split-half reliability coefficients. The KR-20 is used when
there are only two possible responses to each item (e.g., correct, incorrect).

EXHIBIT 5.11   THE PROCESS FOR ESTIMATING SPLIT-HALF
                RELIABILITY

NOTE: One form and one administration of the instrument are
required.

1. Obtain or generate an instrument in which the two halves were
   formulated to measure the same variable.

2. Administer the instruments to the reliability sample.

3. Correlate the summed scores from the first half (often the odd
   numbered items) with the summed scores from the second half
   (often the even numbered items).

4. Compute the Spearman-Brown prophecy formula* to correct for
   splitting one instrument into halves.

$$*Spearman-Brown\ Prophecy\ formula:\quad r\ corrected = \frac{n(r_{xx})}{1 + (n-1)r_{xx}}$$

where: r_{xx} = uncorrected reliability

         n = number of splits (for two halves, $n = 2$)

A second formula called KR-21 is often used because of the faster
computations. It underestimates KR-20 slightly and is also used with two
response items [43].

COEFFICIENT ALPHA

Definition: *Coefficient Alpha:* A reliability estimate similar to the
Kuder-Richardson Formula 20 for items which are not scored
dichotomously.

Comment: Because instruments such as rating scales are widely used
in business research, Coefficient Alpha is frequently used to estimate
reliability.

The formulas KR-20 and KR-21 for dichotomous responses were derived
by Kuder and Richardson in 1937 [43]. In 1951 Cronbach derived the more
general formula, Coefficient Alpha, for use with nondichotomous responses
[20]. The formula for Coefficient Alpha is identical to that of the KR 20

EXHIBIT 5.12   THE PROCESS FOR COMPUTING KR-20 RELIABILITY ESTIMATES

NOTE: One form and one administration of the instrument is required.

1. Generate or select an instrument.

2. Administer the instrument to the reliability sample.

3. Compute the variance ($\sigma_x{}^2$) of the scores.

4. Compute the proportion of correct responses to each item.

5. Compute the proportion of incorrect responses to each item.

6. Compute the KR-20 formula.*

$$*r_{KR20} = \left(\frac{k}{k-1} \right)\left(1 - \frac{\Sigma pq}{\sigma_x{}^2} \right)$$

Where: k   = number of items

$\sigma_x{}^2$ = variance of total scores

p   = proportion of correct (passing) responses

q   = proportion of wrong (not passing) responses or 1-p

except that the sum of the individual item variances ($\Sigma \sigma_i{}^2$) is substituted for the Σ_{pq} [71]. A computer is usually used for these computations.

INTERRATER RELIABILITY

The types of reliability discussed previously have all been concerned with assessing the consistency of measurement of instruments. Interrater reliability is concerned with the consistency of people in the way they observe or rate objects or events.

Definition: *Interrater Reliability:* The degree to which two or more judges (raters) rate the same variables in the same way.

Purpose: To assess the consistency of agreement when there are two or more raters judging the same variables independently of each other.

Comment: It is very important to have an assessment of interrater reliability for any research project in which two or more raters will be observing or rating the same variables.

EXHIBIT 5.13   THE PROCESS OF ESTIMATING INTERRATER
RELIABILITY

1. Select or generate an instrument.

2. Randomly select a number of objects or events to be rated.

3. Train the raters.

4. Have rater #1 judge each object or event independently.

5. Have rater #2 judge each object or event independently.

6. Correlate the scores of the two raters.*

*Other statistical techniques may be used if there are more than two raters. The statistical technique also depends on the level of measurement of the rating instrument used. See Chapter 13 to determine the appropriate measure of association for a specific instrument.

WHERE YOU ARE NOW

At this point you should have:

1. Determined the level of measurement for each variable,

2. Decided if the level of measurement could and should be changed to a higher level,

and recognized that:

3. The level of measurement determines the statistical techniques,

4. Evidence of validity is extremely important before you use an instrument,

5. Evidence of instrument reliability is also important,

6. There are several types of validities and reliabilities, each with its own purpose,

7. It is the researcher's responsibility to ascertain that the instruments used evidence validity and reliability. If the researcher designs an instrument, the researcher provides this information.

6

REVIEW THE RELATED INFORMATION

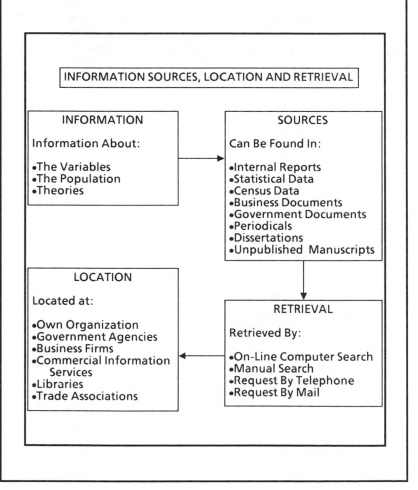

INFORMATION SOURCES, LOCATION AND RETRIEVAL

INFORMATION

Information About:

- The Variables
- The Population
- Theories

SOURCES

Can Be Found In:

- Internal Reports
- Statistical Data
- Census Data
- Business Documents
- Government Documents
- Periodicals
- Dissertations
- Unpublished Manuscripts

LOCATION

Located at:

- Own Organization
- Government Agencies
- Business Firms
- Commercial Information Services
- Libraries
- Trade Associations

RETRIEVAL

Retrieved By:

- On-Line Computer Search
- Manual Search
- Request By Telephone
- Request By Mail

TERMS DEFINED IN CHAPTER SIX

CHAPTER SIX

REVIEW THE RELATED INFORMATION

STEPS TO TAKE AFTER READING THIS CHAPTER

1. List the information needed concerning the variables of interest and their relationship.

2. List the possible sources and locations of the information.

3. Search for and retrieve the related information.

4. Review, record and synthesize the information found.

5. Determine how the information supports or contradicts the hypotheses or research questions.

6. Make a decision about the next step.

   6.1   Revise the hypotheses or research questions, if necessary, to construct the FINAL hypotheses or research questions, or

   6.2   Change the direction of the research or

   6.3   Abandon the research project if there is sufficient evidence on the variables and their relationship in the literature.

After the variables are determined, the relationship between them posited and either a preliminary hypothesis or preliminary research question stated, a review of information related to the hypothesis or research question is conducted.

Definition: *Review of Related Information*: Systematic examination of general information, research studies, data and theories which have been discovered over the years related to the variables of interest and the relationships among them.

Synonym: *Review of the Literature*

Purpose: To determine what knowledge and data pertinent to the variables and their relationship exist, in order to generate appropriate hypotheses and research questions. To determine if the hypotheses or research questions have already been examined sufficiently to warrant a decision not to continue with the study of the same variables and same relationship. To examine any theories applied to or developed from previous research and to assess any controversies relating to the variables and their relationships.

Comment: This is called review of related information to emphasize it may well include information from the organization which is sponsoring the research, business firms, government agencies, commercial information services or trade associations.

LIST THE VARIABLES, POPULATION AND THEORIES

In this era there are massive amounts of information available about a great variety of topics. While some of this information will be pertinent to your project, a large amount of information will not be directly related to your project. The problem is how to determine which, of all this information, is useful for your specific research. It is helpful to begin with a list of the variables and the population you have selected to study and any theories you think might help in generating hypotheses or explaining relationships between variables.

Comment: This focuses the review of related information on areas of direct interest so you will not have to examine materials which are not related to the research topic.

The variables and population are listed so that they can be used in the search of related literature. For example, if you hypothesized that single men in the western United States would purchase more housing then single men in the east, the list might include the descriptors: single men, unmarried men; purchasing behaviors, purchasing behaviors of unmarried men, purchasing behaviors by geographical regions, and housing patterns and sales.

General theories are useful for explaining why one variable might be related to another. Assume that an advertising manager wishes to examine the relationship between amount of advertising and sales of the product. He feels that the actor used in the advertisements may not appeal to all consumers, but does not have any concrete evidence to back up this feeling. Theories are useful in a situation like this.

For example, there are several theories under the name of "balance theories." In general, balance theories posit that given an unbalanced internal state, people will take actions or change attitudes to bring internal states into balance. Applied to the advertising situation, the theories would suggest that if consumers liked the product but did not like the actor advertising the product, one of their actions might be to stop purchasing the product.

Now the advertising manager can use these theories as a rationale for conducting a study on consumers' product purchases and their feelings about the actor. Another way the theories might be used is to conduct a study on consumer purchases and the amount of advertising using different actors.

EXHIBIT 6.1   THE PROCESS FOR REVIEWING RELATED INFORMATION

1. Examine the preliminary hypotheses or research questions.

2. List the variables contained in the hypotheses or research questions to use as key words (descriptors) in the review.

3. Add the type of population to be used in the study (e.g., food stores) and types of theories which might account for the posited relationship between the variables to the list.

4. Determine the most appropriate sources of the desired information, such as government documents or internal reports.

5. Determine the location of the information.

6. Determine the best way to retrieve the information.

   6.1   Search the organization's files to determine if similar studies have been conducted previously which might be useful.

   6.2   Conduct a library search, hopefully via on-line computer, of the key words you have listed to generate specific literature to examine.

   6.3   Contact business firms, trade associations or government agencies, if necessary.

7. Retrieve and examine the materials.

8. Write on index cards the information gathered from each source, as you read it. This information should include title, author, publisher, date of publication, volume number, page numbers, information about the study and the findings.

9. Review and synthesize all the index cards to assess the support or nonsupport for the hypotheses or research questions.

10. Make a decision about the next step.

   10.1   Abandon the research project if the same study has been examined the same way and the evidence supports the findings or

   10.2   Change the direction (variables and their relationship) if the review of the literature so indicates or

   10.3   Retain the original hypothesis or research question.

There are many theories in the social (and physical) sciences which are useful for hypothesizing and explaining relationships in research. If exploration of the theories is desirable for the research project, go to a library and use the descriptors listed (e.g., role theory, change theory). If you do not know where to start, try the descriptors "social science theories" or "physical science theories."

Recommended References: Selltiz, Wrightsman and Cook [56]. Kerlinger [37].

Organization Files

If the research being conducted is specific to an organization, the first place to search for related information is within the organization. Millions of dollars have been spent conducting research which has already been done but the reports were filed away and forgotten. The same research project might have been conducted 5 years ago and perhaps it would be more useful to use the same variables and methodology to assess progress.

There are many reasons to make a thorough search of the organization's files for related information, including the procurement of existing sales and cost reports, rather than attempting to gather this data. Unfortunately, too many researchers ignore these vital sources of information: internal reports and records of the organization itself.

DETERMINE SOURCES OF THE DESIRED INFORMATION

Although there are millions of sources of information, they can be categorized into general and specific types of information. Exhibit 6.2 indicates general categories of information useful for research.

EXHIBIT 6.2   GENERAL CATEGORIES OF SOURCES USEFUL FOR RESEARCH

1. Internal organization reports and records.

2. Statistical data.

3. Census data.

4. Business documents.

5. Government documents.

6. Periodicals and journals.

7. Dissertations.

8. Unpublished manuscripts.

Comment: The literature can also be categorized as: (1) research literature in which the actual conduct and findings of research are reported and (2) nonresearch literature which includes opinions, theories and statistical information.

The most useful sources for acquiring information quickly are abstracting and indexing services, particularly if computer searches are available. Examples of specific sources are given in Exhibit 6.3.

EXHIBIT 6.3   EXAMPLES OF SPECIFIC SOURCES FOR RESEARCH

1. Business Periodicals Index

2. Psychological Abstracts

3. Sociological Abstracts

4. Social Sciences Index

5. Government Reports Annual Index

6. Applied Science and Technology Index

7. Dissertation Abstracts International

8. Bibliographic Index

9. Statistical Abstract of the United States

10. Census of Population

11. Census of Housing

12. Census of Manufactures

13. Federal Reserve Bulletin

14. Business Conditions Digest

15. Survey of Current Business

DETERMINE THE LOCATION OF THE INFORMATION

The sources of information which you select can be located in a variety of places. Most of the sources useful for research are found in the locations listed in Exhibit 6.4.

It should be noted that several of these locations have access to the same sources. For example, commercial information services and libraries

EXHIBIT 6.4   LOCATION OF SOURCES USEFUL IN RESEARCH

1. Your own organization.

2. Government agencies.

3. Business firms.

4. Commercial information services.

5. Libraries at universities.

6. Public libraries.

7. Trade associations.

usually contain sources from government agencies, business firms and trade associations.

Commercial information services are particularly useful because of the wide variety of information available and their ease of access via on-line computers. These information services are available in libraries or can be purchased by your own firm.

DETERMINE HOW TO RETRIEVE THE INFORMATION

Once the sources and the location of the desired information is determined it is necessary to decide the most cost-efficient method of retrieving it. You will be using on-line computers or manual methods, and sometimes both, to retrieve the information.

THE ELECTRONIC LIBRARY -- AVAILABLE ALMOST ANYWHERE

Retrieval of massive amounts of information is no longer confined to libraries. With on-line computer facilities and many databases widely available, most large organizations, some smaller organizations and even individuals have access to a great amount of information. Any organization or person with a computer and the appropriate equipment can subscribe to an ever increasing number of information services, just as libraries do.

Definition: *Database*:   A collection of information assembled in computer accessible form.

Databases are produced by both public and private organizations. These databases might be distributed by a number of on-line computer services. The number of database producers and distributors is increasing very rapidly. The number of databases offered by a single distributor is also increasing. For example, Dialog Information Services has available over 200 databases with over 100 million records [23].

EXHIBIT 6.5 EXAMPLES OF DATABASES USEFUL FOR RESEARCH

DATABASE	CONTAINS	NUMBER OF RECORDS EXCEEDS	UPDATED	VENDOR
ABI/INFORM ®	Information relevant to Business from over 500 Publications in Business and related fields.	250,000	Weekly	Data Courier, Inc. Louisville, KY
BLS: (1) Consumer Price Index (2) Employment, Hours, and Earnings (3) Producer Price Index	Time Series of Consumer Price Indexes, Employment, Hours of Work and Earnings Data, and Producer Price Indexes	1. 10,000 2. 29,000 3. 6,000	Monthly	Bureau of Labor Statistics U.S. Dept. of Labor, Washington, D.C.
Economics Abstracts International	Economic Data and Research from World's Literature	154,000	Monthly	Netherlands Foreign Trade Agency, The Hague, Netherlands
Economic Literature Index	Index of Journal Articles and Book Reviews from over 200 Economics Journals. Some Abstracts	103,000	Quarterly	American Economic Association Pittsburgh, PA
Moody's Corporate News - U.S.	Financial Data and Business Information on Publically-Held U.S. Corporations	96,000	Weekly	Moody's Investors Service, Inc. New York, NY
NTIS	Technological and Business Information from Government Sponsored Research, Development and Engineering	1,000,000	Biweekly	National Technical Information Service, U.S. Dept. of Commerce, Springfield, VA

EXHIBIT 6.5 (cont.)   EXAMPLES OF DATABASES USEFUL FOR RESEARCH

DATABASE	CONTAINS	NUMBER OF RECORDS EXCEEDS	UPDATED	VENDOR
PsycINFO	Information from over 1300 Sources in Psychology and Related Fields	473,000	Monthly	American Psychological Association, Washington, DC
PTS: (1) International Forecasts (2) International Time Series (3) U.S. Forecasts (4) U.S. Time Series	Economic Forecasts for all Countries of the World. Time Series for 50 Major Countries	1. 517,000 2. 126,000 3. 342,000 4. 47,000	1. Monthly 2. Quarterly 3. Quarterly 4. Quarterly	Predicasts, Inc. Cleveland, OH
Social Scisearch ®	Multidisciplinary Information from 1,500 World Social Science Journals and 3,000 other Journals	1,430,000	Monthly	Institute for Scientific Information, Philadelphia, PA
Sociological Abstracts	Information from World's Literature in Sociology and Related Fields	148,000	3 times per year	Sociological Abstracts, Inc. San Diego, CA
Standard and Poor's News	Up-to-Date Financial Information and News on more than 10,000 Publically owned U.S. companies	364,000	Daily	Standard and Poor's Corporation New York, NY
Standards and Specifications	Government and Industry Standards, Specifications and Related Information	100,000	Monthly	National Standards Association, Inc. Bethesda, MD

Source: *DIALOG Database Catalog.* Dialog Information Services, Inc., 1985.

Examples of databases and their producers are given in Exhibit 6.5. Examples of database distributors are given in Exhibit 6.6. Remember there are hundreds of others not included in the lists.

EXHIBIT 6.6   EXAMPLES OF INFORMATION SERVICES WITH
                DATABASES USEFUL FOR RESEARCH

INFORMATION SERVICE	PROVIDES
DIALOG Information Service	More than 200 databases with over 100 million records. Much of this useful for business.
Bibliographic Retrieval Services (BRS)	Coverage of business and other social science topics included.
Reader's Digest (THE SOURCE)	Coverage of stocks and bonds, news, employment. One of the first services accessible to individuals as well as organizations
Dow Jones News Retrieval (DJNR)	Wide variety of financial information and news.

ON-LINE AND MANUAL SEARCHING AND RETRIEVAL OF INFORMATION

It is almost always more cost effective to use on-line computer searching and retrieval of information because it is so much faster than manual searching. In addition, a more thorough search is usually possible with the number of databases available.

Recommendation: Begin with an on-line search using the descriptors from your list of variables. This is particularly useful if you feel you don't know where to start.

Computer searches are conducted by inputting key words (descriptors) into an appropriately programmed computer. The program then searches out specific literature and prints out various information such as titles and abstracts of articles and publications in which these key words appear. Manuals are available to help you with the various on-line searches.

If you do not have access to computer facilities in your organization, usually the next place to try is a library.

Libraries today are much changed from former years because of the addition of new technology which makes the search task much easier. Two of the most useful facilities are on-line computer searches of databases and microfiche readers.

If the library has on-line computer facilities, by all means use them. If not, you may have to conduct a manual search and are likely to be using microfiche readers.

Microfiche is a small piece of material on which print is reduced to a very small size. The researcher searches a directory of the information desired and obtains a microfiche from the librarian. The microfiche is then inserted in a special microfiche reader which enlarges the print so it can be read.

A different aspect of a manual search is contacting business, government or other agencies for information which has not yet appeared in a publication or database. These contacts can be made by phone or mail. In all cases, give information on why you desire this unpublished material, ask if the information is confidential and, if you wish to quote it, obtain permission in writing.

CONDUCT THE REVIEW OF INFORMATION AVAILABLE

Usually, the quickest way to acquire some immediate information is to have a computer search conducted, and then locate the articles for reading. However if this is not practical begin by referring to the abstracts noted above. In particular, the Bibliographic Index is useful because it includes references to publications which include bibliographies on specific subjects.

Periodicals are usually good sources for research information and the Business Periodicals Index is a useful index. Books are good sources for theoretical information but journals and periodicals are better for accessing the most recent research studies. However, the most up-to-date information is found in newspapers, news magazines or on-line databases which are updated daily.

Comment: Note that while research studies are reported in journals and periodicals, many of the articles in these publications report opinions of the authors rather than research studies.

Remember you are looking for information related to the variables of interest, the population being studied or the theoretical basis for predicting the relationship. Thus the search should be limited to these concerns unless your review leads into a different direction.

How do you know when you have reviewed sufficient information? Generally the most recent information is reviewed first. Most of these articles will be accompanied by a bibliography which will aim the review at other related information. If the authors have completed adequate reviews of the literature, there will be a wealth of information available for you to review. Eventually, all the pertinent articles noted will be covered.

READ THE LITERATURE

After the appropriate publications are located you will be faced with the somewhat arduous task of reading the articles. Critique the material as you read it, particularly the research literature. Did the researcher use appropriate sampling, design and other methods? Are the findings supported by the data? You need to make some judgment on the quality of the research since poor research adds little to knowledge. Also judge the pertinency of the research to what you wish to do. You will soon discover that not all the reviewed research is "good," nor is all of it pertinent to your project, nor will all of it be significant.

RECORD THE INFORMATION

While reviewing the literature, record the pertinent information in some systematic fashion. It is common to use 5x8 index cards. It is important to include an assessment of the study's quality because many studies lack adequate research methodology. Exhibit 6.7 indicates the type of information which should be recorded.

EXHIBIT 6.7   INFORMATION TO RECORD WHILE READING THE
               LITERATURE

1. Author's name.

2. Title of article.

3. Publisher's name.

4. City and state or country in which published.

5. Year of publication.

6. If article appears in a periodical, also include the name of the periodical, the volume number, the page numbers and the month and year of publication.

7. Variables used in the study.

8. The hypotheses or research questions.

9. The type of subjects used.

10. The type of research design used.

11. The findings and conclusions.

12. Your rating of the quality of the study.

Recommendation: For some information you may wish to purchase the entire article or set of data.

SYNTHESIZE THE INFORMATION AND
DETERMINE THE NEXT STEPS

When a thorough review of related information is completed, the recorded information is reviewed to acquire an overall picture of what has been done and found in the area.

A synthesis of the information reviewed requires that the researcher examine the information and compare it. This is particularly so when a synthesis of the information is being written as part of a report. As Dyer [24] notes, similarities and differences in the studies must be pointed out.

After synthesizing the information reviewed, the researcher makes a decision to: (1) abandon the project, or (2) change the direction of the research by selecting different variables or a different relationship between the current variables or (3) retain the preliminary hypothesis or research questions.

ABANDONING THE PROJECT

It is not uncommon for the researcher to abandon a specific research project after reviewing related information. One of the major purposes of the review is to discover what has been found in the area in order to modify or abandon the project. IF THERE IS SUFFICIENT EVIDENCE IN THE LITERATURE TO SUPPORT THE HYPOTHESIS, DO NOT HESITATE TO ABANDON THE PROJECT.

CHANGING DIRECTIONS OF THE PROJECT

Often after the review researchers will find themselves saying something like "I don't really want to study variables A and B but variables X and Y instead," thus changing the direction of the research. Again, this is one of the purposes of the review of related information.

Another decision which might be made is to change the hypothesized relationship between variables. For example, prior to the review two researchers had stated a preliminary hypothesis that television advertisements would contain more information than magazine advertisements. After the review of literature the researchers altered that relationship and their final hypothesis was that magazine advertisements would contain more information than television advertisements. This illustrates the power of conducting a review of related information.

RETAINING THE PRELIMINARY HYPOTHESIS OR RESEARCH QUESTION

The synthesis of the literature may well lead you to retain your preliminary hypotheses or research questions. If this is so, the preliminary hypotheses or research questions become the ones you will use in your project.

WHERE YOU ARE NOW

After a thorough review of related information you should have:

1. Records (perhaps on index cards) of studies, theories and other information related to the variables of interest and their relationship.

2. A written synthesis of this information.

3. A decision to abandon the project, or change or retain the preliminary hypotheses or research questions.

4. If the project is not abandoned, a FINAL hypothesis or research question which is either the same as the preliminary one or has been changed.

5. Additional knowledge and understanding of the various research methodologies; a byproduct of reviewing the literature which will help you in your own project.

7

DETERMINE THE SAMPLING METHOD AND PROCEDURES

TERMS DEFINED IN CHAPTER SEVEN

CHAPTER SEVEN

DETERMINE THE SAMPLING METHOD AND PROCEDURES

STEPS TO TAKE AFTER READING THIS CHAPTER

1. Define the population to be used in the study.

2. Determine the sampling unit.

3. Determine the sampling frame.

4. Determine the appropriate sampling method for the study.

5. Determine the size of the sample.

6. List the procedures to be used in the sampling plan.

7. Review the selected sampling method for later use.

Most research projects are conducted with samples rather than populations because it is usually too expensive and impractical to use populations. Occasionally a population is used if it includes small numbers of Ss and it is feasible to do so. If a population is used, then sampling from that population does not occur unless the researcher wishes to compare some subgroups of that population.

Definition: *Sampling*: The process of selecting subgroups from a population of elements such as people, objects or events.

Purpose: To avoid the time and cost of using all the elements in a population. To avoid using up all the elements in the population -- if Kelloggs tested the shelf life of every package of cereal they produced they wouldn't have any left to sell!

Related Definition: *Population*: All members of a defined category of elements such as people, events or objects. All Walmart stores in the United States could comprise a population while selected Walmart stores might be a sample from that population.

Related Definition: *Sample*: A portion of a larger category of elements called the population.

Related Definition: *Parameter*: A population characteristic or value such as a mean, variance, proportion, etc. For example, average gross sales might be the population characteristic of interest.

Related Definition: *Statistic*: A numerical index of a characteristic (e.g., mean, variance, etc.) computed from sample data, usually to estimate the corresponding population characteristic. For example, average gross sales of the population might be estimated by using gross sales figures from a sample of Walmart stores. Also used to indicate results of a statistical test (e.g., a t test, chi square test, etc.) with phrases such as the "test statistic" or the "chi square statistic."

DEFINE THE POPULATION

The population is defined in terms which specify exactly the limits of the elements, objects or people to be studied. For example, a population defined as "all net worth statements on file with the First National Bank on April 15, 1990" would yield much different net worth statements than "all net worth statements filed with the First National Bank from April 15, 1985 through April 14, 1990."

When defining the population you are specifying what is and what is not included. A population defined as "managers who have been employed by the company for a minimum of three years on Dec. 31st" would eliminate all managers who completed 3 years on Jan. 1st. The definition "annual gross sales for military use between 1978 and 1988" would eliminate nonmilitary sales, but would include foreign military sales since there is no mention of country of sales.

DETERMINE THE SAMPLING UNIT

Definition: *Sampling Unit*: The element or object to be sampled or a larger unit containing the objects.

In many research projects the sampling unit is the object itself. For example, in studying opinions of comptrollers, a list of comptrollers could be obtained and a sample selected directly from the list and the comptroller would be the sampling unit. If this were not feasible, a listing of organizations containing comptrollers would be obtained and the organizations would be selected as the sample and the organization becomes the sampling unit.

CAUTION: In selecting larger units which contain the object of interest the size of the sample needs to be increased as the appropriate statistical analyses would include the large unit as a single subject regardless of the number of objects of interest within the larger unit.

DETERMINE THE SAMPLING FRAME

Definition: *Sampling Frame*: A list or other representation of the elements in a population from which the sample is selected.

The elements in a population must be represented in some way. Lists, such as membership names, are often used. Other examples include completed application forms, organization directories, city and county directories or maps, and telephone directories.

CAUTION: To lessen the amount of error involved it is important that the sampling frame be accurate, include all members of the defined population and exclude nonmembers of the population.

DETERMINE THE SAMPLING METHOD

In order to determine the most appropriate sampling method, a clear understanding of two concepts, randomness and probability, is necessary.

Definition: *Random events*: Events whose individual outcomes cannot be predicted because they occur by chance. However, given a sufficiently large number of these events, the outcomes for a random sample can be predicted for the aggregate with a high degree of accuracy because they tend to occur with the same probability as they do in the population.

With random events, including random numbers, there is no regularity or system. Thus, they are unpredictable -- at least on an individual basis. However, given a random sample and a large number of elements, the outcomes can be predicted for the aggregate [37, p. 71]. For example, if a sample of 100 were drawn from a population of 1,000, 500 of whom were males and 500 females, whether a single draw will yield a female or male cannot be predicted. Yet it can be predicted, with very high accuracy, that there will be 50 females and 50 males in the sample.

The idea of randomness is important in research because random selection of elements is an unbiased (no systematic errors) sampling method which is most likely to yield a representative sample, just as the 50 males and 50 females would be representative of the above sample.

HAVING A REPRESENTATIVE SAMPLE IS THE MOST DESIRED GOAL IN SAMPLING. With nonrandom sampling methods a sample may or may not be representative but with random methods the probability is high that the sample will represent the population.

A representative sample is usually more important than size of the sample. There have been some classic prediction errors made when using very large samples which were not representative (e.g., the 1936 Literary Digest's prediction that Alfred Landon would win the presidency over Franklin D. Roosevelt).

Comment: Random sampling methods are unbiased METHODS. The resulting sample is not necessarily unbiased, especially with a small sample size. However, the probability of the sample being unbiased is very high, given a sufficiently large sample. A sufficiently large sample size depends on a number of variables which are explained in the section "Determine the Sample Size."

Definition: *Probability Sampling*: Sampling in which the probability of each element in the population being selected is known and can be specified, and each element has a chance of being selected.

There is little certainty in research. Instead results are usually couched in probabilistic terms. The probability of tossing a coin and having heads is .50. The probability of a researcher being wrong in the inferences might be .05. In sampling it is very helpful to use probability sampling because not only is the probability of each element known, it is also the only type of sampling which can yield estimates of differences between the sample and the population.

TYPES OF SAMPLING METHODS

There are several types of sampling methods. These can be categorized into two major types: random and nonrandom. In determining which method to use for your study it is important to remember that IN ORDER TO DRAW ACCURATE INFERENCES FROM THE SAMPLE ABOUT CHARACTERISTICS OF THE POPULATION THE SAMPLE MUST BE REPRESENTATIVE OF THAT POPULATION. The best chance for a sample to be representative is to use random methods.

Simple random sampling and stratified random sampling are the two most basic and strong forms of sampling because of their advantages and the consequent strength of the inferences. Kerlinger [37, p. 152] notes that of the several ways to draw samples "the only one that gives reasonable and general assurance of being representative is some form of random sample."

The most commonly used sampling methods are listed in Exhibit 7.1.

EXHIBIT 7.1   EXAMPLES OF COMMONLY USED SAMPLING
                METHODS

RANDOM METHODS

1. Simple random sampling.

2. Stratified proportional sampling.

3. Stratified constant sampling.

NONRANDOM METHODS

1. Systematic sampling.

2. Convenience sampling.

3. Purposive sampling.

4. Quota sampling.

EXHIBIT 7.2 SELECTING THE SAMPLING METHOD

SELECTED SAMPLING METHODS	BIAS FREE METHOD*	MAJOR ADVANTAGE	MAJOR DISADVANTAGE
RANDOM METHODS: Simple Random	Yes	High Probability of Sample Representing Population	Requires Sizeable Number of Ss
Stratified Random	Yes	Controls for Stratification Variables	Often More Time and Cost Than for SRS
NONRANDOM METHODS: Systematic	No	Cheaper, Easier and Faster with Large Population	Potentially Biased Method
Convenience	No	Quicker and Cheaper than other Methods	Potentially Biased Method
Purposive	No	Ss Possess Characteristics desired by Researchers	Potentially Biased Method
Quota	No	Sample is Proportional to Population in the Selected Characteristics	Potentially Biased Method

*Since the most desired goal of sampling is to have a sample which is representative of the population, which can only be expected with unbiased methods, only random methods can be highly recommended. If other methods must be used sometimes, remember that the generalizations to a population are questionable.

Recommendation: A sampling method is not necessarily a "good" method because it is commonly used. Review the explanations, advantages and disadvantages of each method before selecting the one which is appropriate for your specific research project.

RANDOM SAMPLING METHODS

SIMPLE RANDOM SAMPLING

Definition: *Simple random sampling*: A probability sampling method in which each element in the population has an EQUAL, known and nonzero chance of being selected.

Abbreviation: *SRS*

Purpose: To yield a sample which has a high probability of being representative of the population from which it was drawn.

EXHIBIT 7.3   THE PROCESS FOR RANDOM SAMPLING

1. Define the population (e.g., all retail stores in three contiguous counties)

2. Determine the method for selecting the random numbers.

    2.1   Random numbers table, found in statistics books.
    2.2   Computer generated random numbers.
    2.3   Objects drawn from a hat, bowl or other container, as is done in lotteries.

3. Assign consecutive numbers to each member of the population.

4. Select the appropriate number for the sample using the method chosen in step 2.

5. Use each number only once.

6. Oversample numbers. It is often useful to draw more numbers than specified for the sample. If some Ss cannot be located or refuse to participate in the study, the sampling process will not have to be repeated.

Advantages: The sampling method is bias free, thus the sample has a high probability of being representative of the population. The random nature of the sampling is expected to control for all variables. For example, two groups randomly selected from the same population would be expected to have approximately the same average of physical, psychological, social and demographic characteristics.

Disadvantages: Requires a sizeable number of elements to attain representativeness.

Rating: Excellent.

The easiest way to obtain random numbers is to use a computer to generate them. Computer software usually includes a program for random number generation and you simply follow the directions in the computer reference manual.

Drawing numbers from a container is time consuming since you have to number a piece of paper (or other object) for each member of the population. This is not recommended unless you have a small sample.

For those people who do not have computer facilities available, instructions on use of a random numbers table are given in Exhibit 7.4. Random numbers tables can be found in statistics books which most researchers have and in the Appendices of this book.

EXHIBIT 7.4   HOW TO USE A RANDOM NUMBERS TABLE

1. Determine in which direction to proceed in the random numbers table. Horizontally or vertically? To the left or to the right? Where to start after the completion of one line? These can all be specified by giving positions such as "lower left to upper right."

2. Determine the starting point. One method is to close your eyes and place a finger somewhere on the page.

3. Read the numbers using the number of digits required by the largest number in the population. If the population consists of 1,000 members, all numbers used must be four digits (e.g., 0019), if the population consists of 80 members, use two digit numbers (e.g., 19).

4. Use each number only once.

5. Oversample numbers. It is often useful to draw more numbers than specified for the sample. If some Ss cannot be located or refuse to participate in the study, the sampling process will not have to be repeated.

STRATIFIED RANDOM SAMPLING

Definition: *Stratified Random Sampling*: A probability sampling method in which elements are randomly selected from EACH designated subpopulation (stratum) of a population. The strata are determined according to differing types or amounts of a variable which the researcher decides may be associated with the major variable. For example, a population of food stores may be divided into strata on the basis of size:

large, medium and small, and a sample randomly selected from each of these strata.

EXHIBIT 7.5   THE PROCESS FOR STRATIFIED RANDOM SAMPLING

1. Determine the type of stratified random sampling.

    1.1   *Proportional*. The number in the sample is determined by selecting from each stratum in a predetermined proportion to the size of that stratum in the population, thus representing the real world situation.

    1.2   *Constant*. The same number of elements is selected from each stratum regardless of the size of the stratum in the population. This is sometimes used to assure that a small stratum is represented in the study. However, if constant stratified sampling is used, the sample may not be representative of the population which would reduce the generalizability of the results.

2. Determine the stratification variable (e.g., brand name).

3. Determine the number and type of strata (e.g, three brands: Del Monte, Green Giant and Van Camp's).

4. Number consecutively the elements in the population FOR EACH STRATUM.

5. Randomly select the appropriate number of elements from each stratum using a random numbers table, computer generated random numbers or objects placed in a container.

Purpose: To incorporate all the advantages of random sampling plus increase the precision of the analysis because of the homogeneous groupings (subgrouping results in reducing the variance within each subgroup while maximizing the variance between groups).

Advantages: Controls for variables which are possible sources of influence on the major variable. For example, in a study examining the relationship of cost of advertising and gross sales the variable "type of advertising" might make a difference. To control for this factor the population of advertisements is stratified into 3 types: T.V., magazine and radio, and a sample is randomly drawn from each of these 3 strata. This process controls for the variable "type of advertising." The incorporation of strata also increases the precision of the analysis.

Disadvantages: It is often more time consuming and consequently usually more costly than SRS because information on the stratification variable is needed for each element in the population. For example, if stratifying on age, the age of each person in the population would need to be available before stratification could take place.

Rating: Excellent. It ensures a bias free sampling method plus controls for the variables used for stratification.

EXHIBIT 7.6   EXAMPLE OF PROPORTIONAL STRATIFIED RANDOM SAMPLING

There are 1,000 advertisements in the population. The researcher decides to use proportional stratified random sampling and a sample of 300 with stratification of the type of ad. Of the 1,000 ads in the population, 50% are T.V. ads, 30% magazine and 20% are radio ads. The researcher numbers the T.V. ads from 001 to 500, the magazine ads from 001 to 300 and the radio ads from 001 to 200. To maintain the same proportions in the sample as in the population, 150 T.V. ads, 90 magazine ads and 60 radio ads are randomly selected as illustrated below.

TYPE OF AD	POPULATION		SAMPLE	
	N	%	n	%
Television	500	50	150	50
Magazine	300	30	90	30
Radio	200	20	60	20
	1,000	100%	300	100%

HELPFUL STRATEGIES

Small Strata. In proportional sampling the sample size may need to be increased if one of the strata is a small proportion of the population. For example, if a population of 1,000 advertisements included 60% TV ads, 39% magazine ads and 1% radio ads and a sample of 300 was originally selected, only 3 radio ads would be included in the research. To increase the number of radio ads and maintain proportionality in the sample, a larger sample could be drawn. Another alternative for small strata is to omit the stratum, radio ads, from the research. This would change the definition of the population to TV and magazine ads.

It may not be desirable for the purpose of a specific research project to omit a stratum. If a study on characteristics of Chief Executive Officers (CEO's) used annual earnings as a stratification variable, the stratum "over $1,000,000" might be small but may be important to the research because characteristics of CEO's with earnings over $1,000,000 may be very different from those of CEO's who earn less.

Number of Strata. Keep the number of strata small. Because stratification is a useful and efficient technique some researchers attempt to use several variables for stratification. It usually becomes impractical beyond stratifying on one or two variables. If the stratification variable "cost of ad" with four strata were added to the variable "type of ad" with three strata, 3x4 = 12 subgroups would be needed. If a third stratification variable "season of the year" with 4 seasons were added, 48 (12x4) subgroups would be needed!

NONRANDOM SAMPLING METHODS

The following nonrandom sampling methods are discussed because they are so widely used. They are all given a rating of "poor" because their nonrandom nature leads to a high probability of creating a biased sample; one that is not representative of the population. There is little doubt that random sampling methods could be used more frequently. Usually, but not always, random methods are more time consuming and costly. If a random method is at all feasible, it is far preferable and may be worth the additional cost and time in order to make stronger inferences. Remember that a nonrandom sample is a potentially biased method which can easily yield nonrepresentative samples.

If a random sampling procedure is simply not feasible then examine several sample characteristics (demographic, social, etc.) which are related to the major variable to see if the sample characteristics are similar to the population characteristics.

Generally, the more critical the research the more likely it is to incorporate either random sampling or random assignment to groups.

Comment: It should be noted that organizations which specialize in survey research usually use very sophisticated sampling techniques which sometimes incorporate nonrandom sampling methods. However, the people involved are experts in sampling and use a variety of control techniques to enhance the probability of drawing representative samples. For more information on sampling see the recommended references.

Recommended References: Kish [40], Chein [13], Cochran [16].

SYSTEMATIC SAMPLING

Definition: *Systematic Sampling:* A nonrandom sampling method in which every nth element is chosen from a list of numbered elements. Thus, every element does NOT have a chance of being drawn once the starting point is selected. The start is often chosen randomly and sometimes changed several times during the selection process to improve the chances of representativeness, especially in ordered lists. In practice a systematic sample is often treated like a simple random sample and is usually referenced as a probability sampling method if there is a random start.

Advantages: Easier, faster and less expensive to carry out, particularly with a large population (all residences in the New York telephone book) than is simple random sampling.

Disadvantages: A potentially biased sampling method. Bias and consequent misleading conclusions are particularly likely if lists are ordered (e.g., from large incomes to small incomes) or periodicity exists (e.g., sampling one day of seven days). Remember, if selecting every 10th name in a list, once the start is selected every 10th name has a 100% probability of being selected and the nine names in between have zero probability of being selected.

Rating: Poor unless random starts are used and careful attention is given to overcoming the possible nonrepresentativeness resulting from ordered or periodic lists.

Recommendation: Shuffle ordered or periodic lists. Use random starts.

CONVENIENCE SAMPLING

Definition: *Convenience Sampling*: A nonrandom sampling method in which the researcher uses some convenient group or individuals as the sample.

Synonyms: *Grab Sampling, Accidental Sampling, Incidental Sampling, Haphazard Sampling, Chunk Sampling.*

Advantages: Easy access to a sample. Usually quicker and cheaper than other methods.

Disadvantages: Nonrandom, potentially biased method. Often the population has not been defined and results cannot be generalized to a nondefined population.

Rating: Very poor. It is not defensible to use a convenience sample except possibly for exploratory research.

PURPOSIVE SAMPLING

Definition: *Purposive Sampling*: A nonrandom sampling method in which the sample is arbitrarily selected because characteristics which they possess are deemed important for the research. For example, purposely selecting certain Ford managers because they have 10 years of managerial experience. In contrast, in simple random sampling the population would be defined as "Ford managers with 10 years of managerial experience" and the managers would be randomly selected from the defined population. Judgment (expert choice) sampling, when Ss are judged by experts to be appropriate for a study, is also usually considered purposive sampling.

Advantages: Ss possess the characteristics desired by the researcher.

Disadvantages: It is a nonrandom, potentially biased method which can lead to large sampling errors [40].

Rating: Poor compared with random sampling. Purposive sampling is usually used only when random sampling is not feasible.

Recommendation: The researcher can achieve the advantages of purposive sampling by defining the population as Ss who possess the characteristics and then randomly sampling from that population. For example, a population is defined as "all corporations headquartered in New York which have more than 9,000 employees and are listed on the New York Stock Exchange." Then a sample of such corporations would be randomly selected from the list. Thus a random sampling method is used instead of a nonrandom method and the desired characteristics are still represented.

QUOTA SAMPLING

Definition: *Quota Sampling*: A nonrandom sampling method in which elements of the sample are selected until the same proportion of selected characteristics which exists in the population is reached. For example, a population of clients includes 65% females, 35% males; 30% over 65 years old and 70% 65 and younger; and the sample would include these same proportions. While this appears similar to proportional stratified random sampling they are NOT the same because the Ss are not randomly selected from each stratum in quota sampling. Quota sampling is also usually considered purposive sampling.

Advantages: The sample is proportional to the population in selected characteristics.

Disadvantages: A nonrandom, potentially biased sampling method which can lead to large sampling errors.

Rating: Poor compared with random sampling. Quota sampling is usually used only when random sampling is not feasible.

Recommendation: In place of Quota sampling, see if it is feasible to use proportional stratified random sampling.

CLUSTER SAMPLING

Cluster sampling appropriately carried out is a random sampling procedure. However many researchers use a nonrandom procedure which they call cluster sampling. The difference between the two approaches is that with random sampling the clusters are selected randomly from a population of such clusters and the CLUSTER itself, not the individual elements within the cluster, is considered the sampling unit and the unit of analysis.

Definition: *Cluster Sampling*: A sampling method in which the sampling unit is a GROUP of population elements rather than a single element. Often sampling is carried out in two (or more) stages. In the first stage the clusters are sampled; in the following stages the elements are sampled. Sometimes all the elements in each cluster are used.

Advantages: It is usually cheaper and faster, particularly in sampling over large geographical areas. Often city blocks are used as the sampling unit and interviews are conducted at specified dwellings.

Disadvantages: Can lead to biased samples if carried out carelessly. Cluster sampling of 20 blocks from 200 blocks with food stores within the blocks used for interviews could miss certain types of stores which might appear on blocks which were omitted. Sampling error is usually greater, thus requiring a larger sample size than simple random sampling to reduce error.

CAUTION: Clusters are usually NOT random. For example, people of the same social class tend to live in certain housing areas by choice, not randomly. Managers are selected for promotions because they are qualified, not by some random process. Because of the nonrandom processes which create most clusters, a larger sample size is usually needed for cluster sampling to achieve the same level of precision as in simple random sampling.

Recommendation: Select more small size clusters rather than fewer large size clusters since "a number of clusters of small size are likely to produce more precise estimates than fewer clusters of a larger size" [24, p. 98].

CONCEPTS RELATED TO SAMPLE SIZE

All sorts of hints are heard when discussing sample size. Some are good and some are not. An extremely large sample size is not necessary for representativeness -- in fact, many major predictions based on samples of millions have been drastically wrong because the samples, while large, were not representative. However, given all other equal factors, a large sample randomly drawn will have less sampling error than a smaller sample. Many authors suggest a minimum sample size of 30 for each group, based on the distribution approaching a normal distribution with a size of 30. Some researchers decide to use a 10% or 5% sample of the population based on no rationale at all.

Factors which usually determine sample size are: (1) cost, (2) how much confidence in the results is desired, (3) how much error can be tolerated and (4) information about the population. Costs of sampling are real and can affect the choice of sampling method. The other three factors require more explanation.

POINT AND INTERVAL ESTIMATION

Two types of estimates, called point estimates and interval estimates, are used in estimating population characteristics from a sample.

Definition: *Point Estimate*: A sample statistic such as a mean or proportion used to estimate the corresponding population parameter. Point estimates estimate a single population value.

If a random sample of 50 receipts is selected from a population of 600 receipts, the best estimate of the population average (mean) amount is the mean of the 50 in the sample. This is a point estimate used to estimate the exact mean if the total population of 600 had been used. However, if 5 different samples of 50 receipts were drawn and the means of each computed, they would probably differ: e.g., $10.56, $11.02, $9.95, $10.04, $11.52. If the population mean is $10.91, each of these sample means would differ from the population mean. This difference between a sample mean and the population mean is termed sampling error.

Definition: *Sampling Error:* The difference between the parameter value and the sample estimate of the parameter value which occurs when sampling from a population.

Because point estimates are rarely exact, interval estimates are often used to establish confidence intervals within which the exact population parameter is expected to be.

Definition: *Confidence Interval:* A range of values which have a specified probability of including the parameter estimated and are computed from values gathered from a sample of the population.

Definition: *Confidence Limits:* The upper and lower boundaries of the confidence interval.

Definition: *Confidence Level:* The specified probability that the confidence interval will include the true value of the parameter estimated. In interval estimation this is often specified when using the term "confidence interval," e.g., "the 95% confidence interval."

In order to compute a confidence interval the researcher must decide what the level of confidence should be. The most commonly used confidence levels are the 95% and the 99% levels which represent the percent of the area under the normal curve. For computational purposes the confidence level chosen is expressed in the form of z scores which, in sampling, represent the standard error of the sampling distribution. Selected z scores and the corresponding area under the normal curve are given in Exhibit 7.7. The Table of the Normal Distribution in the Appendices may also be used.

EXHIBIT 7.7 COMMONLY USED CONFIDENCE LEVELS:	
% of Area Under the Normal Curve	No. of Standard Errors (z)
99%	2.58
95%	1.96
90%	1.65
68%	1.00

Definition: *Standard Error:* The standard deviation of a sampling distribution which is computed for sample statistics such as a mean or proportion. It is based on the concept that the sampling errors of a series of samples from the same population will form a normal distribution. A standard deviation of this distribution of errors (standard error) could then be computed. However, instead of using many samples, this standard deviation of errors (or standard error) is usually estimated by using data from a single sample with the appropriate formula.

Symbol: Standard errors are usually indicated by the symbol σ or s with an appropriate subscript. See following formulae.

Abbreviation: *SE*

Formula:

$$\text{Standard Error of a Mean: } \sigma\bar{x} = \frac{\sigma}{\sqrt{n}}$$

where $\sigma\bar{x}$ = *standard error of a mean,* n = *sample size,*

σ = *population standard deviation*

Formula:

$$\text{Standard Error of a Proportion: } \sigma p = \sqrt{\frac{pq}{n}}$$

where σp = *standard error of a proportion,* n = *sample size,*

p = *proportion of incidences in the population,* $q = 1\text{-}p.$

Comment: If the population values in these formulae are unknown, they are estimated by using the sample values: e.g., the population standard deviation (σ) is estimated by using s, the sample standard deviation.

DETERMINE THE SAMPLE SIZE

In order to determine sample size for simple random sampling the researcher must specify: (1) the level of confidence required, (2) the amount of error which can be tolerated, and (3) values or estimates of population characteristics such as the standard deviation or proportion. If the population characteristic is unknown, a sample is taken to provide an estimate.

EXHIBIT 7.8   THE PROCESS OF ESTIMATING CONFIDENCE INTERVALS FOR
               MEANS

FORMULAE: (a) if population s.d. known (b) if population s.d. unknown

$$(a)\ \sigma \bar{x} = \frac{\sigma}{\sqrt{n}} \qquad (b)\ s\bar{x} = \frac{s}{\sqrt{n-1}}$$

where $\sigma \bar{x}$ = *standard error of the mean,* n = *sample size,*

σ = *population standard deviation,* s = *sample standard deviation*

1. Compute the mean and standard deviation of the sample.

2. Compute the standard error of the mean using formula a or b.

3. Specify the desired confidence level.

4. Look up the z score for the selected confidence level in Exhibit 7.7.

5. Multiply the z score by the computed standard error.

6. Add the result in step 5 to the sample mean to compute the upper limit of the confidence interval.

7. Subtract the result in step 5 from the sample mean to compute the lower limit of the confidence interval.

8. Conclude that the population mean is within the specified limits with the probability (confidence) specified in step 3.

EXHIBIT 7.9   EXAMPLE OF ESTIMATING A CONFIDENCE INTERVAL FOR A MEAN

1. n = 64 receipts, $\bar{x}$ (mean) = \$4.20, s = \$2.05, σ unknown.

2.

$$s\bar{x} = \frac{2.05}{\sqrt{63}} = \frac{2.05}{7.937} = \$.2582$$

3. Confidence level = 95%

4. Tabled z = 1.96 standard errors for 95% confidence level.

5. (1.96) (\$.2582) = \$.5060

6. \$4.20 + \$.51 = \$4.71.

7. \$4.20 - \$.51 = \$3.69.

8. Conclude: There is a 95% probability that the population mean lies between \$3.69 and \$4.71.

EXHIBIT 7.10   PROCESS FOR ESTIMATING SAMPLE SIZE WHEN
                 MEANS ARE INVOLVED

FORMULAE*: (a) if population s.d. known   (b) if population s.d.
unknown

$$(a) \quad n = \frac{z^2 \sigma^2}{e^2} \qquad (b) \quad n = \frac{z^2 s^2}{e^2}$$

Where: z = no. of standard errors for specified confidence level
         n = sample size,
         e = tolerable error specified by the researcher
         σ = population standard deviation
         s = sample standard deviation

         * Assumes infinite population. If using finite population
         use:

$$n = \frac{\sigma^2}{\dfrac{e^2}{z^2} + \dfrac{\sigma^2}{N}}$$

where   N = size of the finite population.

1. Compute standard deviation of sample if population's unknown

2. Determine the level of confidence required.

3. Look up the z score for the specified confidence level in
    Exhibit 7.7.

4. Determine the amount of error which can be tolerated.

5. Compute formula a or b to determine sample size.

EXHIBIT 7.11   EXAMPLE OF ESTIMATING SAMPLE SIZE WHEN
                MEANS ARE INVOLVED

1. $57.80 = the standard deviation, s, of a sample of receipts, the
   population standard deviation is unknown.

2. 90% = specified confidence level.

3. 1.65 = z.

4. $20 = specified tolerable error.

5.

$$n = \frac{(1.65)^2 \, (57.80)^2}{20^2} = \frac{9095.44}{400} = 23 \; receipts \; needed \; in \; the \; sample$$

If error thought to be too large and changed to $10, n =   91

If confidence level too low and changed to 95%,   n =   32

If error still too large and changed to $5,   n =   364

If confidence level changed to 95% and error to $5, n =   513

If confidence level changed to 95%, error to $0.10,   n = 1,282,883

Note how selecting different confidence levels and tolerable errors
changes the estimated sample sizes. You pay for more confidence
and less error by increased sample size.

EXHIBIT 7.12   PROCESS FOR ESTIMATING SAMPLE SIZE WHEN
                 PROPORTIONS ARE INVOLVED

FORMULA*: $n = (z/e)^2$ (p) (1-p)

where: z = no. of standard errors for a specified confidence level
           p = proportion of incidence of the variable in the population
           e = proportion of tolerable error

          * For infinite populations. For a finite population use:

$$n = \frac{(p)\,(1-p)}{\dfrac{e^2}{z^2} + \dfrac{p\,(1-p)}{N}}$$

where N = size of the population.

1. Determine the proportion of the variable in the population.

2. Determine the confidence level.

3. Look up the z score for the specified confidence level.

4. Determine the proportion of error which can be tolerated.

5. Compute the formula above to estimate sample size.

EXHIBIT 7.13   EXAMPLE OF ESTIMATING SAMPLE SIZE WHEN
                 PROPORTIONS ARE INVOLVED

1. 40% = proportion of males in the population

2. 95% = confidence level

3. 1.96 = z

4. .10 = proportion of tolerable error*

5.

$$n = \left(\frac{1.96}{.10}\right)^2 \left(.40\right)\left(.60\right) = 93$$

*   This means the researcher has decided tolerable error can be + or - .10.

LIST THE SAMPLING PROCEDURES

The final step in the planning process for sampling is to list all the planned sampling procedures including the unit, frame and method, how size of the sample was determined and procedures for carrying out the sample. This is particularly important for use when interviewers are involved. Each interviewer needs to use the same procedure which should be written down so they can follow the sampling plan. A brief example of procedures for interviewers is given in Exhibit 7.14.

EXHIBIT 7.14　　EXAMPLE OF INSTRUCTIONS TO INTERVIEWERS
　　　　　　　　　AFTER TRAINING

1. Review separate instructions for uncompleted interviews.

2. Go to location marked #1 on your map.

3. Turn right.

4. Begin interviewing at the dwelling marked on the map.

5. Continue interviewing at each dwelling marked on the map for that block.

6. Go to location #2 when interviews at block #1 are completed.

Written instructions to interviewers can be very complex, given a complex sampling situation. In such cases it is important that the interviewers are trained in the procedures as well as trained for conducting interviews.

Recommended References: Kish [40], Chein [13], Cochran [16].

WHERE YOU ARE NOW

At this point you should have:

1. Defined the population,

2. Determined the sampling unit and sampling frame,

3. Selected the sampling method,

4. Determined the sample size,

5. Listed procedures in the sampling plan

and recognized that:

6. Sampling is used to avoid the cost and time of using the population,

7. Characteristics of the sample are ESTIMATES of population characteristics,

8. Random sampling methods are unbiased methods,

9. The major goal in sampling is to have a sample which is representative of the population and

10. The appropriate sample size depends on several factors including (a) costs, (b) how much confidence in the results is desired, (c) how much error can be tolerated and (3) data about the population.

8

SELECT THE RESEARCH DESIGN

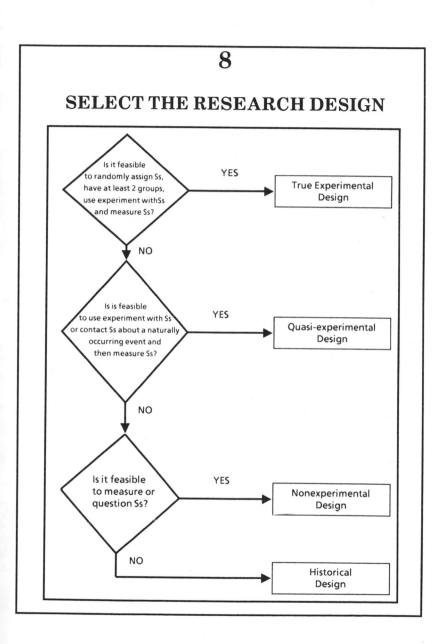

TERMS DEFINED IN CHAPTER EIGHT

CHAPTER EIGHT

SELECT THE RESEARCH DESIGN

STEPS TO TAKE AFTER READING THIS CHAPTER

1. Determine which type of design is appropriate for the research project.

2. Specify the different treatments, if using experimental or quasi-experimental design.

Definition: *Research Design*: A plan for conducting research which usually includes specification of the elements to be examined and the procedures to be used.

Purpose: To have the most appropriate and feasible methods for testing hypotheses or answering research questions.

SELECTING THE TYPE OF RESEARCH DESIGN

Research designs can be categorized into four types: (1) true experimental, (2) quasi-experimental, (3) nonexperimental and (4) historical. These four types of research designs differ in the amount of control the researcher has over the research situation.

CAUTION: Note that neither nonexperimental nor historical designs includes experiments but are distinguished by the ability (non-experimental) or inability (historical) to impose measures on Ss. Thus, historical designs require a separate category because they are unique in the total lack of control over the original research situation.

Comment: The concept of random assignment is important in understanding the different designs. Random assignment is different from random selection although both use random numbers.

Definition: *Random Assignment*: The assignment of subjects to different experimental or control groups, using random procedures, for the purpose of equating groups prior to conducting the experiment.

Purpose: To provide an unbiased method for placing Ss in groups so that there is a high probability of characteristics such as age, education, etc. being about the same for each group.

Recommendation: If you are randomly selecting Ss and randomly assigning them to groups, it can be done in the same process. Simply number each subject and generate the appropriate random numbers. As the numbers appear on the list assign each to a different group. For example, the first number drawn is 05; place subject number 05 in Group A. The second number drawn is 24; place subject number 24 in Group B. The third number drawn is 39; place subject number 39 in Group A and continue this process.

CAUTION: Random selection is not always necessary to conduct an experimental design but random assignment is necessary. For example, you wish to conduct an experiment using the 42 department heads in your own organization. Simply randomly assign 21 of them to the experimental group and 21 to a control group (or to a second experimental group).

The type of research design is selected on the basis of the type of information desired, the availability of resources, the degree of control the researcher has over the selection and assignment of subjects and the ability to manipulate the independent variable(s).

As illustrated in Exhibit 8.1 and at the front of this chapter, if the researcher is able to randomly assign subjects to at least two comparison groups and is free to manipulate the subjects in some way, a true experimental design is likely to be used. This affords the maximum control and, if the project is conducted properly, the researcher can talk about cause and effect.

If the researcher is free to manipulate the Ss (experiment) but perhaps is not able to randomly assign them, a quasi-experimental design is likely to be used. Sometimes the experiment is a naturally occurring event, such as a merger of two companies rather than a researcher manipulated experiment. Quasi-experimental designs afford less control than true experimental designs and thus the conclusions cannot be as strong as with true experimental designs.

With nonexperimental designs, the researcher only has control over the measurement of Ss and perhaps the time and place of the measuring process, but is unable to manipulate the subjects. This type of design has very little control and the conclusions reflect this lack of control. Often the conclusions are based on correlational procedures which reflect the association or relationship between or among variables but never that one variable causes another.

With historical designs, the researcher had absolutely no control over the data collection, the subjects or anything at all at the time the events took place. Often the researcher does not know if all the data have been found, if the existing data are accurate or if some data were deliberately destroyed or distorted. This total lack of control renders conclusions from historical research as tentative.

QUALITY AND SIGNIFICANCE QUESTIONS IN DESIGN SELECTION

No one type of research design is better or worse than any other. They are different and used for different purposes. If researchers are concerned about cause and effect, they will arrange to have true experimental designs, if possible. If a researcher is interested in what happened in 1892,

EXHIBIT 8.1   CHARACTERISTICS OF FOUR TYPES OF RESEARCH DESIGNS

TYPE OF RESEARCH DESIGN	SUBJECTS RANDOMLY ASSIGNED TO TREATMENTS	REQUIRES MINIMUM TWO COMPARISON GROUPS	MANIPULATE INDEPENDENT VARIABLE (EXPERIMENT)	IMPOSE MEASURE ON SUBJECTS	AMOUNT OF CONTROL
True Experimental	X	X	X	X	Maximum
Quasi-Experimental	?	?	X*	X	Less
Non-Experimental	-	-	-	X	Very Little
Historical	-	-	-	-	None

X = Possesses Characteristic
? = May or May Not Possess Characteristic
- = Does Not Possess Characteristic

*EXPERIMENT OFTEN OCCURS NATURALLY BUT MAY ALSO BE MANIPULATED BY RESEARCHER.

historical research must be conducted. This does not make historical research "worse" than experimental, but different from experimental. There have been good and bad studies in each of the four design categories just as there have been significant and not very significant research in each of the four categories.

EXPERIMENTAL DESIGN

Definition: *Experimental Design*: A specific plan for a research study which includes: (1) methods of selecting and assigning subjects and (2) number and types of treatment variables. Experimental designs must include at least two comparison groups with at least one group receiving a treatment (some amount of the independent variable.)

Purpose: To design an experimental situation with sufficient controls to conclude that the independent variable(s) cause the dependent variable.

Related Definition: *Treatment Variable*: The independent variable which is manipulated by the researcher so that different groups of subjects receive different kinds or amounts. For example, each of 3 groups of managers receives a different number of days of training.

Synonyms: *Experimental Variable. Manipulated Variable.*

Related Definition: *Treatment*: One type or amount of the independent variable. For example, 3 groups of managers receive either 1, 2 or 3 days of training. Each of these training periods is a treatment.

Synonyms: *Condition. Experimental Treatment.*

Related Definition: *Experimental Group*. A group of subjects which is administered some form of the experimental variable. There may be more than one experimental group in an experimental design, each receiving differing amounts or kinds of the treatment variable(s).

Related Definition: *Control Group*: A group of subjects which, usually through random assignment, is equated to -- and thus assumed comparable to -- the experimental group but which does NOT receive an experimental treatment. In experimental design a control group is not necessary unless the researcher is interested in a "no treatment condition" because a second (third, fourth, etc.) experimental group can serve as the comparison group instead of a control group.

In experimental design the variables are now termed independent and dependent, the presumed cause and the presumed effect.

CONTROL MECHANISIMS

Control is the keyword in experimental situations, as the researcher attempts to control as much as possible to rule out extraneous variables as an interfering cause of the dependent variable. Control can occur in several ways as illustrated in Exhibit 8.2.

EXHIBIT 8.2   CONTROL MECHANISMS FOR EXPERIMENTAL DESIGNS

For maximum control* the researcher must be able to:

1. Have a sufficient number of subjects available to form at least two comparison groups.

2. Randomly assign subjects to treatments.

3. Manipulate the independent variable (apply differing amounts of the treatment to the different groups).

*   Control can also be enhanced by the use of statistical techniques such as covariance or by blocking on other independent variables.

Comment: Note that the three points listed in Exhibit 8.2 are also characteristics of true experimental designs which are the most highly controlled designs.

In an experiment, the experimenter manipulates the independent variable and administers it to the Ss. True experimental designs always have at least two groups of Ss. The group which receives the independent variable is called the experimental group. Some designs have more than one experimental group, each receiving differing amounts or kinds of the treatment variable.

Often there is a control group, a group which is equated to the experimental group prior to the experiment. A control group does not receive the treatment variable. A control group is not necessary unless the researcher is interested in the effect of no treatment. Instead of a control group receiving none of the independent variable, there are often several experimental groups. The choice of including a control group or more experimental groups depends upon what information the researcher desires.

You can imagine how difficult it is to assure that two or more groups are equated. This is done by random assignment of Ss to the various groups. The power of random procedures to enhance the probability of groups being equal on all possible variables was demonstrated by Fisher [29] and has been illustrated many times over the years.

INTERNAL AND EXTERNAL VALIDITY OF EXPERIMENTAL DESIGNS

The validity of various designs can be affected by many factors. If these factors are not controlled then the researcher does not know if the experimental treatment accounted for the results or if some other factor caused the results. Also of concern is if the results of a specific experiment will generalize to (be the same for) populations, settings and treatment variables. Campbell and Stanley [12] have specified these factors and placed them into two categories, internal and external validity. These are given in Exhibit 8.3.

EXHIBIT 8.3   THREATS TO VALIDITY IN RESEARCH DESIGN
Internal Validity

	FACTOR*	EXPLANATION*	EXAMPLE	SUGGESTIONS FOR CONTROLLING FACTOR
1.	History	Events which occur between 1st and 2nd measurement.	Researcher collects gross sales data before and after a 5 day 50% off sale. During the sale a hurricane occurs and results of the study may be affected because of the hurricane, not the sale.	Use control group. Effects of events should be the same for both experimental and control group.
2.	Maturation	Ss changing because of time passing (tireder, hungrier, etc.).	Ss become tired after completing a training session and their responses on the Posttest are affected.	Use control group. Maturation should affect experimental and control group equally.
3.	Testing	Effects on scores of 2nd measure from taking a prior measure.	Ss take a Pretest and think about some of the items. On the Posttest they change to answers they feel are more acceptable. Experimental group learns from the pretest.	Avoid Pretests or use designs with unpretested groups. Use control group as testing effects should be the same for both experimental and control groups.
4.	Instrumentation	Changes in measurement because of changes in instruments or observers.	Interviewers are very careful with their first two or three interviews but on the 4th, 5th, 6th become fatigued and are less careful and make errors.	Do not allow interviewer or observer to know which Ss are in experimental and control groups. Randomly assign interviewers to Ss if possible.
5.	Statistical Regression	Occurs when groups are selected on extreme scores.	Managers who are performing poorly are selected for training. Their average Posttest scores will be higher than their Pretest scores because of statistical regression, even if no training were given.	Use random assignment. Assign Ss to experimental and control groups randomly from pool of Ss with extreme scores or include Ss with average performance in the pool and randomly assign to experimental and control groups.
6.	Selection	Differential selection of groups.	A group of Ss who have viewed a T.V. program is compared with a group which has not. There is no way of knowing that the groups would have been equivalent since they were not randomly assigned to view the T.V. program.	Use random assignment. Assures high probability of the experimental and control groups being equated on variables prior to the experiment.
7.	Experimental Mortality	Differential loss of Ss from comparison groups.	Over a 6 month experiment aimed to change accounting practices, 12 accountants drop out of the experimental group and none drop out of the control group. Not only is there differential loss in the two groups but the 12 dropouts may be very different from those who remained in the experimental group.	Examine the number who drop out of both experimental and control groups to assess differential loss. If experimental group mortality exists, attempt to follow up Ss who dropped out to assess differences between them and the remainder of the experimental group.

*Source: Campbell, D.T. and Stanley, J.C. *Experimental and Quasi-Experimental Designs for Research.* Rand McNally and Co., 1966.

EXHIBIT 8.3 (cont.)   THREATS TO VALIDITY IN RESEARCH DESIGN
External Validity

	FACTOR*	EXPLANATION*	EXAMPLE	SUGGESTIONS FOR CONTROLLING FACTOR
1.	Reactive or Interaction Effect of Testing	Pretest might increase or decrease Ss response or sensitivity to treatment.	Prior to viewing a film on Environmental Effects of Chemicals a group of Ss is given a 60 item antichemical test. Taking the Pretest may increase the effect of the film. The film may not be effective for a nonpretested group.	Use designs with unpretested groups.
2.	Interaction of Selection and Experimental Variable	May occur if there is bias in the selection procedures.	Researcher, requesting permission to conduct experiment, is turned down by 11 corporations but the 12th corporation grants permission. The 12th corporation is obviously different than the others because they accepted. Thus Ss in the 12th corporation may be more accepting or sensitive to the treatment.	Try to increase the representativeness of the sampling by reducing the number of Ss from one organization and increasing the number of organizations participating.
3.	Reactive Effects of Experimental Arrangements	Ss may react in some unknown way to conditions of the experiment.	Department heads realize they are being studied, try to guess what the experimenter wants and respond accordingly rather than respond to the treatment.	Avoid Pretests. Do not allow Ss and observers to know that an experiment is being conducted, for example, by using unobtrusive measures such as gross sales, net profit or absenteeism rate. Incorporate experiment into naturally occurring events such as regularly scheduled sales meetings, evaluation periods or training sessions.
4.	Multiple-Treatment Interference	There may be effects from prior treatments when the same Ss are given multiple treatments.	A group of CPA's is given training in working with managers followed by training in working with comptrollers. Since training effects cannot be deleted the first training will affect the second.	Avoid multiple treatments.

*Source: Campbell, D.T. and Stanley, J.C. Experimental and Quasi-Experimental Designs for Research. Rand McNally and Co., 1966.

EXHIBIT 8.4   SOURCES OF INVALIDITY FOR SELECTED RESEARCH DESIGNS*

SOURCES OF INVALIDITY

RESEARCH DESIGN	INTERNAL							EXTERNAL			
	History	Matura-tion	Testing	Instrumen-tation	Regres-sion	Selec-tion	Mor-tality	Interaction of Testing and X	Interaction of Selection and X	Reactive Arrange-ments	Multiple Treatment Inter-ference
TRUE EXPERIMENTAL											
1. Pretest-Posttest Control Group	+	+	+	+	+	+	+	-	?	?	
2. Posttest Only Control Group	+	+	+	+	+	+	+	+	?	?	
3. Solomon Four Group	+	+	+	+	+	+	+	+	?	?	
QUASI-EXPERIMENTAL											
1. Multiple Time-Series	+	+	+	+	+	+	+	-	-	?	
2. Time-Series	-	+	+	?	+	+	+	-	?	?	

Minus = Definite Weakness   ? = Possible Source of Concern
Plus = Factor is Controlled   Blank = Factor is not Relevant

*Source: Campbell, D.T. and Stanley, J.C. Experimental and Quasi-Experimental Designs for Research, Rand McNally and Co., 1966.

Definition: *Internal Validity*: The ability to conclude that the experimental (independent) variable did indeed create changes in the dependent variable. (In a measurement context internal validity refers to how well an instrument measures what it should measure.)

Definition: *External Validity*: The ability to generalize the results of the research to populations, settings, treatment variables and measurement variables; representativeness.

Both types of threats to validity are important and the ideal situation is to select designs which control for the threats to internal and external validity. However, internal validity is necessary for experimental design. Without internal validity the results of an experiment cannot be interpreted because the researcher does not know what caused the effects. The questions of generalizability, external validity, while "never completely answerable" [12, p.5] are enhanced with designs controlling for factors which affect external validity.

Experimental designs are considered ideal designs because they are so highly controlled that the researcher can rule out most threats to validity and consequently make stronger inferences about cause and effect. However, many experiments are conducted in laboratory settings rather than in the "real world" or natural settings.

For some studies the artificial nature of the settings and the lack of generalizability outside of the laboratory weakens the results. Note, however, that: (1) many research projects conducted in laboratory settings do yield results which generalize to natural settings and (2) true experimental designs can be carried out in natural settings more frequently than is the current practice.

The choice of using true experimental designs or other designs depends on many factors including: (1) the nature of the treatment variable, (2) the availability of Ss, (3) the ability to randomly assign Ss to treatments, (4) the ability to make observations and (5) the amount of resources available.

CAUTION: Some variables cannot be studied with experimental design because it would not be ethical. For example, it would not be ethical to require nonsmokers to smoke cigarettes.

TRUE EXPERIMENTAL DESIGNS

Three designs, called true experimental designs, are recommended as the best experimental designs to control threats to internal and external validity. All three designs control for all the threats to internal validity because of random assignment of Ss to more than one group and the presence of comparison groups.

Of the external validity threats to these three designs: (1) multiple treatment interference is not relevant as there are not multiple treatments, (2) interaction of selection and treatment and reactive measurements are always possible in specific research situations and (3)

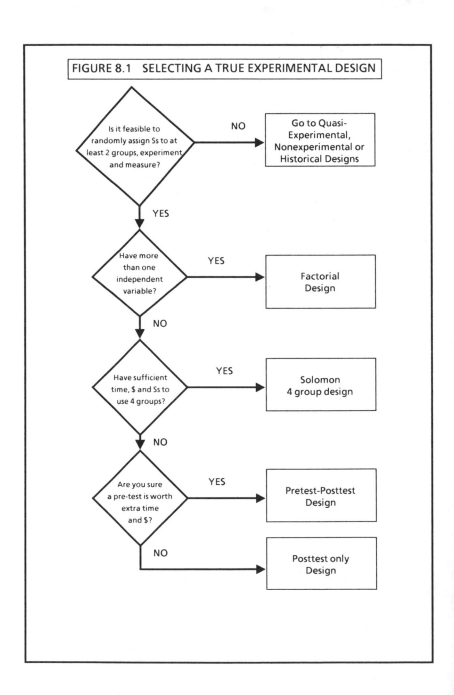

FIGURE 8.1   SELECTING A TRUE EXPERIMENTAL DESIGN

Is it feasible to randomly assign Ss to at least 2 groups, experiment and measure? — NO → Go to Quasi-Experimental, Nonexperimental or Historical Designs

YES

Have more than one independent variable? — YES → Factorial Design

NO

Have sufficient time, $ and Ss to use 4 groups? — YES → Solomon 4 group design

NO

Are you sure a pre-test is worth extra time and $? — YES → Pretest-Posttest Design

NO → Posttest only Design

EXHIBIT 8.5 TRUE EXPERIMENTAL DESIGNS

EXPERIMENTAL DESIGN	SYMBOLIC FORM	POSSIBLE THREATS TO EXTERNAL VALIDITY*	EXAMPLE
1. Pretest-Posttest Control Group	R O X O R O O	1. Interaction of testing & treatment. 2. Interaction of selection and treatment. 3. Reactive arrangements	1. 100 clerical workers are randomly assigned to either the control group (n = 50) or the experimental group (n = 50). Pretests on attitudes toward using computers are given to all Ss. Ss in the experimental group are trained to use computers and use them for four weeks. At the end of the four week period the attitude posttests are given to both experimental and control groups Ss and a comparison of attitude between the two groups is made using pretest and posttest information.
2. Posttest Only Control Group	R X O R O	1. Interaction of selection and treatment. 2. Reactive arrangements.	2. Same as design 1 except no pretest is given and comparison is based on the posttest only.
3. Solomon Four-Group**	R O X O R O O R X O R O	1. Interaction of selection and treatment. 2. Reactive arrangements.	3. Same as Design 1 and Design 2 combined. There will be 25 Ss in each of the four groups. Comparisons are made between pretested and unpretested groups and experimental and control groups.

Where: R = Random assignment to groups
        X = Experimental treatment
        O = Observation

*ALL THREATS TO INTERNAL VALIDITY ARE CONTROLLED
**Design 3 combines designs 1 and 2

interaction of testing and treatment is a threat only in one design, the pretest-posttest control group design.

Comment: Note that true experimental designs do not require a control group but do require at least one comparison group which may be a control group receiving none of the treatment or may be a second experimental group receiving a differing amount or type of the treatment.

In discussing experimental designs the symbols which Campbell and Stanley [12] initiated are used. R indicates random assignment of Ss to groups, X indicates a treatment and 0 indicates an observation (measurement). Examples are given in Exhibit 8.5 and each design is discussed separately.

Recommended References: Campbell and Stanley [12]. Churchman [14]. Rosenthal [54]. Festinger [28]. Blalock [8].

PRETEST-POSTTEST CONTROL GROUP DESIGN

Design: R O X O
          R O   O

Threats to Internal Validity: All are controlled.

Threats to External Validity: Interaction of testing and treatment; also possibly interaction of selection and treatment and reactive arrangements.

Disadvantages: Since interaction of testing and treatment is not controlled it is possible that the pretest could sensitize the experimental group to the treatment, thus confounding the experimental results.

Cost: More than the posttest only design because of the pretest.

Rating: Very Good

EXHIBIT 8.6 THE PROCESS FOR A PRETEST-POSTTEST DESIGN

1. Randomly assign Ss to two groups.

2. Administer a pretest to both groups.

3. Administer the treatment to the experimental group but not to the control group.

4. Administer the posttest to both groups.

POSTTEST ONLY CONTROL GROUP DESIGN

Design: R   X O
R   O

Threats to Internal Validity: All are controlled.

Threats to External Validity: It is always possible that interaction of selection and treatment and reactive arrangements could be threats.

Advantages: Controls for interaction of testing and treatment since there is no pretest. This is the same design as the pretest-posttest design with the pretest omitted. Despite the wide use of pretests it should be remembered that PRETESTS ARE NOT NECESSARY WHEN RANDOM ASSIGNMENT IS USED. The possible effects of pretests should be considered prior to their use.

Cost: Less than the pretest-posttest design because there is no pretest.

Rating: Excellent. This is a strong design and should be used more frequently than it is.

EXHIBIT 8.7 THE PROCESS FOR THE POSTTEST ONLY CONTROL GROUP DESIGN

1. Randomly assign Ss to two groups.

2. Administer the treatment to the experimental group but not to the control group.

3. Administer the posttest to both groups.

SOLOMON FOUR-GROUP DESIGN

Design: R O X O
R O   O
R   X O
R   O

Note that this design is a combination of the other two designs.

Threats to Internal Validity: All are controlled.

Threats to External Validity: Possible interaction of selection and treatment and reactive arrangements.

Advantages: This is the only one of the three designs where the researcher can actually MEASURE the interaction of testing and treatment by comparing the pretested experimental group's scores with the non-pretested experimental group's scores (the posttest only design controls for this by randomization but it cannot be measured).

Disadvantages: More costly and time consuming because of the requirement of four groups. However, the increased strength of the inferences and conclusions make it worth the added cost in some instances.

Cost: Highest cost of the 3 true experimental designs.

Rating: Excellent. Very strong design.

EXHIBIT 8.8   THE PROCESS FOR THE SOLOMON FOUR-GROUP DESIGN

1. Randomly assign Ss to the four groups.

2. Administer pretests to groups one and two.

3. Administer the treatment to groups one and three.

4. Administer posttests to all four groups.

EXTENSIONS OF THE TRUE EXPERIMENTAL DESIGNS

The true experimental designs can be extended by adding other groups, each with differing kinds or amounts of the treatment (levels of the treatment), resulting in a design with two or more conditions (levels) of the independent variable. For example, in a study of the nutritional effects of different types of milk, there could be four levels of the independent variable "type of milk": skim milk (X_S), 2% butterfat milk (X_2), homogenized milk (X_H) and buttermilk (X_B). A posttest only design would be symbolized as:

$$R \quad X_S \quad O$$
$$R \quad X_2 \quad O$$
$$R \quad X_H \quad O$$
$$R \quad X_B \quad O$$

A fifth condition of "no milk" could be added as a control group IF the researcher needs to compare effects of receiving no milk with receiving milk. However, as indicated by the design, it is not necessary to include a "no milk" condition unless it is of interest to the researcher.

Remember this design still has only ONE independent variable (type of milk) with 4 conditions or levels of the treatment.

FACTORIAL DESIGNS

Definition: *Factorial Design*: An extension of the true experimental designs which has more than one independent variable.

Purpose: To assess the effects of each of two or more independent variables on the dependent variable and to assess the interaction effects (joint influence) of the independent variables.

Related Definition: *Main Effect*: The effect of one independent variable on the dependent variable computed by averaging over all other independent variables. In a factorial design there is one main effect for each independent variable.

Related Definition: *Interaction Effect*: In designs with two or more independent variables, the effect created when different combinations of the independent variables result in differences in the dependent variable. For example, given an experiment with two independent variables, color of numbers (green or white) and shape of dials (round or square), accuracy of reading dial numbers (dependent variable) might be higher for round dials with green numbers and square dials with white numbers than for the other combinations (round, white and square, green).

Comment: Factorial designs are discussed in terms of the number of levels in each factor. Thus, a 2x2 factorial design will have two levels for each of two independent variables. A 4x6 design will have four levels of one independent variable and 6 levels of another independent variable. A 2x2x2 design will have three independent variables, each with two levels.

The number of groups of Ss required for each design can be computed by simply multiplying these numbers. A 2x2 design will require 4 groups of Ss, a 4x6 design, twenty-four groups and a 2x2x2, eight groups of Ss.

Rating: Excellent. One experiment yields information on the main effect of each of the independent variables on the dependent variable plus assessing any joint interaction effects -- that is, if different combinations of the independent variables yield differences in the dependent variable. A strong design.

EXHIBIT 8.9 THE PROCESS FOR FACTORIAL DESIGNS

1. Determine the number of levels of each independent variable.

2. Lay out the design so that each level of one independent variable is combined with each level of every other independent variable.

3. Randomly assign subjects to each condition created in step 2.

4. Administer the various treatments.

5. Administer posttests to all Ss*

6. Analyze for main effects and interaction effects.

* A pretest-posttest design may also be used.

EXAMPLE

A researcher wishes to study the effects of heat and size of integrated circuits on the performance of integrated circuit boards. Amount of heat has two levels: warm and very warm, size of circuits has three levels: large, medium and small. Because there may be an interaction between the levels of heat and size of circuits, a factorial design is used as follows:

EXHIBIT 8.10   PERFORMANCE OF CIRCUIT BOARDS UNDER DIFFERING CONDITIONS OF SIZE AND AMOUNT OF HEAT

Size of Circuits

	Small	Medium	Large	
Amt of Heat Warm	*Performance Scores of 15 Circuit Boards under small, warm conditions*	*Performance Scores of 15 Circuit Boards under medium size, warm conditions*	*Performance Scores of 15 Circuit Boards under large size, warm conditions*	**Main effect of**
Very Warm	*Performance Scores of 15 Circuit Boards under small, very warm conditions*	*Performance Scores of 15 Circuit Boards under medium size, very warm conditions*	*Performance Scores of 15 Circuit Boards under large size, very warm conditions*	**Amount of Heat**

Main Effect of Size of Circuits

A 3 x 2 Factorial Design

Note the amount of information this factorial design generates. There will be information about the main effect of the independent variable "size of circuit" on the dependent variable "performance of integrated circuit boards." There will be information about the main effect of the independent variable "amount of heat" on the dependent variable. Also the design allows examination of possible interaction effects -- e.g., is there a difference in performance of integrated circuit boards for the conditions of large circuits with warm heat, small circuits with warm heat, etc. for each of the 6 conditions.

QUASI-EXPERIMENTAL DESIGNS

For those situations in which full experimental control is not feasible, and consequently the better true experimental designs are not possible, there are a series of quasi-experimental designs listed by Campbell and Stanley [12] which control for some of the threats to validity. Two of the most frequently used ones are discussed here.

Comment: If an experiment is desired and the true experimental designs cannot be used, the researcher should incorporate as many control aspects as feasible.

Definition: *Quasi-experimental Design*: A research design which lacks the full control of a true experimental design. The treatment variable often occurs naturally but sometimes the researcher may be able to manipulate it. Observations take place but random assignment of Ss to treatments is usually not feasible. As much control as possible is attempted.

Example: A researcher learns that the XYZ Corporation will install a Management Information System in 6 months and designs a study to measure the flow of information before and after the MIS is installed. A control group from the STR Corporation which does not have MIS will be used as a comparison group.

MUTLIPLE TIME-SERIES DESIGN

Design: 0   0   0   0X0   0   0   0
            ‾   ‾   ‾   ‾‾‾   ‾   ‾   ‾
            0   0   0   0 0   0   0   0

Comment: Note there is no symbol R because the time-series designs are usually used because random assignment of Ss is not feasible. The broken lines indicate a nonequivalent control group. The treatment (X) can be interjected at any time. There can be any reasonable number of pre and post observations; four are used in the design for illustrative purposes.

Threats to Internal Validity: All are controlled.

Threats to External Validity: Interaction of testing and treatment and interaction of selection and treatment are NOT controlled. Reactive arrangements are possible.

Advantages: This design is especially useful for study of institutions such as businesses, prisons or universities where random assignment of Ss is often not feasible.

There are two comparisons of the treatment, one with the pre and post measures of the treatment group and a second comparison of the treatment group with the control group. This adds strength to the design.

Disadvantages: All time series designs are subject to extensive invalidity because the multiple observations may interfere with the treatment.

Cost: Depends upon the complexity of the observation procedure.

Rating: Excellent quasi-experimental design. This is probably the best quasi-experimental design because of the two comparisons of the treatment.

EXHIBIT 8.11   THE PROCESS FOR A MULTIPLE TIME-SERIES DESIGN

1. Select two similar groups of Ss.

2. Make observations of the Ss at regular time intervals.

3. Introduce the treatment in the middle of the series of observations
    for one group but not for the other. (Or wait for a naturally
    occurring event.)

NOTE: It is preferable to randomly assign one of the groups to the
treatment, if feasible.

TIME-SERIES DESIGN

Design: 0 0 0 0X0 0 0 0

Note that the number of observations does not have to equal 8 but is
determined by the purpose of the study.

Threats to Internal Validity: Lack of control for history.
Instrumentation is a possible threat. All others are controlled.

Threats to External Validity: Interaction of testing and treatment is
not controlled.   Interaction of selection and treatment and reactive
arrangements are possible.

Advantage: A possible design when no better controlled design is
feasible.

Disadvantage: Several internal and external threats to validity. All
time-series designs are subject to extensive invalidity because the multiple
observations may interfere with the treatment. Noncontrol of history is a
considerable weakness since some event which occurs at approximately the
same time as the treatment could also account for any changes from
pretest to posttest measures.

Cost: Less expensive than multiple time-series.

Rating: Fair-poor. Campbell and Stanley point out that the time-
series design should only be used "WHERE NOTHING BETTER
CONTROLLED IS POSSIBLE" [12, p. 42] and should be replicated many
times in various settings before drawing conclusions.

Process: Take measurements (observations) at regular time intervals
before and after introduction of the experimental treatment to one group.

PATCHED UP DESIGNS

You can generate your own "patched up" designs by placing the most
control possible on a feasible design. If unable to use true experimental
designs, try to use quasi-experimental or add controls to the design. Ways

to do this include: (1) randomly assign Ss to treatments, (2) replicate the study in different settings at different times, (3) replicate the study several times or (4) use a comparable but not equated control group.

Patched up designs do not yield results as clear cut as the designs discussed. The major idea is to add some degree of control which will rule out the various threats to validity.

OTHER QUASI-EXPERIMENTAL DESIGNS

Campbell and Stanley [12] and Cook and Campbell [17] discuss several other quasi-experimental designs which are beyond the scope of this book. If the researcher is considering quasi-experimental designs, reference to these sources is highly recommended.

PRE-EXPERIMENTAL DESIGNS

There are three designs which have been used by researchers which are considered "bad" examples of research design and are termed pre-experimental designs. They are: (1) the One-Shot Case Study, diagrammed as X O, (2) the One-Group Pretest-Posttest Design, diagrammed as O X O and (3) the Static Group Comparison, diagrammed as

$$\frac{X O}{O.}$$

These designs have so many sources of invalidity that they are rarely worth the time and money to carry out and are not recommended.

NONEXPERIMENTAL DESIGNS

Nonexperimental research is just as important as experimental but it does not include the highly controlled aspects which allow the researcher to assume cause and effect. Thus, the inferences, conclusions and recommendations of nonexperimental research are not supported with as much confidence as they are in experimental research.

In some research projects it is not feasible or desirable to carry out experiments which often intrude upon the natural setting, are perhaps more costly or perhaps Ss are not available in a laboratory situation. The research problem still needs to be explored but under nonexperimental conditions. Most of the research processes are the same. The major difference lies in the inability to conclude cause and effect because of the lack of control.

Definition: *Nonexperimental Design:* A research design in which an experimental variable is NOT introduced by the researcher but measures can be taken. Sometimes random selection is feasible. The researcher usually has control over who or what to measure, when the measurement takes place and what to ask or observe. Sometimes the researcher is interested in reactions to a specific event, such as a business merger, a tornado, hostage taking, etc., which occurred PRIOR to the current study (Ex Post Facto research).

Synonyms: *Ex Post Facto Design. Nonmanipulative Design. Correlational Design. Association Design. Relationship Design. Survey Design.*

Purpose: To observe or measure Ss to assess the relationship between or among variables.

Advantages: Does not require an experiment. Can be carried out in natural settings.

Disadvantages: Results lead only to conclusions about associations, not cause and effect.

Comment: A data analysis frequently used for nonexperimental designs is correlation. Although a high correlation does not indicate causation, correlational analyses are very useful because the absence of or a low correlation provides the information that one variable has a very low probability of causing the other variable [37]. This information saves time and money on further studies of the specific hypothesis and channels the researcher into different directions. (In an experimental study, if there is a significant effect there will also be a correlation between the major variables.)

Examples: Measuring attitudes toward the IRS of CPA's and non-CPA managers to assess the relationship of attitude and job position; administering questionnaires regarding purchasing behaviors to male and female customers to assess the relationship of purchasing behaviors and sex of customer; conducting exit polls to assess the relationship of voting behaviors and party affiliation; conducting telephone interviews to assess the relationship of the number of visits to shopping malls and the distance of the shopping malls from the residence.

CAUTION: Even though you might be comparing two groups of Ss, if you are not conducting an experiment you are examining associations among variables, not the effect of an independent variable on a dependent variable.

Comment: The differing types of nonexperimental research are almost endless. The important concept to remember is that the researcher does not conduct an experiment but is able to impose measures of the variables of interest.

EXHIBIT 8.12   THE PROCESS FOR NONEXPERIMENTAL RESEARCH

1. Administer the measure to the Ss.

2. Analyze the relationships among the variables under study, using appropriate statistical procedures.

PREDICTION STUDIES

A great many nonexperimental designs are used in order to predict the degree of probability that something might happen in the future. Correlational analyses are very useful and much used for prediction. With a sufficient amount of evidence, a high correlation between two variables indicates that one variable can be used to predict the other variable (within a range of error) even though it cannot be assumed to "cause" the other variable. Indeed both variables may be related to a third variable which, under experimental research, may turn out to be the "cause" of both.

Prediction studies range from assessing the ability of one variable to predict a criterion variable, to the use of several variables in predicting a criterion variable. An example of the first is to predict gross sales (the criterion) by using an average of the last four years' gross sales as a predictor. An example of the second, using several predictor variables, would be to predict gross sales using the average of the last four years' gross sales plus the expected unemployment rate and amount of current savings.

OTHER CORRELATIONAL STUDIES

Correlation based procedures are widely used in research in a variety of ways. For example, a researcher may have gathered questionnaire information on a large number of variables and wishes to condense these into a smaller number of variables. Factor analysis, including principal components analysis, is frequently used for condensing many variables into a fewer number. These techniques have particularly useful applications for marketing to identify latent dimensions of consumer preferences [68, p. 542].

The presentation of factor analysis is outside the scope of this book and reference to other readings is recommended.

Recommended References: Kim & Mueller [38]. Kim & Mueller [39].

Another use of correlation based procedures is when placing people or objects into classifications on the basis of predictor variables. The purpose is to be able to correctly classify most of the subjects. This technique has wide application in various areas. Imagine being able to correctly predict which people will buy Del Monte vegetables and which will buy other brands, or what type of individuals invest in stocks rather than treasury bills.

Discriminant analysis is the statistical technique often used for prediction of group membership. As discussion of discriminant analysis is outside the scope of this book, see the recommended reference if additional information is desired.

Recommended Reference: Tatsuoka [63].

THE RETROSPECTIVE PRETEST

Campbell and Stanley [12, p. 66] point out that, in a two group comparison of survey items, it is often useful to incorporate a retrospective pretest. That is, in addition to the items of major interest, ask the respondents to RECALL what their attitudes, values or whatever variables you are measuring were prior to the natural occurrence of the variable of interest. The purpose of this is NOT to assess differences in the pre and post observations because data based on memory or recall are usually distorted and not worth using. The purpose is to ascertain if the two groups are similar in recalled observations -- any distortion because of memory should be equal for the two groups. If the two groups are similar in recall of the variables of interest, the findings of the research are strengthened.

HISTORICAL DESIGNS

Conducting research on the relationship of last year's (or even this morning's) sales and oil exploration costs or on the relationship of the last six months' absenteeism rate and seniority of employees is historical research. Anytime the researcher has data which already exist they are called historical data.

Definition: *Historical Design*: A research design for which the data or physical artifacts already exist and thus cannot be changed or manipulated. The researcher had no control over how or when or with what instruments the data were collected.

Purpose: To assess the probable relationships among variables using prerecorded or existing documents, materials or artifacts.

Advantages: Historical design is the only method for studying the past.

Disadvantages: The representativeness of the data is often questionable because the researcher often does not even know if all the existing data are known or how much data may have been destroyed (consider the Nixon White House tapes) or distorted. The researcher had no control over data collection methods, instruments used, accuracy of the recordings, etc.

Related Definition: *Primary Sources*: Sources of information who made direct firsthand recording or reporting of events or which are the physical artifacts themselves. Primary sources were present during the event, experience or time.

Related Definition: *Secondary Sources*: Sources of information who were not present at the time of the event and whose information about events or physical artifacts was gathered from other sources.

PRIMARY SOURCES

Primary sources are firsthand recordings of data or the actual data themselves, as with physical artifacts. Such factors as sales figures, minutes of meetings, video and audio tapes of events, gold mines, office buildings and the ship the ANDREA DORIA are all primary sources.

The chief characteristics of primary sources are: (1) being present during the experience, event or time and (2) consequently being close in time with the data. This does not mean that data from primary sources are always the best data. Remember that the researcher had no control over how the data were collected or what data were collected. Physical artifacts can experience major changes in form over time. Data from human sources are subject to many types of distortion because of such factors as selective recall, selective perceptions, and purposeful or nonpurposeful omission or addition of information. Thus, DATA FROM PRIMARY SOURCES ARE NOT NECESSARILY ACCURATE DATA even though they came from firsthand sources.

SECONDARY SOURCES

Secondary sources differ from primary sources in that they were NOT present at the event (a news reporter's presentation of the President's European trip last month). Thus, a secondary source also differs from a primary source in terms of both time (further in time from the event) and the introduction of a SECOND PERSON'S INTERVENTION between the event and the recording of it. The second person brings a second set of selective perceptions, selective recall, etc., adding the possibility of even more distortion. Imagine the possible distortion of events recorded fifth or sixth hand or even more!

Secondary sources are not necessarily worse than primary sources and can be quite valuable. A secondary source may include more information about more aspects of the event than did a primary source. However, as with a primary source, the data are not necessarily accurate.

MAJOR PROBLEMS WITH PRIMARY AND SECONDARY SOURCES

Since the researcher had no control over the data collection of historical events or artifacts there are many uncertainties about the representativeness of the records being used. Exhibit 8.13 gives examples of possible problems.

THE RESEARCH PROCESS FOR HISTORICAL DESIGNS

Most of the steps of the research process are the same as for any other type of research design. This is emphasized here because so many novice researchers seem to believe that hypothesis testing cannot be used with historical data. Hypothesis testing may be used with data that are generated during the research project or data which already exists.

One difference may lie with the sampling procedures. Occasionally, in historical research there are so little existing data that the researcher uses the total population of recordings of the event. However, it is more usual to have a large amount of material which the researcher samples in an unbiased way.

EXHIBIT 8.13   POSSIBLE PROBLEMS WITH PRIMARY AND
                  SECONDARY SOURCES

1. All existing data may not be known.

2. All existing data may not be available.

3. Some data may have been destroyed, purposefully or non-
    purposefully.

4. Some data may have deteriorated and/or changed.

5. Some data may have been distorted, purposefully or non-
    purposefully.

6. Primary sources may not exist.

7. Primary sources may not be available.

8. Primary and secondary sources may not be accurate

WHERE YOU ARE NOW

At this point you should have:

1. Selected the type of research design for your project,

2. Specified the treatments, if using an experiment,

and recognized:

3. The power of random assignment in equating groups.

4. The difference in the amount of control in the four types of research designs,

5. The difference between experimental and control groups,

6. Why it is important to control for threats to internal and external validity,

7. How to control for threats to internal and external validity,

8. The power of true experimental designs in controlling,

9. The usefulness of quasi-experimental designs when true experimental designs cannot be used,

10. The concept of "patched up" designs to increase control,

11. That pre-experimental designs are not recommended,

12. That nonexperimental designs are widely used but incorporate very little control,

13. That historical designs are widely used but there was no control over the original research situation,

14. That primary and secondary sources may be inaccurate, distorted or lacking vital information, and

15. A major difference in the four types of research designs is in the strength of the conclusions resulting from the amount of control. This does not mean that any one type of design is better or worse but different and the researcher selects the most appropriate research design for the specific project.

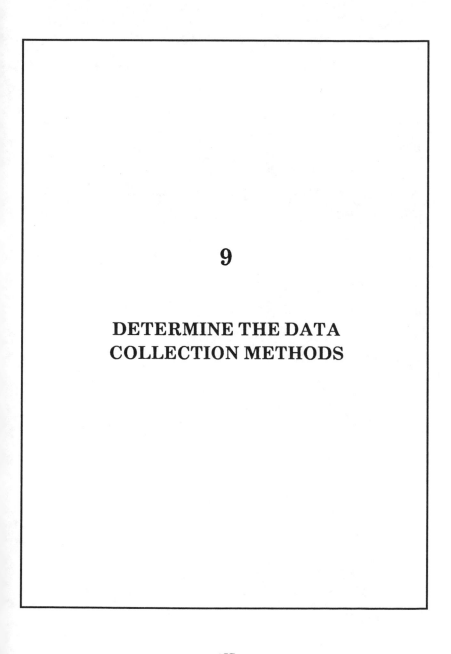

9

**DETERMINE THE DATA
COLLECTION METHODS**

TERMS DEFINED IN CHAPTER NINE

CHAPTER NINE

DETERMINE THE DATA COLLECTION METHODS

STEPS TO TAKE AFTER READING THIS CHAPTER

1. Determine the type of data collection method for each variable in the study.

2. Review each method selected to ascertain that any subjects of the study will not be affected by the data collection method.

3. Change the data collection method if subjects will be affected by it.

4. Determine the type of sampling (event or time) or a census of phenomena, if observation methods are used.

5. Determine the type of sampling or a census of all phenomena, if examination of documents, materials or artifacts is used.

The variables of interest in a research project are measured by some type of instrument. A wide variety of instruments are used including questionnaires, rating scales, checklists, thermometers and weight scales.

Regardless of the type of instrument used, there has to be some way of gathering the data. These are called data collection methods.

Definition: *Data Collection Method*: The means by which information about variables is collected.

Comment: Note that data collection and instrumentation are two different processes. Data collection is the process by which information is gathered and instrumentation is the process by which variables are measured. Instrumentation is discussed in Chapters 10, 11 and 12.

CAUTION: Often the data collection method is determined first and the instrument follows. For example, a researcher decides that in-depth information is desired which can only be obtained from interviewing people and an interview schedule is then designed.

However, data collection and instrumentation work together. Some instruments require a specific data collection method. For example many standardized performance measures, such as preemployment skills tests, require that a person administer the instrument to the subject. Thus, you may wish to read about instrumentation in Chapters 10, 11 and 12 before determining the data collection method.

EXHIBIT 9.1   TYPES OF DATA COLLECTION METHODS

1. **Interviewing**

A person (interviewer), usually trained, asks respondents questions via telephone, on-line computer, interactive television or in a face-to-face situation. Respondents' answers are usually recorded by the interviewer on a previously prepared* interview schedule. Sometimes the respondent completes a written questionnaire first and the interviewer then probes for more detailed answers.

2. **Instrument Administration**

A person (administrator) gives instruments* (questionnaires, attitude scales, tests) to subjects and then collects them after the Ss have responded. Or the administrator attaches an instrument, such as a lie detector, to the Ss and collects all their responses. Or the administrator asks the Ss to complete a task such as fitting parts together, drawing a diagram or writing memos.

In some situations the contact between administrator and Ss is minimal. Often the administrator simply reads the directions, provides the materials and monitors the Ss while they are responding.

In many of these situations the administrator is face-to-face with the Ss but questionnaires are often mailed or transmitted by electronic means and interactive television can also be used to ask Ss to complete certain tasks.

3. **Observation**

A person (observer) watches Ss (people, animals, etc.) and records characteristics (observations) of the situation on a previously prepared instrument.* Sometimes Ss are recorded on film or video or audio tape. Other times the observer views the situation directly.

4. **Examination of Documents, Materials or Artifacts**

A person (researcher or assistant) examines documents, materials or physical artifacts and records the data on previously prepared instruments.*

*Note that previously prepared instruments usually include opportunities to record unanticipated or unique findings.

TYPES OF DATA COLLECTION METHODS

There are four types of data collection methods:

1. Interviewing.
2. Instrument administration.
3. Observation.
4. Examination of documents, materials and artifacts.

Interviewing, instrument administration and observation all require subjects such as people, animals, etc. Examination of documents and artifacts is used for existing materials.

One or all of these data collection methods might be used in a single study. Examples of these processes are given in Exhibit 9.1.

> In determining the appropriate data collection method one of the first decisions is whether people are your best source of information or whether documents, materials or artifacts might be more error-free sources. Despite the tendency of researchers to send out survey after survey, people are not always the best source of information.

> For example, if your research deals with opinions, attitudes, beliefs or values, your best source is probably people. If you are interested in finding out if people voted, if they drink liquor, if they read certain magazines, if they buy certain products, then the best source is usually "hard data" such as sales figures. Exhibit 9.2 gives some suggestions for selecting a data collection method.

THE INTERVIEWING METHOD

Definition: *Interviewing Method:* A data collection method in which an interviewer questions people to elicit self-reports of their opinions, attitudes, values, beliefs or behaviors. Interviews are usually carried out in face-to-face situations although interactive television and on-line computers are also used.

Advantages:

1. Elicits information directly from people.

2. Allows opportunity for probing; finding out why people feel or respond the way they do.

3. Allows opportunity to clarify information as it is given.

4. Allows opportunity to explain complex information.

5. Allows opportunity to clarify previously collected data.

EXHIBIT 9.2   SUGGESTIONS FOR SELECTING THE DATA COLLECTION METHODS

1. Use the INTERVIEWING method ONLY when people's SELF-REPORTS of their
    opinions, attitudes, values or beliefs are the best source of information AND
    desired information is complex or probing is required or it is necessary to clarify
    previously collected information.

    If people's reports are the best source of information but none of the other
    conditions hold, use instrument administration. Interviewing is too costly for
    data which can be acquired by other methods.

2. Use INSTRUMENT ADMINISTRATION when people's self reports or subject's
    responses to an instrument are the best source of information. For example,
    obtaining attitudes via questionnaires, giving performance tests, attaching
    devices to people and requesting people to conduct tasks or create items.

3. Use the OBSERVATION method ONLY when subjects are the best source of
    information and it is important or necessary to observe the behavior of the
    subjects. This method is often used in natural settings; for example, observing
    shoppers' purchasing behaviors or characteristics of communication during a
    conference.

    The observation should be as unobtrusive as possible so that Ss do not react to
    it and change their normal behaviors.

4. Use EXAMINATION OF DOCUMENTS, MATERIALS AND ARTIFACTS when these
    are the best or only sources of the desired information. This method often
    yields more valid data than questioning people about such variables as
    absenteeism, theft, and sales ability. It is much better to examine the actual
    figures on these.

    This method also has the advantage of being unobtrusive (the Ss don't know
    their behaviors are being examined) and thus nonreactive (if the Ss don't
    know, they won't change their behaviors). Historical research requires this
    method.

5. Direct measurement of a variable usually results in the most valid data. If you
    need to know the number of products sold, look at sales figures rather than
    asking people how many they bought. If you want people's opinions, ask
    them. The more indirect the measure, the higher the probability of error.

6. Use unobtrusive methods whenever possible. They often yield more valid data,
    particularly with sensitive items, even though though they are indirect
    methods.

Disadvantages:

1. Very costly because of the time required for each interview and the required training of interviewers.

2. Less information can be gathered than by other methods because of the time requirements.

3. Probability of inaccurate data because people may lie, omit information or use selective recall (see Exhibit 9.3).

4. Possibility of inaccurate data because of interviewer bias or the interaction of interviewer and respondents (see Exhibit 9.3).

INSTRUMENT ADMINISTRATION

Definition: *Instrument Administration:* A data collection method in which Ss respond to questionnaires, tasks, scales, tests or other devices used to measure variables. The instruments are administered by a variety of means including mail, telephone, on-line computer or in face-to-face situations to all Ss in a group or to individual Ss.

Characteristics of this method are: (1) contact between administrator and Ss is usually kept to a minimum, (2) Ss are given oral or written instructions, (3) the device is given (or in the case of some physical instruments, attached) to the Ss and (4) the Ss responses are measured.

Advantages:

1. There are many existing instruments, measuring a variety of variables, which have sufficient evidence of validity and reliability to warrant their use.

2. Well designed written instruments often are excellent measures of variables and some of these create minimal negative reactions from Ss.

3. Physical instruments, such as those which measure galvanic skin response, weight and temperature, have a long history of use in research.

Disadvantages:

1. Ss may react to the intrusion of being measured and lie or distort information or change their behavior.

2. If good existing instruments are not available the researcher may have to generate an instrument. This is time consuming and can be costly.

There is a wide variety of forms of instrument administration. Some examples are given below.

EXHIBIT 9.3   REASONS TO AVOID QUESTIONING PEOPLE*

1. **Lying**. People sometimes lie, particularly with sensitive items such as income, age, frequency of sex and if they are ashamed of doing or not doing something. Items such as "have you ever stolen anything from a retail store?" or "did you vote in the last presidential election?" inevitably elicit some lying. Some people lie on all items because they resent being questioned.

2. **Omission**. People will often omit or refuse to answer sensitive items like those in #1. If too many people omit the same item, which is likely to occur with sensitive items, the item cannot be analyzed and important data will be missing.

3. **Inaccurate Recall**. What did you eat for lunch last Thursday? What clothing did you wear to work Monday? With whom did you speak at work last week? The responses to questions like these depend on how well the respondent remembers. Memory deteriorates rather rapidly over time, particularly with items which are not significant to the respondent.

4. **Insufficient Information**. Some people do not know and never knew the answer to a question or they may have only pieces of information but not the whole. What corporations do you feel have the best environmental policies? People who are unfamiliar with organizations' environmental policies will tend to either omit the item or lie rather than admit insufficient information.

5. **Interviewer Bias**. The interviewer might "lead" the subject to a certain response, either consciously or unconsciously.

6. **Interviewer-Respondent Interaction**. Sometimes the respondent and interviewer clash, creating respondent resentment which affects responses.

7. **Item Bias**. Sometimes questionnaire items are worded so that they "lead" the respondent to specific responses.

*All these reasons greatly lower the validity of the data. The best way to overcome these problems is to avoid questioning people and use other data collection methods.

Examples of Instrument Administration

1. Researcher asks CPA's to rate a sample of the Fortune 500 companies on public accessibility of financial information, over the telephone.

2. Researcher administers a written instrument which measures anxiety level to a group of aircraft controllers gathered in one room.

3. Researcher asks personnel assistant to administer an instrument, which measures honesty, to job applicants at the same time they are filling out their applications.

4. Researcher mails questionnaires asking for opinions of the local savings and loan institutions.

5. Researcher has an experimental group of Ss view a film about cooperative behaviors between business and government and then gives them an "attitude toward government" scale.

SOME COMMENTS ON QUESTIONING PEOPLE

Note that the interviewing method requires questioning people and that questionnaires are one form of the instrument administration method. Prior to selecting a data collection method you should consider the advantages and disadvantages of questioning people. The primary advantage of questioning people is that it is the only way to elicit SELF-REPORTS of people's opinions, attitudes, beliefs and values.

Far too many researchers, particularly those in marketing research, think of questioning first when much of the time other methods will yield far more accurate data. If you want to know how many gallons of ice cream were purchased last month, look at the sales figures, don't ask people. If you want to know why people purchased ice cream last month, ask them.

Some reasons for avoiding questioning people are given in Exhibit 9.3. All these reasons, if they should occur, lower the validity of the data and it is impossible for an organization to plan appropriately with invalid data.

The reasons to avoid questioning are only some of the most commonly occurring factors which can affect responses in a questioning situation. Given the number of these factors and their serious effects on the validity -- and consequently the results -- of the research it is recommended that questioning be used only when it is appropriate and the data yielded has a high probability of being valid.

Cost: Some people think that questioning methods are cheaper than other methods. Sometimes that is true but often it is not. A close examination of the costs versus validity of the data should be done prior to selection of one of the data collection methods. Often other procedures are cheaper, take less time and yield more valid data. It takes a considerable amount of time and money to generate a GOOD questionnaire, print the forms and have someone administer them or mail them. If interviewers are used they must be trained and, because interviewing is very time consuming, the data collection is usually very costly and usually yields less data because of time.

OBSERVATION

Definition: *Observation Method:* A data collection method in which a person (usually trained) observes Ss or phenomena and records information about characteristics of the phenomena.

EXHIBIT 9.4   THE PROCESS FOR DATA COLLECTION BY OBSERVATION

1. Define the variables of interest precisely. It is not sufficient to say the variable is "communication" or "nonverbal communication" or even "gestures" but rather "type of gesture" with specification of the various types.

   1.1   If there is insufficient a priori knowledge of the variable to define it precisely, conduct a pilot study by observing Ss like those selected for the study.

   1.2   If a pilot test is not feasible and film, video or audio recorders are available, the observations for the study can be recorded. A content analysis can then be conducted on random samples of the observations to determine the most appropriate way to define the variables and then design the instrument to measure the variables.

2. Determine the procedure for sampling observations, if not observing all specified phenomena.*

   2.1   Sample events or

   2.2   Sample time or

   2.3   Sample both time and events.

3. Obtain or design an instrument to record the observations.

4. Train the observers.

*Observing all phenomena is often expensive and time consuming. The added time and expense may be justified when using video, audio or film recordings because of the increased validity and reliability of the laboratory analysis.

Advantages:

1. Useful in situations where Ss must be observed in their natural settings.

2. Includes a variety of techniques for making observations.

2.1 NASA personnel use telecommunication techniques, biologists use microscopes, psychologists sometimes use one way vision mirrors to observe Ss.

2.2 Video or audio tapes or films are useful tools as observations can be made at one time and analysis of the data at a later time.

2.3 Video taping has several advantages including: (1) produces both audio and visual information, (2) can be run over and over, stopped for a "freeze frame" and enlarged if desired, (3) is relatively inexpensive, (4) creates an enduring record and (5) data can be collected in natural settings and analyzed in the laboratory, thus increasing validity and reliability. However analysis of video tapes is usually time consuming and there is a limited amount of recording time on each tape which may require changing tapes unless there are two video recorders.

Disadvantages:

1. Ss who are aware of being observed tend to change their behavior.

2. Ethical considerations include the Ss right to privacy, informed consent and confidentiality of data. This means that, in many research situations, Ss must agree to or be informed of the observation.

3. Observations are usually time consuming.

EVENT SAMPLING

Definition: *Event Sampling*: The process of selecting a subgroup of events from a population of events specified by the researcher.

Definition: *Event*: An occurrence of a specific phenomenon such as a verbal expression, two-way communication, conference, or television commercial. Events are those situations which include the variable(s) to be observed.

Advantages:

1. As events are naturally occurring situations they "possess an inherent validity not ordinarily possessed by time samples" [36, p. 512].

2. Because events are natural and complete units they include a complete set of behaviors which piecemeal time samples do not.

3. Because events are sometimes infrequent (e.g., a stockholders' meeting) they could be missed by time sampling.

Disadvantages: If it is not known when the event will occur there may be a long (and possibly expensive) wait. In this situation time sampling is not feasible because of the possibility of missing the occurrence.

TIME SAMPLING

Definition: *Time Sampling:* The process of selecting specific time periods for observing phenomena. Time periods can be selected randomly or systematically. For example, in observing T.V. commercials the researcher might select systematic time samples of 3 minutes, beginning at one minute before the hour to two minutes after the hour, between the time periods of 6.59 and 11.02 p.m. For sampling of continuous behavior, such as observation of the interaction of a group of robotics technicians, the researcher might designate five samples of ten minutes each, selected randomly from a specified population of ten minute periods.

Advantages: With regularly recurring phenomena, time samples are representative samples of the phenomena.

Disadvantages:

1. Time sampling is not useful for infrequent events. The research must deal with phenomena which occur throughout the time span in order to "catch" the event.

2. A time sample may cut in on the event in the middle and miss much of the advantages of the natural setting. If the time set for observing commercials began at 7:03 the commercial might be halfway completed or even completed and there would be no observation for that time period.

EXAMINATION OF DOCUMENTS, MATERIALS AND ARTIFACTS

Examination of Documents, Materials and Artifacts is a widely used data collection method in research because so many variables of interest are regularly recorded. For example, businesses regularly record gross sales, cost figures, number of rejects, absenteeism rates and a large number of other variables.

Definition: *Examination of Documents, Materials and Artifacts:* A data collection method in which a person (often trained) examines and records characteristics of phenomena which already exist.

Advantages:
1. Ss do not react to the data collection method because the data already exist.

2. The only possible method for historical research.

3. Many artifacts (e.g., buildings) can be examined in their natural settings.

4. Many documents and artifacts (e.g., moon rocks) can be transported to a laboratory where they can be examined at leisure.

5. Enduring records can be created. Documents can be copied and artifacts can be filmed.

Disadvantages:

1. The phenomena found may not be representative of all existing phenomena.

2. The phenomena may have deteriorated to a point where examination becomes difficult.

3. The researcher, having NOT been present at or during the event in which the phenomena occurred, may not recognize erroneous information or changes in the phenomena.

EXHIBIT 9.5 THE PROCESS OF DATA COLLECTION BY EXAMINATION OF DOCUMENTS, MATERIALS AND ARTIFACTS

1. Define the known population of phenomena very specifically.

2. Determine the method for sampling the phenomena.

    2.1   The sampling unit for a document might be a page, a paragraph or even a sentence.

    2.2   The sampling unit for physical artifacts is usually the artifact itelf or a group of such artifacts.

3. Find an existing instrument or generate a new instrument to record the pertinent information about the variables.*

4. Examine primary and secondary sources for desired information.

5. Evaluate the authenticity of the source and, for human sources, their expertise and reputation.

*Sources may need to be examined prior to generating an instrument.

UNOBTRUSIVE MEASURES

One way to avoid subjects' awareness and reaction to data collection procedures is to collect unobtrusive measures. These are measures of variables which the subjects are unaware or minimally aware they are providing.

Definition: *Unobtrusive Measure:* A measure of a variable which is collected in such a way that subjects are usually unaware that they are being measured. This is also called a nonreactive measure because if Ss are not aware they are being measured they cannot react to the measurement.

Comment: This discussion of unobtrusive measures is placed here so you can consider using them before you decide on a data collection method.

They are well worth considering because of their strong advantage of being nonreactive.

Advantages:

1. Ss are usually unaware that data about them is being collected.

2. Thus, Ss cannot react to the measurement.

3. Unobtrusive measures often yield more valid data than questioning people.

Disadvantages:

1. Researcher may be making erroneous inferences from the data. For example, assuming that a subject drinks milk because milk cartons are found in the garbage but the subject is feeding the milk to pets, not drinking it.

2. Sometimes collecting unobtrusive measures is uncomfortable. For example, sorting through trash or standing out in inclement weather while making observations of the type of people entering a restaurant.

Webb et al [70] wrote a classic book on unobtrusive measures and they give many examples. Some of the most interesting unobtrusive measures used in various studies have been physical traces. Physical traces might be the wear on a museum floor to indicate popularity of a display, materials collected from garbage cans to assess what Ss are eating, drinking or reading and examination of materials donated to charities to assess quality of products purchased.

Many of the unobtrusive measures used fall into the data collection methods of examination of documents, materials and artifacts or observation. For example, observing and counting the number of people who place coins or bills in a Salvation Army donation pot or examining products on the shelf to see which have deteriorated.

Unobtrusive measures are especially useful in replacing surveys when variables to which people are sensitive are being measured. For example, people tend to lie about or minimize their consumption of alcohol and food, and their use of drugs; exaggerate their voting participation, levels of contributions and reading behaviors; and not respond to questions about their spending behaviors and sexual preferences.

Thus, data from surveying people on these variables is often invalid. Unobtrusive measures might include examining trash for bottles, cans and containers, asking for donations of used books and magazines and observing spending behaviors. These measures are likely to be more accurate than those obtained by questioning.

Recommended Reference: Webb et al. [70] is highly recommended for additional information on unobtrusive measures.

WHERE YOU ARE NOW

At this point you should have:

1. Determined the type of data collection method for each variable in your study,

2. Reviewed each method to ascertain that Ss will not be affected by it,

3. Determined the type of sampling if you are using the observation method or examination of documents or materials,

and recognized that:

4. Instrumentation and data collection are two different processes,

5. Interviewing is very costly and should be used only when probing is desirable, complex information is involved or clarification is needed,

6. When people respond to questions, either in interviews or questionnaires, errors tend to occur because of such factors as lying, omission of information and insufficient knowledge,

7. Observation methods are very useful when natural settings must be used,

8. Examination of documents and materials is widely used in research and should probably be used even more frequently because of the many variables of interest which are regularly recorded and

9. When reaction to the data collection method or the measure might affect Ss responses, unobtrusive measures should be considered.

10

DETERMINE THE INSTRUMENTS TO MEASURE THE VARIABLES

TERMS DEFINED IN CHAPTER 10

CHAPTER TEN

DETERMINE THE INSTRUMENTS TO MEASURE THE VARIABLES

STEPS TO TAKE AFTER READING CHAPTERS 10, 11 AND 12

1. Determine the type of information desired and variables to be measured.

2. Review the types of instruments listed in Chapters 10, 11 & 12.

3. Determine the type of instrument desired.

4. Examine existing instruments for selection of one appropriate for measuring the variables.

5. Design an instrument, if an appropriate existing one cannot be found.

6. Examine the validity and reliability estimates of the instrument.

7. Examine the instrument to ensure that the levels of measurement it yields are sufficiently appropriate to answer the research questions or hypotheses and for the statistical analysis.

8. Pilot test the instrument if it is a new design or a modification of an existing instrument.

9. Select or design another instrument if the pilot test indicates.

INSTRUMENTS

All variables are measured by some type of instrument. An instrument is whatever device is used to measure variables. Instruments can range from written or oral materials to physical devices. Examples of instruments include: (1) questionnaires (e.g., asking opinions of recent mergers), (2) rating scales (e.g., rating major corporations on the social goals), (3) skills tests (e.g, a typing test), (4) checklists (e.g., checking cities which have a high "quality of life") and (5) materials created by Ss (e.g., Ss designing parts for a computer).

Definition: *Instrument*: Any type of written or physical device which is purported to measure variables.

CAUTION: Note that by definition an instrument is a measuring device. This says nothing about the quality of the device -- it can be very good (valid, reliable, yielding appropriate data and easy to administer, respond to and interpret) or very bad or somewhere in between these extremes.

CAUTION: Using an instrument may affect Ss responses. For example, giving a skills test may increase Ss anxiety level and affect their responses. Giving a pretest prior to an experiment may sensitize Ss to the experiment and affect the posttest scores. Ss may become nervous while waiting to be interviewed. The instrument itself may be inaccurate. The instrument administrator may have poor rapport with Ss.

Any unnatural situation in which Ss are placed may affect their responses. These conditions are known as instrumentation effects and can create major or minor distortions of the data. The best way to guard against these effects is to have the instrument administrator, the instrument and the environment in which it is administered as natural and unobtrusive as possible.

Definition: *Instrumentation Effects*: Effects created by subjects' responses to an instrument, the administration of the instrument or the environment in which the instrument is administered. These effects can cause major or minor distortions of the data.

INTERRELATIONSHIP BETWEEN DATA COLLECTION METHODS AND INSTRUMENTS

Now that you have selected a data collection method the next step is to acquire an instrument (or instruments) either by selecting an existing instrument or by designing a new one. Before you make the choice of selecting or designing, remember that the data collection method selected often determines the type of instrument used. For example, if you have decided to interview people you will need an interview schedule.

Exhibit 10.1 gives some typically used instruments for each type of data collection method. Note that these instruments can be used for more than one type of data collection method. For example, rating scales might be used in an interview schedule, a questionnaire or when the researcher is observing Ss.

The most important factors in acquiring an instrument are that it: (1) measures the variables appropriately, (2) is sufficiently valid and reliable, (3) yields the appropriate level of measurement for each variable, (4) requires an appropriate amount of time, (5) is easy to acquire Ss response, (6) is easy to administer, (7) is easy to interpret and (8) costs an amount which is within the researcher's budget.

SUGGESTIONS FOR DETERMINING THE TYPE OF INSTRUMENT

Because there is such a wide variety of instruments it is helpful to examine the choice of type of instrument in terms of the data collection method as given in Exhibit 10.1.

EXHIBIT 10.1   TYPICAL TYPES OF INSTRUMENTS FOR EACH DATA
COLLECTION METHOD

Data Collection Method	Typical Type of Instrument
Interview	* Interview Schedule
Instrument Administration	* Questionnaire
	* Rating Scale
	* Checklist
	* Skills Test
	* Original material created by Ss such as written materials or drawings
Observation	* Forms for observer rating or recording Ss behaviors
Examination of Documents or Artifacts	* Forms for recording pertinent data.

Interviewing requires some type of interview schedule. An interview schedule is simply a questionnaire which is directed toward the oral interaction between the interviewer and the respondent. With the advent of the computer some interview schedules are directed toward the electronic interaction of interviewer and respondent.

Sometimes interviewers give the respondent a brief questionnaire and then the interviewer reads the completed questionnaire and probes deeper to find out why the respondent made specific responses. Sometimes rating scales are used; for example, when conducting a telephone survey asking opinions of various retail stores.

Information on designing interview schedules and questionnaires is given in Chapter 11.

Instrument Administration has the widest variety of possible types of instruments to use. The variation is so great it is almost impossible, in this short space, to give the reader a sufficient picture of the numbers and kinds of instruments.

Questionnaires might be used to measure attitudes toward Fortune 500 companies. Rating scales might be used to measure how Ss rate the newest line of personal computers. Skills tests might be used to assess how much job incumbents learned from training or how well applicants might perform in specific jobs. Ss may be asked to design a house, a robot or a prospectus. The variety of instrument types is extensive.

Questionnaires are covered in Chapter 11. Examples of other typically used instruments are given in Chapter 12.

Observation requires that some type of form be selected or designed so that the observer can record the observations. **Examination of Documents and Artifacts** requires a form for the researcher to record information found upon examining the data. Information on these forms is given in Chapter 12.

THE MOST IMPORTANT ASPECT IN ACQUIRING AN INSTRUMENT IS THAT IT MUST ALLOW THE BEST POSSIBLE MEASUREMENT OF YOUR VARIABLES.

SELECT OR DESIGN AN INSTRUMENT

There are hundreds of existing instruments available to the public which measure a variety of variables including performance, attitudes, values, beliefs, perceptions, interests and intelligence. It is good use of your time to examine existing instruments for selection of one appropriate to your research rather than trying to design an instrument. The time and money spent on designing a GOOD instrument usually is far greater than purchasing existing instruments.

SELECTING AN EXISTING INSTRUMENT

Purpose: To select an instrument where: (1) the content measures the variable(s) of interest, (2) evidence of acceptable kinds and degrees of validity and reliability is provided, (3) interpretation manuals are provided, (4) the levels of measurement are appropriate, (5) clear directions and administration procedures are provided and (6) costs are within the allocated budget.

In order for the researcher to select an instrument which meets all the criteria listed in the purpose, several types of information are examined. These are given in Exhibit 10.2, which indicates the process for selecting an existing instrument.

DESIGNING AN INSTRUMENT

Purpose: To design an instrument where: (1) the content measures the variable(s) of interest, (2) acceptable levels of appropriate types of validity and reliability are yielded, (3) the appropriate levels of measurement are produced, (4) interpretation of the instrument is easy, (5) the time for administration is appropriate and (5) costs are within the allocated budget.

EXHIBIT 10.2   PROCESS FOR SELECTING AN EXISTING INSTRUMENT

1. List the variables to be measured by the content of the instrument.

2. Examine sources of information about existing instruments.

   2.1   Buros' *Mental Measurement Yearbooks* [10]. Lists published instruments in print at time of publication and provides descriptions and critiques of the instruments. Found in libraries. Published periodically, not annually.

   2.2   *Tests In Print* [11]. Provides title, publication date, authors, publishers and comments. Found in libraries.

   2.3   Publishers' catalogs. Provide information about instrument's purpose, content, administration time, cost and scoring services available. Acquired from publisher.

   2.4   Specimen sets. Usually includes a specimen instrument, technical manual, administrator's manual, answer sheets and information on ordering, costs and additional services such as scoring and/or interpretation. Acquired from publisher.

   2.5   Professional journals. Occasionally new instruments are available from authors of journal articles who usually have conducted studies using these instruments. Many of these have insufficient evidence of validity and reliability.

3. Examine the technical manual to assess the evidence provided for validity and reliability. Check that types, magnitudes and sampling for validity and reliability are appropriate.

4. Examine the information on interpretation of the instrument. There should be sufficient information for the user to interpret the results correctly.

5. Examine the directions to assess their clarity and ease of use.

6. Examine administration procedures including the time necessary for Ss to complete the instrument.

7. Examine the scoring procedures for sufficient detail, ease and clarity to avoid errors.

Exhibit 10.3 indicates the process for designing an instrument.

EXHIBIT 10.3   THE PROCESS FOR DESIGNING AN INSTRUMENT

1. List the variables which will be measured by the content of the instrument.

2. Select the type of instrument you wish to use after referring to Chapters 11 and 12 or other references.

3. Follow the design procedures for the type of instrument selected.

4. Check that the content measures the selected variables.

5. Check that the level of measurement for each variable is appropriate for the research question or hypothesis and statistical analysis.

6. Pilot test the instrument with a sample similar to the study sample but not included in the study.

7. Assess the appropriate validities and reliabilities using the pilot test data (see Chapter 5).

8. Evaluate the time required for Ss to take the instrument and the ease of interpretation of results, using the pilot test data.

9. Redesign the instrument if it does not yield the desired information in appropriate form or if validity and reliability coefficients are too low or if directions or sequencing yield poor results or if it takes too much time.

GENERAL CATEGORIES OF INSTRUMENTS

Although an instrument is used to measure specific variables it has become common practice to refer to instruments as measuring general categories of variables such as performance or attitude variables. This is often shortened to performance instrument or attitude instrument.

CAUTION: Despite the loose language usage remember you are measuring specific variables; these may fall into a general category of variables.

Many instruments are categorized using common terms. Thus, in order to locate existing instruments for review or even to design your own instrument you should be aware of the most commonly used categories. Exhibit 10.4 gives types of measures associated with these categories.

EXHIBIT 10.4:   TYPES OF MEASURES AND TYPICAL ITEM FOCUS

MEASURES	TYPICAL ITEM FOCUS
1. Performance	Items focus on Ss knowledge or skills or information on organization related performance such as product durability.
2. Attitudes/Opinions Values/Beliefs	Ss are usually asked to respond to questions, statements, concepts or objects according to their preferences or perceptions.
3. Interests	Items are based on those interests expressed by people in specific occupations which are different from interests of people in other occupations.
4. Intelligence	Items often require Ss to select objects which do not belong in a set of objects, complete a sentence with a word or phrase, provide the next number in a series of numbers or interpret written material.
5. Personality	Items often use unstructured and ambiguous stimuli such as pictures, ink blots or written materials to which Ss respond.
6. Demographic	Items are focused on information about Ss such as income, marital status, age, sex, religious preference, home ownership or group affiliation.

CAUTION: Some variables are not easily classified into only one category. For example, the variables "dogmatism" and "authoritarianism" are considered personality variables by some people and attitude variables by other people.

Instruments can be categorized generally as measuring: (1) performance, (2) attitudes or opinions, (3) beliefs, (4) values, (5) interests, (6) intelligence, (7) personality or (8) demographic characteristics. Instruments measuring physical phenomena such as weight, heat, etc. are not within the scope of this book.

PERFORMANCE MEASURES

Definition: *Performance Measure*: A measure which assesses the degree to which Ss (e.g., people, animals) demonstrate mastery of knowledge or skills, or physical devices (e.g., spacecraft) demonstrate capabilities. Variables such as amount of gross sales or costs are also called performance measures.

Comment: Note that performance TESTS are usually defined as tests in which subjects manipulate objects.

Advantages:

1. Can assess to what degree Ss possess specific knowledge or skills.

2. Useful in predicting job performance if the measure is directly related to job tasks.

3. Many good existing standardized instruments are available in various performance areas.

Disadvantages: Care must be used in selecting existing instruments as some will not measure the variables the researcher desires and some do not have sufficient evidence of validity and reliability.

CAUTION: Because there are so many existing instruments which measure a variety of skills and knowledge, it is worthwhile to examine various instruments and their psychometric qualities to ensure that you select one of the better instruments.

Comment: Performance measures are widely used in research to assess people, parts, mechanisms, etc. When assessing performance of such phenomena as electronic devices special technical instruments are often used. For information on these instruments refer to the associated professional societies.

MEASURES OF ATTITUDES, OPINIONS, BELIEFS AND VALUES

Definition: *Attitude Measure*: An instrument which purports to measure a person's predisposition to perceive, feel and behave toward someone or something.

Comment: Some authors distinguish between attitude and opinion while others do not. Thurstone [66] defined opinions as "verbal expressions of attitudes." Many experts, for example, Anastasi [4], treat "attitude" and "opinion" as interchangeable concepts.

Comment: Attitude measures are widely used in marketing research and for assessing employee attitudes.

Definition: *Beliefs Measures*: An instrument which purports to measure a person's closely held opinion about someone or something.

Definition: *Values Measure*: An instrument which purports to measure a person's preference for someone or something.

Advantages: As beliefs are difficult to change (some last a lifetime) measures of beliefs are usually good predictors of future behaviors.

Disadvantages:

1. As attitudes are changeable, the use of attitude measures may be useful for short term predictions but are questionable for long term predictions.

2. Values are largely developed through a culturization process. As values change when awareness of differing values occurs or when changing cultures, measures of values are sometimes of limited usefulness in predicting future behavior.

Comment: There are several existing instruments for assessing values such as economic values and work values. See Buros [10].

MEASURES OF INTERESTS, INTELLIGENCE AND PERSONALITY

MEASURES OF INTERESTS

Definition: *Interest Measure*: An instrument which purports to measure vocational or occupational interests of people.

Synonym: *Interest Inventory*.

Disadvantages: Interests may change over time and interest inventories are not always useful for long range predictions.

Comment: Two well known interest inventories [4] are the KUDER OCCUPATIONAL INTEREST SURVEY and the STRONG-CAMPBELL INTEREST SURVEY. Both have acceptable evidence of validity and reliability and have the Ss respond to activities supposedly related to different occupations or vocations.

MEASURES OF INTELLIGENCE

Definition: *Intelligence Measure*: An instrument which purports to measure general factors which are related to a person's capability to learn, adapt, integrate and deal with complex and abstract activities.

Abbreviation: I Q measure.

Advantages: Many of the standardized intelligence measures demonstrate acceptable validity and reliability indices.

Disadvantages: Some intelligence measures require trained administrators.

Comment: Some areas of social science research (e.g., business research) have not often included IQ measures but their use appears to be increasing. IQ measures have a long history and most of the well known instruments are quite good in format, validity, reliability, instructions and ease of use.

PERSONALITY MEASURES

Definition: *Personality Measure*: An instrument which purports to measure affective characteristics of individuals such as introversion or dominance.

An individual's personality is comprised of a whole set of traits, attitudes, beliefs, values and perceptions. While attitudes, beliefs and values are considered part of the personality, their measurement is usually placed in a separate category, as is done here, because of the frequency of use by researchers.

Disadvantages:

1. Personality measurement is the most complex of all the psychological measurements.

2. Many personality measures have little or no evidence of adequate validity.

3. Reliability of personality measures is often too low to be considered adequate. Note the low interrater reliability in opposing opinions of the same personality instrument given by psychologists and psychiatrists in court cases.

4. Many personality instruments require professionally trained administrators and/or interpreters.

CAUTION: The use of personality instruments for research should be confined to situations where their use is absolutely crucial to the project. Professionally trained personnel should be available to administer and interpret some personality instruments.

DEMOGRAPHIC MEASURES

Definition: *Demographic Measure*: An instrument which purports to measure demographic characteristics such as age, national origin, sex of respondent or family size.

CAUTION: Geographic location is often considered a demographic variable but some researchers place it in a separate category.

Comment: It is very common to include items measuring demographic characteristics in an instrument whose major purpose is to measure some other group of variables such as attitudes. It is a relatively rare occurrence to use an instrument measuring only demographic variables.

Advantages:
1. Demographic variables are very useful in segmenting groups. For example, market segmentation studies use demographic information to aim product advertising toward groups which are most likely to use the products.

2. Demographic information is useful in determining nonusers of products so that appropriate steps might be taken to "capture" the nonusers.

3. Many service industries require demographic information in order to target their services or to improve them.

Disadvantages: The major disadvantage in using demographic variables TO WHICH Ss ARE ASKED TO RESPOND is that many of the items require information sensitive to the Ss. Thus, Ss are less likely to respond to items such as "what is your annual income" or sometimes lie, thus distorting the data.

Comment: Demographic variables are widely used in all types of research and heavily used in marketing research.

These general categories of instruments were presented here to aid the researcher in thinking more deeply about what is being measured and to help in directing the researcher toward appropriate information.

For example, if you want to measure attitudes, reading about the measurement of attitudes would be advisable before attempting to select or design an instrument.

Note that there are other ways to categorize instruments than the categories given here. For example, the category "occupational instruments" usually includes instruments which measure performance such as typing skills and mechanical skills. An examination of Buros *Mental Measurements Yearbook* [10] will give the reader a grasp of the wide variety of categories and terms used in connection with existing instruments.

WHERE YOU ARE NOW

At this point you should have:

1. Determined the types of instruments which might be used with your selected data collection method,

2. Examined existing instruments to assess their appropriateness for your study,

3. Decided to design an instrument if no appropriate existing instruments were found,

    and recognized that:

4. Using an existing instrument is usually much less expensive and time consuming, if an appropriate one can be found and

5. Instruments are often categorized by the types of variables they measure and the categories are useful in locating information about the measurement of these variables.

11

DESIGNING QUESTIONNAIRES OR INTERVIEW SCHEDULES

TERMS DEFINED IN CHAPTER ELEVEN

Term   **Page**

CHAPTER ELEVEN

DESIGNING QUESTIONNAIRES OR INTERVIEW SCHEDULES

STEPS TO TAKE AFTER READING THIS CHAPTER

1. List the variables and their operational definitions.

2. Consider including demographic variables, if relevant.

3. Specify the type of respondents.

4. Select mail, telephone or personal approach

5. Determine the amount of structure for the questionnaire or interview.

6. Determine the level of measurement desired and the type of response format for each item.

7. Write the questionnaire items.

8. Check the items for invalidating factors and appropriate levels of measurement.

9. Determine the placement and sequencing of items.

10. Write the introduction, directions and ending.

11. Determine the degree of interviewer direction to respondent, if interviewing.

12. Train the questionnaire administrator or interviewer.

13. Compute the interrater reliability, if interviewing.

14. Use techniques for increasing response, if using the mail.

15. Conduct a pilot study.

16. Check that questions elicit appropriate measures of the variables, desired levels of measurement, ease of response, ease of administration and that time of response for the instrument is appropriate.

17. Revise the instrument, if necessary.

REMINDERS

Remember that questionnaires and interview schedules should be used only when people's attitudes, values, beliefs or self-reports are desired or to clarify information. Check to make sure how your variables will be best measured before proceeding with a questionnaire or interview schedule.

If you determine that a questionnaire or interview schedule is the best instrument for your study, check to see if an appropriate existing instrument is available. It is much less expensive and time consuming to use an existing instrument (either by purchasing copies or having the author's written permission) than to design and pilot test one.

Sometimes an existing instrument might be modified to meet specific project needs. Again, you must have the author's written permission to modify an instrument.

If you should decide to use an existing instrument, simply list the variables, operational definitions and the type of respondents. Then start searching for appropriate instruments using the suggestions in Chapter 10 and refer to selected sections of this chapter as needed.

LIST THE VARIABLES

Before beginning to write the questionnaire items, the research questions or hypotheses should be specifically stated and the variables operationally defined. The variables as defined in the operational definitions are then listed. For example, the hypothesis "frequency of men's use of aftershave lotion is positively related to their educational level" would result in two operational definitions to be included in the list. These might be:

Frequency of use of aftershave lotion: The number of times per week the respondent places aftershave lotion on his face.

Educational level: The level of education completed categorized as: less than high school, high school or equivalent diploma, less than four years of college, four year college degree, some post college education, master's degree, some post master's education, doctoral or professional degree.

You can see how these operational definitions will lead you directly to the item writing and type of responses.

CAUTION: Make sure information is needed about each variable as questionnaire design, construction, administration and analysis is too costly to generate unnecessary information.

CONSIDER DEMOGRAPHIC VARIABLES

Often it is useful to include demographic variables in the questionnaire. This is particularly important for marketing research where some products are aimed at target populations such as pregnancy tests for young and middle aged women and special airline fares for ages 55 and older.

The demographic variables used most frequently include sex of respondent, age, educational level and income level. Remember that these are sensitive items which need to be handled carefully.

Items measuring demographic variables are not a necessary part of the questionnaire but consider them if their inclusion would enhance the usefulness of the results. If demographic variables are included be sure to add them to the variable list.

SPECIFY THE CHARACTERISTICS OF THE RESPONDENTS

Do not begin a questionnaire until the population to which the results are targeted is specified. Reasons for this include: (1) people who have experienced whatever is being asked need to be included, and (2) types of items, item formats and words used are different for different groups of people.

For example, if asking about the effects of smoking marijuana, people who have smoked it need to be included and probably certain age groups (children under 5 years old) could be excluded. If studying the effect of TV ads on preschool children, written items cannot be used and with older children difficult words cannot be used. Young adults cannot be asked to recall World War II because they were not living at the time. The definition of the population should be clearly specified to include appropriate respondents and to help with the wording, format and type of questionnaire.

SELECT MAIL, TELEPHONE OR PERSONAL APPROACH

Three commonly used methods of conducting interviews and distributing questionnaires are by: (1) mail, (2) telephone or (3) personal (face-to-face) contact. When to use each and their disadvantages are given in Exhibit 11.1. Note that on-line computers and interactive television are also now being used for interviews.

INCREASING RESPONSE RATE OF MAILED QUESTIONNAIRES

The possibility of a high nonresponse rate is a major problem with mailed questionnaires. Some researchers consider a 35% to 40% response rate as acceptable. However, consider the question "have you ever shopped at K-Mart?" If 40% of the sample responded and all of them said "yes," the possibility remains that the other 60% who did not respond might have said "no." Thus, there has been a considerable amount of examination of methods to increase response rate. Some of these suggestions are given in Exhibit 11.2.

EXHIBIT 11.1   SELECTING THE TYPE OF QUESTIONNAIRE OR
                  INTERVIEW APPROACH

USE WHEN: **MAJOR DISADVANTAGES***
                         MAIL

1. Questionnaire can be easily   1. Possible high non-
   answered by respondent.   response rate.

2. No need to probe deeper.

3. Respondents are geographically
   scattered.

                      TELEPHONE

1. Need to save costs.   1. Lack of control over
                                       sampling.

                       PERSONAL

1. Desired information is   1. Interviewer bias and
   complex.   influence on responses.

2. Probing is required   2. Interviewer/respondent
                                       interactions.

                                    3. Interviewer training time
                                       and costs.

                                    4. Need for interviewer
                                       reliability checks.

                                    5. Time consuming.

                                    6. Costly.

                                    7. Less data because of time
                                       required.

*One method of avoiding some of these disadvantages is to administer
the questionnaire to a "captive" group, such as conference
participants who are in one room, and wait in the room while the
group completes the questionnaires. However, this is appropriate
ONLY when the group comprises the desired Ss and sampling
procedures appropriate to the specific project have been considered,
e.g., conference participants would not be representative of
nonparticipants.

EXHIBIT 11.2   SELECTED WAYS TO INCREASE RESPONSE RATE OF
                 MAILED QUESTIONNAIRES

1. Include a cover letter which appeals to respondent's affiliation such as "as a graduate of Michigan State University we feel you will want to _____."

2. Mail a reminder postcard about 10 days after the first mailing. Every respondent will have to receive this postcard unless Ss who have returned questionnaires are identified.

3. Mail a second questionnaire about one week after the postcard.

4. Contact nonrespondents by telephone.

5. Enclose a token, such as a pencil, pen or coin, with the questionnaire.

6. Write clear directions.

7. Mention how little time is required to complete the questionnaire.

8. Avoid open-ended items, if possible. People are more likely to respond to a format in which they can check items rather than generate responses.

9. Structure item responses so respondent can answer quickly and easily.

10. Structure the entire questionnaire so respondent can complete it easily and quickly. Make placement and sequencing of items logical and easy to follow.

11. Ensure that the questionnaire is professionally typed and printed so that its appearance gives the impression of credibility and professionalism.

USE OF MAILING LISTS

Mailing lists can be purchased from several organizations. While these lists are convenient, their use poses serious potential sampling problems. Most mailing lists are not generated with the precision required in defining a research population. This makes it difficult to define the population other than saying it consisted of ABC's mailing list. It is hazardous to use mailing lists if the researcher wishes to generalize research results to a specified population.

TELEPHONE SURVEYS

Telephone surveys have become increasingly popular because a large proportion of people in the United States can be reached by telephone. The major disadvantage -- and it is a serious one -- is lack of control over sampling.

People who do not own phones and people with unlisted numbers tend to differ from those people who are listed in the phone book on a number of significant variables such as income level, type of housing and degree of mobility. If the phone book comprises the listing of the possible population elements (the sampling frame) remember that certain groups will be overrepresented and other groups will be underrepresented. This plays havoc with inferences to an appropriate and specified population, even when simple random sampling is used.

THE PERSONAL APPROACH

A face-to-face interview is useful when the information desired is complex or when probing is required. These are probably the two major reasons for personal interviews to be considered. There are so many disadvantages to personal interviews that they are rarely used if budgets are tight.

Personal interviews are usually very costly because so few people can be questioned by one interviewer in one day, compared with mail and telephone surveys. In addition interviewer influences and interviewer/respondent interaction may bias the data.

After training interviewers it is necessary to have reliability estimates on how consistently the interviewers rate items in a similar manner. This is done by computing interrater reliability estimates between or among interviewers as illustrated in Chapter 5. If the reliability estimates are not sufficiently high, retraining of interviewers should be conducted.

To cut costs of interviewing, interview schedules can combine open-ended items for probing and structured items. It is useful to add as much structure as possible and use open-ended items only for probing and complex items, thus saving interviewer time and consequently costs.

DETERMINE THE AMOUNT OF STRUCTURE

Definition: *Structured Questionnaire*: A questionnaire which includes fixed items, fixed response categories and fixed sequencing of items.

Purpose: To restrict the respondent to specific questions with specific answers in a specific ordering.

Advantages: The more the respondent is restricted to specific questions with specific responses, the more likely it is the researcher has responses to the questions desired and in the form desired.

Disadvantages: Structured items and responses do not allow creative responses from respondents.

> **Comment:** Using a highly structured questionnaire is the least expensive and fastest method of acquiring the information needed when there is sufficient knowledge to write the items and responses and there is no need for creative responses.

Many questionnaires are fully structured but varying degrees of structure can be used within a single questionnaire. Open-ended items to which the respondent can respond freely are often included, usually at the end of the questionnaire.

DETERMINE THE RESPONSE FORMAT

It may seem strange to determine the response format before you write the item. However, writing the response format first saves a great deal of time because the item stem and item responses must be compatible.

Determine the level of measurement desired for each variable prior to selecting the type of response format. Scaled responses are usually at the ratio, interval or ordinal level of measurement but can be analyzed using nominal statistical tests. Ranking responses are considered ordinal level but can also be analyzed with nominal level statistical tests. Categorical responses must be analyzed at the nominal level.

Examples of scaled, ranking and categorical responses are given in Exhibit 11.3.

Definition: *Scaled Responses:* Response categories which indicate gradations or a continuum of the variable being measured.

Definition: *Ranking Responses:* Response categories (or materials) which the respondent is asked to place in order according to some variable such as degree of preference.

Definition: *Categorical Responses:* Response categories which are different from one another but have no assumption of order (that one is better than or larger than another).

Four types of response formats usually considered are: (1) multiple choice, (2) dichotomous, which is a two response multiple choice, (3) ranking or (4) open-ended. Examples of each are given in Exhibit 11.4.

EXHIBIT 11.3	LEVEL OF MEASUREMENT AND TYPICAL EXAMPLES OF THREE TYPES OF RESPONSES		
Type of Response	Description	Allowable Level of Measurement	Typical Example*
1. Scaled	Responses indicate gradations of the variable.	Depends on the responses (see Chapter 5). Usually Ratio, Interval or Ordinal. Can be used as Nominal.	Please rate each of the following cities in terms of its desirability as a place for you to live. 1 I would like living in this city 2 I would neither like nor dislike living in this city. 3 I would dislike living in this city. New York ___ ___ ___ Chicago ___ ___ ___ Los Angeles ___ ___ ___ San Francisco ___ ___ ___
2. Ranking	Responses are ranked in order.	Ordinal. Can be used as nominal.	Please rank each of the following cities from one to four in terms of its desirability as a place for you to live. Mark 1 for the city in which you would most like to live and 4 for the city in which you would least like to live. ___ New York ___ Chicago ___ Los Angeles ___ San Francisco
3. Categorical Response	Categories are different from one another.	Nominal only.	In which one of the following cities would you prefer to live? ___ 1. New York ___ 2. Chicago ___ 3. Los Angeles ___ 4. San Francisco ___ 5. Other (Please Specify)_____

*Note how much more information the scaled response yields compared with ranking and categorical responses. For the many disadvantages of ranking see Chapter 12.

EXHIBIT 11.4   MAJOR ADVANTAGES AND DISADVANTAGES OF DIFFERENT RESPONSE FORMATS

Type of Response Format	Major Advantages	Major Disadvantages	Example
1. Multiple Choice	• Obtain researcher specified responses. • Response easy and fast. • Allows more items than would open-ended in same time span. • Easy tabulation of data. • Can be used for scaled or categorical responses.	• Does not allow respondent creativity or originality. • Requires time to generate "good" items.	How do you feel about the U.S. government funding the so-called "Star Wars" (Strategic Defense Initiative) technology? 1. Strongly Agree: U.S. Should Fund SDI 2. Somewhat Agree 3. Neither Agree nor Disagree 4. Somewhat Disagree 5. Strongly Disagree
2. Dichotomous (two response multiple choice)	• Response easy and fast. • Tabulation easy and fast.	• Severely limited amount of information. • May yield erroneous data if respondents can't decide how to answer.	Have you ever attended a Chicago Cubs baseball game at Wrigley Field? 1. Yes 2. No
3. Ranking	• Forces discrimination among responses.	• Does not yield degree of respondent preference but only preference for selected responses over other responses. • Respondent is not allowed "dislike" responses. • Response more difficult and slower than multiple choice.	Rank each of the following items from 1 to 4 in terms of how frequently you use each. Mark 1 for the item you use most often and 4 for the item you use least often. _____ Video Cassette Recorder _____ Microwave Oven _____ Computer _____ Hand Held Calculator
4. Open-Ended	• Can elicit creative or original responses. • Can measure organization of thought.	• Can generate unpredictable information. • Requires much respondent time. • Requires much respondent effort • Requires much researcher or clerical time for data coding and tabulation.	By the year 2010, what will be the effects on employment of using robots in manufacturing processes?

MULTIPLE CHOICE RESPONSES

Definition: *Multiple Choice Response Item:* A question or statement comprised of: (1) a stem, which is the question or statement itself and (2) the possible responses, sometimes called foils. The responses may form a scale or be categories only. Usually the respondent is instructed to select one response only but, in some situations, is allowed to choose more than one.

Related Definition: *Response Bias:* The tendency of a subject to consistently select or demonstrate one type of response from a series of responses.

Advantages:

1. Restricts the respondent to the questions and choices of responses which the researcher desires.

2. Ease and speed of response by checking or otherwise marking.

3. More items measuring more variables may be used because the format allows the respondent to answer more items in the same time span required for few items requiring written responses.

4. Reduces interviewer bias.

5. Tabulation of data is easier than with other methods.

Disadvantages:

1. Limits the respondent to researcher determined responses.

2. Does not allow for respondent's original or creative ideas.

3. Possible respondent resentment if fixed responses do not include alternatives the respondent considers viable.

4. Requires time and effort to write unbiased stems which best measure the variable appropriately and responses which are mutually exclusive, inclusive and appropriate.

5. Potential for invalid data from poorly written items exists.

6. The potential for response bias exists.

Comment: Response bias can be somewhat alleviated by changing the response categories in sequential items. For example, number five responses to an item from 1 to 5 with 1 indicating the most positive response and 5 indicating the most negative response. On the next item again number the responses 1,2,3,4,5 but reverse the responses with 1 indicating the most negative response and 5 indicating the most positive response.

Another strategy is to word some item stems positively and other item stems negatively.

CAUTION: Well written multiple choice items are considered far preferable to dichotomous, ranking or open-ended items for many projects because they elicit appropriate information in the desired form.

Level of Measurement: Can be ratio, interval, ordinal or nominal depending on whether the multiple choices represent scales or categories.

EXHIBIT 11.5   WRITING TIPS FOR MULTIPLE CHOICE ITEMS

1. Avoid leading or biased stems.

2. Avoid items which respondents cannot or will not answer, or will not answer truthfully.

3. Ensure that the categories are mutually exclusive -- that the response can only be in one category.

4. Ensure that the categories are inclusive -- that they include all reasonable answers to the question.

5. Add a category "Other, please specify _____ " if uncertain that the categories are inclusive.

6. Read Chapter 12 about instruments, if including a scale.

7. Limit the number of choices. Three to seven alternative responses are usually sufficient with five alternatives commonly used. Beyond seven choices the respondent has some difficulty in discriminating and the time of response increases.

DICHOTOMOUS RESPONSE FORMAT

Definition: *Dichotomous Response Item*: A question or statement for which only two mutually exclusive responses are given.

Advantages:

1. Easy and fast for respondent to answer.
2. Easy and fast for researcher to tabulate.

Disadvantages: The amount of information yielded is limited because there are only two possible responses.

Dichotomous response items are often overused because of lack of awareness that multiple choice items would generate more information. While there are items for which dichotomous responses are appropriate (e.g., sex of respondent, true or false, right or wrong) for most items the researcher should attempt multiple choice rather than dichotomous responses.

For example, "Do you eat cereal for breakfast?" yields yes/no responses. This could be reworded to "how many times per week do you eat cereal for breakfast?" to which multiple choice responses could be:

1. Seven or more times per week
2. Five to six times per week
3. Three to four times per week
4. One to two times per week
5. Less than one time per week
6. Never eat cereal for breakfast

This multiple choice item yields yes/no information on whether the respondent eats cereal for breakfast or not (responses 1 through 5 = yes, response 6 = no) plus information on how frequently cereal is eaten for breakfast. The additional information is often worth the additional time and space needed to generate multiple choice items.

2. Often forces the respondent to give an answer which may not indicate the reality. How would someone who eats cereal for breakfast once or twice a year answer the dichotomous question, "Do you eat cereal for breakfast?" Some would answer yes and some no.

Level of Measurement: Usually nominal as most two responses items are unordered categories. Two responses such as "I read books often" and "I rarely or never read books" would be ordinal if the variable were "frequency of reading books." (Note that more information would be elicited by asking, "How many books did you read last year?" with numerical responses.)

OPEN-ENDED RESPONSE FORMAT

Definition: *Open-Ended Response Item*: A question or statement with no fixed responses, requiring the respondent to generate a written or oral response or create something such as a drawing.

Advantages:

1. Can elicit creative and/or original information.

2. Gives respondent the opportunity of giving opinions.

3. Can measure organization of thought.

4. Can measure writing, grammatical or spelling ability.

5. Can add new information when there is very little existing information about a topic.

6. Allows the respondent to add personal notes or comments.

Disadvantages:

1. Generates unpredictable information which can easily stray from the intent of the question, yielding poor and inadequate data. This is a

serious disadvantage. Years ago the author helped conduct a research study in which 8th graders were asked their father's occupation and one eighth grade boy wrote down "he sells license plates." A year later we discovered that his father was the Secretary of State.

2. Requires much respondent time.

3. Requires much respondent effort.

4. Requires some degree of respondent writing ability, if the responses are written. The illiteracy rate is higher than one may think, and some respondents may be unable to generate written responses.

5. Respondent handwriting is often illegible.

6. Can create respondent resentment about the task, which can create invalid responses.

7. Requires much researcher time to generate an instrument to measure the variables in the responses.

8. Requires much researcher time for coding and tabulation of data.

CAUTION: Open-ended items should be used only for the reasons such as those listed under advantages above, because of their several serious disadvantages.

Level of Measurement: Depends on how variables are categorized. Such categories as "mentions texture of product" and "mentions flavor of product" would be at the nominal level. Categories such as "number of times respondent mentions product" would be at the ratio level.

EXHIBIT 11.6   WRITING TIPS FOR OPEN-ENDED ITEMS

1. "What is your reaction to the current Federal Budget Deficit?" is an open-ended item. This item could elicit responses from "I think it stinks" to a four paragraph treatise on the subject. It would be better to place that item into a multiple choice format and save the open-ended items for measuring variables which require creative responses such as "What would you recommend to decrease the Federal Budget Deficit?"

2. Never use written open-ended items to elicit dichotomous responses such as yes/no or agree/disagree. Provide these responses for the respondent to check to save both respondent and researcher time.

OTHER RESPONSE FORMATS

Response formats other than multiple choice, dichotomous and open-ended can be used in questionnaires and interview schedules. Several of these formats, including ranking, are discussed in Chapter 12.

EXHIBIT 11.7   WRITING TIPS FOR QUESTIONNAIRES AND INTERVIEW SCHEDULES

1. **Use Clear Language.** The respondent must be able to understand the question and the type of response desired. Words should be kept simple and short. Avoid using technical words except for specialized fields where respondents understand them.

2. **Avoid Value Laden Words and Phrases.** Phrases like "RED China" or "WEALTHY corporations" can be interpreted negatively by some respondents. This leads to item bias.

3. **Avoid Suggestive Wording.** Any word or phrase which suggests a specific response to an item results in a biased item. For example, "Given the poor condition of our roads, would you agree that taxes should be raised to resurface them?" would elicit much different responses than "Should taxes be raised to resurface the roads?"

4. **Ask One Question Per Item.** An amazing number of researchers include two or more questions in one item. "Have you ever used or owned a video recorder?" should be two questions.

5. **Specify the Framework of the Question.** Specify the limits within which you want the question answered. These limits can be in terms of time or other types of responses desired. For example, "How often have you attended a theatre" is open to questions on what type of theatre and during what time period. "How many times did you attend a movie theatre last year?" is better.

6. **Consider Adding an Open-Ended Item for Comments.** An open-ended item for respondents' comments is often included, usually at the end of a questionnaire. This allows respondents to add whatever information they wish without researcher directions. It is useful for acquiring novel information the researcher may not have considered and gives the respondents the opportunity of greater participation which often makes them feel more positive about the time spent in completing the questionnaire.

Examples are: "Please feel free to add any comment you wish to make" or simply "Comments." Some questionnaires use "comments" after each item but this is questionable practice unless the researcher is willing to analyze each comment. Research should be parsimonious and data should not be collected unless it will be used.

7. **Limit the Number of Items.** Keep the questionnaire as short as possible so that the respondent will complete it. A lengthy questionnaire is very discouraging to respondents and many will refuse to participate or will stop responding when partially completed or will rush to complete it giving little thought to the responses. Giving respondents an estimate of the time required to complete the questionnaire is helpful.

8. **Write Each Item on a Separate Card or Use a Word Processor.** Items are usually revised several times, discarded or new items added. Placement of items also changes during the design It saves a considerable amount of time if items are written on separate papers or cards such as 3x5 or 5x8 file cards so that items can be modified without changing other parts of the questionnaire and can be shuffled around to achieve the best placement. Using a word processor will help with these problems.

WRITE THE ITEMS

The reason for using a questionnaire is to ask questions. Yet many researchers rush through the writing of the questions with little thought. One criterion should be kept in mind: the question should convey to the respondent what the researcher intended to say. This is not an easy task. Tips for writing questionnaires are given in Exhibit 11.7.

Recommended References: Payne [52]. Kornhauser and Sheatsley [41].

CHECK THE ITEMS FOR INVALIDATING FACTORS

After writing the items check each item for factors which might invalidate the data. Exhibit 11.8 is a checklist for you to use.

EXHIBIT 11.8   CHECKLIST FOR EACH QUESTIONNAIRE ITEM*

1. Will item yield data in the form required by the hypotheses or research questions and the operational definitions?

2. Will item yield data at the level of measurement required for the selected statistical analysis?

3. Does item avoid "leading" respondent to a specific response?

4. Is item unbiased?

5. Will most respondents have sufficient knowledge to answer item?

6. Will most respondents be willing to answer item?

7. Will most respondents answer item truthfully?

*All answers should be yes before proceeding with questionnaire.

WRITE THE INTRODUCTION AND THE ENDING

The introduction and ending of the questionnaire are added after the items are written and checked, because directions and time estimates depend on the number and type of items.

Cover letters are often used to introduce the project to the respondent and persuade the respondent to reply. If costs and space are problems the information usually included in the cover letter is frequently placed on the first page of the questionnaire.

If you can afford to use a cover letter, do so but be sure to include the name and address of the organization conducting the study on the questionnaire itself. Information usually included in an introduction is given in Exhibit 11.9 and an example of a cover letter is given in Exhibit 11.10.

EXHIBIT 11.9   INFORMATION USUALLY INCLUDED IN
                QUESTIONNAIRE INTRODUCTIONS AND
                COVER LETTERS

1. **Name of Organization Conducting the Study**. This is not always
   the same as the sponsor of the study. Often giving the name of
   the sponsor, such as General Motors, will elicit different
   responses than will "The Survey Corporation."

2. **Purpose of the Project**. This should not be a lengthy explanation
   but a brief general statement such as "we are interested in your
   opinions of various products."

3. **How Respondent was Selected**. Phrases such as "your name was
   randomly selected _____."

4. **Expression of Appreciation for Respondent's Help**. Phrases such
   as "We would very much appreciate your help _____."

5. **Estimate of Questionnaire Completion Time**. Phrases such as
   "This should only take about 10 minutes of your time."

6. **Assurance of Nonidentification of Respondent**. Phrases such as
   "you will not be identified by name."

7. **Assurance of Confidentiality of Responses**. Phrases such as "All
   responses will remain confidential."

8. **Directions for Completion**. Complete information on how to
   mark responses should be given such as "Please circle ONE answer
   for each of the following questions." Directions are not included
   in a cover letter but are placed directly on the questionnaire
   where the respondent can easily see them.

EXHIBIT 11.10   EXAMPLE OF A COVER LETTER

Winter, 1987

To: Participants in the 1987 Financial Institutions Study

We would appreciate your help and need a few minutes of your time. We are seeking your views and opinions about financial institutions and their services. From you, and other residents in your region, we hope to secure information about current practices and preferences of consumers who use services of banks and savings and loan associations.

The enclosed survey form will take only a few minutes of your time to complete and return in the postage-paid reply envelope. Most of the questions can be answered with a check mark or a brief phrase of two or three words. PLEASE BE ASSURED THAT YOUR RESPONSES WILL BE HELD IN STRICT CONFIDENCE AND USED ONLY TO SECURE KNOWLEDGE ABOUT CONSUMER PREFERENCES AND USE OF FINANCIAL SERVICES.

Your response is important. Your name was chosen as part of a "random sample" which is representative of residents in your region. The accuracy of the study depends heavily upon your response to assure that the views and opinions reflect residents in your geographical region.

Your prompt cooperation and participation in this important survey is appreciated. Please take a few minutes today to complete the questionnaire and return it to the Center for Business and Economic Research in the envelope provided.

Sincerely,

xxxxxxxxxxxx
xxxxxxxxxxxx

P.S.:   As a token of our appreciation, we have enclosed a crisp $1.00 bill for your participation in this important study.

xxxxxxxx

Enclosures

_____

Reprinted by permission from Michael T. Pledge and Robert W. Jefferson, Western Illinois University.

At the end of the questionnaire always include at least a "thank you" or "thank you for participating." If a summary of the findings is to be returned to the respondent, include this information also. One option is to include the address or phone numbers to be contacted if the respondent desires a summary of the findings. This is less expensive than sending summaries to all respondents as many respondents will not take the trouble to make the contact -- but will still feel pleased at being offered the opportunity.

Also at the end of the questionnaire be sure to repeat directions for mailing or turning it in to the questionnaire administrator.

DETERMINE PLACEMENT OF THE ITEMS

Where items are placed on the questionnaire depends on: (1) the type of variables used, (2) the response formats and (3) the sensitivity of the items. Suggestions for item placement are given in Exhibit 11.11.

EXHIBIT 11.11   SUGGESTIONS FOR ITEM PLACEMENT

1. Place introduction in a separate cover letter or at the top of the first page.

2. Place nonsensitive demographic items at the beginning of the questionnaire because they are easy to answer, nonthreatening and tend to put the respondent at ease.

3. Place items of major interest next, as there is a greater probability of respondents completing the first part of the questionnaire.

4. Sequence items of major interest in logical order, usually with items on the same topic grouped together. Item sequence can lead to biased responses so be careful that one item does not influence the response to the following item.

5. Place sensitive items (e.g., income) last so that resentment of the intrusiveness of these items does not affect other responses.

6. Group items with the same response formats together, if using mixed response formats, unless this interferes with the desired sequencing of items.

COMPLETE THE QUESTIONNAIRE PREPARATION

The questionnaire now needs preparation for the final typing and copying or printing. Combine the items, the introduction and the ending in the appropriate sequence and placement. If the information is on index cards simply place them in order; if already on a word processor instruct the typist about the sequence desired.

EXHIBIT 11.12   TRAINING TIPS FOR INTERVIEWERS AND
                  QUESTIONNAIRE ADMINISTRATORS

1. Give written directions to all questionnaire administrators and interviewers so that each respondent receives the same directions and questions in the same format.

2. If all the directions or items are not included in the questionnaire or if administering questionnaires to young children or adults who cannot read, give the interviewer a card on which the information is written. Instruct the interviewer to read the card in the same way to each respondent.

3. Anticipate respondent questions by using information from the pilot study and instruct interviewers how to respond. A typical interviewer response is: "I'm sorry, I'm instructed not to answer questions so that you can use your own ideas." However, for some research projects, the interviewers will be instructed to clarify items and how to clarify items for respondents.

4. Have the interviewer participate in a simulated situation, answering respondent questions and interviewing respondents. Have judges observe this procedure and give the interviewer their critiques and suggestions for improvement after the simulation.

5. Train interviewers carefully and thoroughly if they will be probing (asking respondents for in-depth answers). Training for questionnaire administration only and for in-depth interviews is quite different, even though their purpose is the same. The major reason for the increased training of interviewers is that they have so many opportunities to influence the respondent by what they say and do. A great deal of training is required to avoid invalid responses.

6. Instruct the interviewer on the amount of direction given to the respondent. The amount of direction an interviewer gives the respondent is a continuum ranging from very little interviewer direction (nondirective) to a large amount (directive interview).

Initially, have a sufficient number of copies made to train people to administer the questionnaires and to conduct a pilot test. If printing the final questionnaire, delay printing until after the pilot test in case there may be changes.

TRAIN THE QUESTIONNAIRE ADMINISTRATOR OR INTERVIEWER

In any situation where a questionnaire will be given directly to the respondent by another person, it is necessary to train that person. Even if all the administrator does is hand the respondent the questionnaire, training on how to answer respondent questions is necessary.

EXHIBIT 11.13   EXAMPLE OF INSTRUCTIONS TO QUESTIONNAIRE ADMINISTRATOR

1. **Say**:
"I'm (name) from the XYZ Company and we are interested in your opinion of our products."

"We would appreciate your filling out this questionnaire which only takes about 3 minutes. The directions are right there at the top."

2. **Hand Respondents the Questionnaires and Pencils**.

3. **If Respondent Has Questions About the Directions**: Clarify them.

4. **If Respondent Has Questions About the Items**: Say:
"Just answer according to how you interpret the question."

5. **Write on the Back of this Sheet**: Respondents' comments and item numbers of items which respondents have questioned.

6. **When the Respondents Turn in the Questionnaires**: Say:
"Thank you. We appreciate your help."

Definition: *Interviewer Training*: Giving instruction and practice to questionnaire administrators or interviewers on exactly what to say and do during administration of the questionnaire or interview schedule.

Purpose: To ensure that the researcher acquires the information needed in the appropriate form with a minimum amount of administrator bias. To control what the administrator does and says to lessen the possibility of interviewer influence on respondent answers.

In nondirective interviewing, the interviewer usually asks the respondent a question and allows the respondent to answer freely while the interviewer maintains contact by comments such as "yes" or "I understand." The more the interviewer directs the questioning, e.g., "Why do you think that is?", the more directive is the interview.

EXHIBIT 11.14   THE PROCESS FOR CONDUCTING A PILOT TEST

1. Select a sample similar to the sample to be used in the study but which will not be included in the study.

2. Copy a sufficient number of questionnaires for the pilot study sample.

3. Instruct the questionnaire administrators to make notes of respondent questions about the items or directions.

4. Administer the questionnaires or interview schedules.

5. Check the results of the pilot test:

    5.1 Did the items yield the desired information in the appropriate form?

    5.2 Did the items yield the selected levels of measurement?

    5.3 Were the directions clear to the respondents?

    5.4 Were respondents able to answer the questions easily?

    5.5 How much time did the fastest 90% of the respondents take to complete the questionnaire or interview?

    5.6 How much time did it take 90% of the fastest questionnaire administrators to give directions and complete the probing phase?

6. Revise the questionnaire if responses to #5 are unsatisfactory.

7. Retrain the questionnaire administrators or interviewers if their performance was unsatisfactory.

CAUTION: GROUP INTERVIEWS

Occasionally interviews are conducted with groups of people as they interact with one another. While this method has the advantage of eliciting creative responses it has the serious disadvantage of lack of independent responses of the individuals in the group.

Any time a subject's response can be influenced by someone or something else, the individual response is said to lack independence. To overcome this, when using group interviews use several groups and consider each group, rather than the individuals within the groups, as one subject. This requires several groups.

CONDUCT A PILOT TEST

Before the questionnaire is administered to the Ss, a pilot test should be conducted to assess any flaws in the questionnaire or its administration. The process for conducting a pilot test is given in Exhibit 11.14.

After the pilot test is conducted and any modifications made, the questionnaires should go through a final typing and copying. Printing questionnaires is advisable as it makes them appear professional and tends to give more credibility to the project. This enhances the probability of potential respondents being willing to participate in the project.

WHERE YOU ARE NOW

At this point you should have:

1. Determined whether to select an existing questionnaire or design one,

2. Listed the variables and their operational definitions,

3. Listed the type of respondents,

4. Selected mail, telephone or personal approach,

5. Determined whether to use multiple choice or other types of response formats for each item,

6. Written each item so that it best measures the variable, using the most appropriate level of measurement and response format,

7. Placed all items, introduction and ending in the most appropriate sequence,

8. Trained the questionnaire administrators or interviewers,

9. Computed interrater reliabilities, if interviewing,

10. Pilot tested the questionnaire or interview schedule,

11. Completed any changes, if necessary and

12. Completed the final typing and printing of the questionnaire.

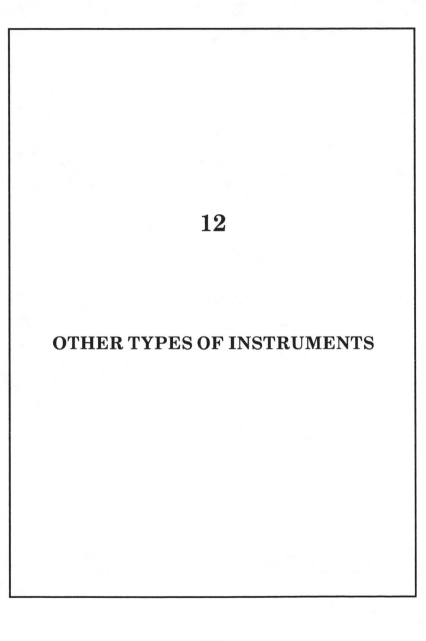

12

OTHER TYPES OF INSTRUMENTS

TERMS DEFINED IN CHAPTER TWELVE

CHAPTER TWELVE

OTHER TYPES OF INSTRUMENTS

STEPS TO TAKE AFTER READING THIS CHAPTER

1. List the variables to be measured.

2. Determine the desired level of measurement for each variable.

3. Determine the type of instrument which will best measure the variables at the desired level of measurement.

4. Select or design the instrument.

5. Conduct a pilot study, if a new instrument is designed or an existing instrument is modified.

6. Revise the instrument, if necessary.

Many types of instruments are used in research. Exhibit 12.1 indicates the most frequently used instruments with ratings of their advantages and disadvantages. Note that these ratings are subjective and the instruments selected depend on a researcher decision on how the variables under study will be best measured within the constraints of the research project.

Comment: While processes and examples of these instruments are given in the text, they are necessarily brief. To fully describe all the ramifications of each instrument would require several books. Refer to the recommended references if you desire additional information.

INDEPENDENT AND NONINDEPENDENT RESPONSES

In determining the type of instrument be aware of the difference between responses which are independent and not independent. With independent items the Ss response to one item has no influence on responses to any other items. Nonindependent items force Ss to select an alternative that "precludes the choice of other alternatives" [36, p. 492] and are called forced-choice items.

Definition: *Forced-choice item*: An item which forces subjects to choose one alternative from a set of alternatives so that the subject is NOT given the opportunity to: (1) express individual opinions on each alternative or (2) select none of the alternatives. Thus, the responses are

EXHIBIT 12.1   MAJOR ADVANTAGES AND DISADVANTAGES OF INSTRUMENTS USED IN RESEARCH

Instrument	Rating*	Major Advantages	Major Disadvantages	Example of Item
1. Rating Scale	Good	• Easy Response • Independent response for each item.	• Susceptible to constant error (response bias).	Please rate the flavor of this Cola drink. 1. Excellent 2. Good 3. Fair 4. Poor 5. Very Poor
2. Summated Rating (Likert-type)	Fair	• Yields a single score by summing or averaging items.	• Assumption of equal value items difficult to meet.	Store: <u>Smiths</u> <u>Agree</u> No <u>Opinion</u> <u>Disagree</u> Low Quality Food: ------ ------ ------ Clean: ------ ------ ------
3. Thurstone Equal Appearing Interval Scale	Poor	• Yields a scale which is usually treated as an interval scale.	• Appropriateness of scale depends on judges' attitudes. • Time consuming to generate. • Costly to generate.	• Large Corporations rob the government. • Large Corporations help the average person.
4. Semantic Differential (SD)	O.K.	• Easy response • Large quantity of data yielded in short amount of time.	• Difficult to generate bipolar adjectives. • Time and expertise required to factor analyze untested adjectives. • Time required for analysis.	<u>President Reagan</u> Large _:_:_:_:_:_:_:_ Small Passive _:_:_:_:_:_:_:_ Active Bad _:_:_:_:_:_:_:_ Good Sharp _:_:_:_:_:_:_:_ Dull

EXHIBIT 12.1 (cont.)   MAJOR ADVANTAGES AND DISADVANTAGES OF INSTRUMENTS USED IN RESEARCH

Instrument	Rating*	Major Advantages	Major Disadvantages	Example of Item
5. Single Anchor Scale	O.K.	• Avoids generating bipolar adjectives. • Response slightly faster than for SD.	• Nuisance and time consuming if negative numbers are used. • Careful selection of unipolar adjectives required.	President Reagan Good +3 / +2 / +1 / Passive -1 / -2 / -3 +3 / +2 / +1 -1 / -2 / -3
6. Multidimensional Scaling (MDS)	Poor	• Helps identify criteria people use in making judgments. • Increased use will lower impact of disadvantages as more trained people will be available.	• Requires specific computer programs. • Requires training Lack of research on the validity of MDS • Difficult to determine the meaning of different dimensions.	Please rate each of the following pairs of cars on their degree of similarity to each other. Very Similar / Some-what Similar / Some-what Dis-similar / Very Dis-similar Ford Escort & Toyota Tercell ----- ----- ----- ----- Ford Escort & Olds Cutlass ----- ----- ----- -----

EXHIBIT 12.1 (cont.) MAJOR ADVANTAGES AND DISADVANTAGES OF INSTRUMENTS USED IN RESEARCH

Instrument	Rating*	Major Advantages	Major Disadvantages	Example of Item
7. Rank Order Method	Poor	• Similar to real world in forcing discrimination.	• Ss do not have opportunity to express "like", "dislike" for each item. • Longer response time. • More difficult for Ss to rank than to rate. • Fewer items because of longer response time. • Can create Ss resentment.	Please rank from 1 to 4 each of the following stores in terms of the quality of their small appliance service. Rank the best quality appliance service 1 and the lowest quality service 4. Sears _____ J.C. Penney _____ Smith's _____ Wilson Co.
8. Constant Sum Method	Poor	• Similar to real world in forcing discrimination.	• Ss do not have opportunity to express "like", "dislike" for each item. • Some Ss have difficulty summing to zero. • Response time longer than for other instruments. • Very few items used because of time and difficulty. • Insufficient research on assumed equal interval properties.	Please assign points to each of the following countries according to how much you would like to live there. The total number of points must add to 100 points. Country Points China _____ Japan _____ Cuba _____ Haiti 100

EXHIBIT 12.1 (cont.)   MAJOR ADVANTAGES AND DISADVANTAGES OF INSTRUMENTS USED IN RESEARCH

Instrument	Rating*	Major Advantages	Major Disadvantages	Example of Item
9. Q Technique	Fair	• Yields both a rank order and a normal distribution.	• Time and costs to generate the cards. • Time and costs to conduct the personal interviews.	Please place each of the 60 cards into one of the eleven piles according to how much you approve of these business practices. The piles to the left reflect practices most approved by you and the piles to the right least approved by you. If you are unsure place the card in the middle.
10. Paired Comparison Method	Poor	• Similar to real world in forcing discrimination.	• Forced choice requires Ss to choose items even if they dislike item. • Can create Ss resentment at task of choosing • Lacks independence of response. • Long response time.	For each pair of vendors, please circle the vendor you consider most reliable. 1 2 3 Gray King Post Post Gray King
11. Checklist	Good	• Easy response • Fast response	• Ease and speed of response may make Ss careless in responding. • Tendency to use when rating scale would be better.	Check the name of the vendor you consider the most reliable. -----1. Gray -----2. King -----3. Post

EXHIBIT 12.1 (cont.)   MAJOR ADVANTAGES AND DISADVANTAGES OF INSTRUMENTS USED IN RESEARCH

Instrument	Rating*	Major Advantages	Major Disadvantages	Example of Item
12. The Delphi Method (Delphic Poll)	Fair	• Reflects most up-to-date consensus of experts. • Anonymity avoids conflict among respondents. • Supposedly encourages innovative thinking.	• Lacks independence of response after first round. • Time consuming to prepare and analyze each round. • Costly.	By what time period do you expect auto production plants to be completely robotized with no human workers. ——1. 1990 ——2. 2000 ——3. After 2000 ——4. Never

13. Projective Techniques	Fair	• Supposedly allows Ss to project inner feelings.	• Low validity often a problem.
			• Low reliability often a problem.
			• Time consuming to administer.
			• Time consuming and often difficult to score.
			• May require highly trained administrators.
			• Costly
				<u>Sentence Completion</u>
				
				People who drive Jaguars ....
				
				           <u>Word Association</u>
				
				Stimuli: IBM
				           AT&T
				           Ford

EXHIBIT 12.1 (cont.) MAJOR ADVANTAGES AND DISADVANTAGES OF INSTRUMENTS USED IN RESEARCH

Instrument	Rating*	Major Advantages	Major Disadvantages	Example of Item
14. Content Analysis Techniques	Good	• Can be used with any type of communication. • Widely applicable. • Usually free of response bias. • Useful when direct observation is not feasible • Usually carried out at researcher's convenience. • The most appropriate method for open-ended items. • Computer programs are available.	• Can be time consuming. • Can be costly depending on number and type of variables analyzed.	For each TV commercial, record the number of verbal and nonverbal references to and the name of each competitive product. Product Advertised: Name of Competitive Product / Number of References (Verbal, Nonverbal) 1. ___ ___ 2. ___ ___ 3. ___ ___ 4. ___ ___

*Researchers should use these ratings as guides not givens.
Each instrument was rated by the author using the following scale:
1. Good: Advantages outweigh disadvantages.
2. O.K.: Advantages and disadvantages about equal.
3. Fair: O.K. for selected situations. May require extra careful construction or interpretation or may be time consuming/costly.
4. Poor: Disadvantages outweigh advantages.
These ratings are obviously subjective as the selection of an instrument depends on the type of research project and variables studied. Generally, forced choice items were rated "poor" because of their serious disadvantages of nonindependence of response, longer response time and possible respondent resentment; other instruments because of time, cost or training requirements.
Researchers should use their own judgments in instrument selection.

nonindependent; the response to one alternative depends on how the subject responded to the others.

CAUTION: Forced-choice items have many disadvantages including (1) nonindependence of response, (2) longer response time, (3) the tendency to create respondent resentment and (4) less information yielded than with independent items. While some experts feel they are useful for reducing response bias, this advantage would not appear to outweigh their many disadvantages.

EXAMPLE OF FORCED-CHOICE (NONINDEPENDENT) RESPONSE ITEM

Listed below are 20 pairs of automobiles. For each pair of automobiles, choose the one you would most prefer to own.

EXAMPLE OF INDEPENDENT RESPONSE ITEM

For each automobile listed below, mark your preference for owning it, using a scale from 1 through 5. 1 indicates "very much like to own it" and 5 indicates "not at all interested in owning it."

RATING SCALES

Rating scales are widely used in research. They might be used to measure such factors as perceptions of products, people, policies or organizations, or performance of people or products. People can rate themselves or others or rate printed materials or physical devices. The variety of applications is very large. Rating scales can be used whenever it is desirable to have someone estimate characteristics of specified factors.

Definition: *Rating*: Estimation of the degree of a characteristic possessed by some phenomenon such as an object or a person.

Definition: *Rating Scale*: An instrument on which the rater (observer) assigns the factor to be rated to one of two or more categories.

CAUTION: Note that rating and ranking are two different processes. Ratings are assigned independently to each factor to be rated. Ranking requires that a set of factors be placed in order.

Kerlinger [36] discusses three types of rating scales: (1) category, (2) numerical and (3) graphic. These three types differ only in the way they are presented to the rater.

Definition: *Category Rating Scale*: A rating scale in which the rater assigns the factor to one of two or more unnumbered categories which have verbal descriptions.

Definition: *Numerical Rating Scale*: A rating scale in which the rater assigns the factor to one of two or more numbered categories. The numbered categories may or may not include verbal descriptions.

EXHIBIT 12.2 EXAMPLES OF CATEGORY, NUMERICAL AND GRAPHIC RATING SCALES

Type of Rating Scale	Response Categories
Category	-----Very Attractive -----Attractive -----Unattractive -----Very Unattractive
Numerical	-----1. Very Attractive -----2. Attractive -----3. Unattractive -----4. Very Unattractive

Graphic*

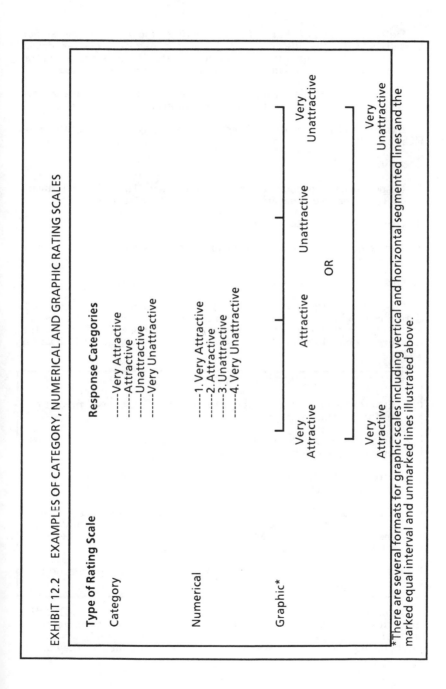

| Very
Attractive | Attractive | Unattractive | Very
Unattractive |

OR

| Very
Attractive | | | Very
Unattractive |

*There are several formats for graphic scales including vertical and horizontal segmented lines and the marked equal interval and unmarked lines illustrated above.

Definition: *Graphic Rating Scale*: A rating scale in which lines and/or bars are added to the categories in order to give the rater a clearer idea of how to respond. The lines tend to remind the rater of a continuum and the bars tend to suggest equal intervals. A variety of forms may be used.

Comment: Graphic rating scales are considered by some researchers as the best of the rating scales because of their graphic features.

Examples of each of these three types of rating scales are given in Exhibit 12.2.

Advantages:

1. Responses are independent for each item rated. Thus, Ss can indicate degree of positive or negative perceptions for each item.

2. Usually easy for Ss to mark or check.

3. Time required for administration and response is shorter than for many other methods.

4. Often less expensive than other methods because of #3.

Disadvantages: Susceptibility to "constant error" (response bias). Errors come about when raters, because of their predispositions, mark each response in a consistent manner thus affecting the validity of the measure. Some of the most serious constant errors are given in Exhibit 12.3.

EXHIBIT 12.3   POSSIBLE CONSTANT ERRORS OF RATERS

1. **Error of Severity**. The tendency to rate objects too low -- no one or nothing is good enough.

2. **Error of Leniency**. The tendency to rate objects too high -- loves everybody, everything.

3. **Error of Central Tendency**. The tendency to rate objects in the middle -- can't stand extreme positions or has no knowledge.

4. **Halo Effect**.* The tendency to rate objects according to how the rater feels about it in general -- rating politicians high on honesty because of liking their appearance, rating a product low because someone they dislike advertises it.

*The halo effect is probably the most frequently occurring reason for constant errors.

Another possible source of constant errors might be called the numerical effect. Some Ss appear to have the tendency to attach values to the numbers regardless of the anchors. For example, the number "1" might be considered first or best by some raters. Consequently, they might mark a "1" even when the verbal description is "very unsatisfactory." In this case the numbering system overrides the verbal descriptions.

One commonly used technique to attempt to reduce constant errors is to reverse the responses by placing positive responses first for some items and last for others.

CAUTION: Rating scales give the appearance of being easy to design. Because of this apparent ease of design, inexperienced people tend not to give the required thought and care in designing rating scales. The results can be disastrous.

Recommended Reference: Guilford [32], a classic reference, has excellent descriptions of rating scales.

SUMMATED RATING (LIKERT-TYPE) SCALES

Purpose: To estimate the Ss overall attitude, opinion, etc. toward an object by summing, and sometimes averaging, over all items.

In order to use the sum or mean in this manner each item must be considered of "equal value" to each of the other items and the response categories, usually degrees of agreement and disagreement, must be the same for all items. The results position the Ss score on a continuum of scores. As this yields individual scores the individuals can be rank ordered according to the variables under study.

Advantages:

1. Yields a single score from several items.

2. Ss can be rank ordered on the variables, which may be useful for certain types of research projects.

Disadvantages: A major disadvantage is the assumption of equal value items. It is very difficult to originate items which can be assumed to be of equal value because it indicates that the rater will value each item in the same way and all raters will value the items equally.

CAUTION: DO NOT USE SUMMATED RATING SCALES IF THE ASSUMPTION OF EQUAL VALUE ITEMS CANNOT BE MET.

Exhibit 12.4 shows an example of a rating scale with items which are probably of differing values and consequently should not be used as a summated rating scale. It is unlikely that each of the six items is of equal value to respondents. Many people consider food quality and cleanliness more important than lighting and parking, for example.

Referring to Exhibit 12.4, assume that a researcher mistakenly summed the items and both restaurants A and B received the same numerical rating. Yet A's food quality and cleanliness were rated high and B's low (B had high ratings on attractiveness and parking). If the ratings are summed this valuable information about the differences in the two restaurants is hidden.

EXHIBIT 12.4   EXAMPLE OF A RATING SCALE WITH ITEMS WHICH DIFFER IN VALUE* TO RESPONDENTS AND SHOULD NOT BE SUMMED

Please indicate your opinion of this restaurant by marking your selected category for each item.

Restaurant name: _____

	Strongly Agree	Agree Somewhat	Neither Agree nor Disagree	Somewhat Disagree	Strongly Disagree
1. Attractive	___	___	___	___	___
2. Low Quality Food	___	___	___	___	___
3. Clean	___	___	___	___	___
4. Poor Lighting	___	___	___	___	___
5. Poor Service	___	___	___	___	___
6. Adequate Parking	___	___	___	___	___

*   It is not likely that each of the six items has the same value to respondents. Many people consider quality of food and cleanliness far more important than lighting and parking. Thus, a rater's responses to the 6 items should not be summed. A summated rating scale should be used only when the items have equal value.

Comment: Summated rating scales are usually associated with attitude measurement but have been used to measure other types of variables.

EXHIBIT 12.5   STEPS FOR DESIGNING A SUMMATED RATING SCALE

1. Specify the variable of interest, e.g., degree of favorableness toward Coca-Cola.

2. Write both positive and negative items of equal value.

3. Select the response categories.

4. Conduct a pilot study.

5. Analyze the item responses with correlational analysis.

6. Throw out items which do not correlate with the other items.

7. Keep those items which intercorrelate for the final scale.

8. Redesign the scale, if necessary.

Recommended Reference: Edwards [26].

THURSTONE EQUAL APPEARING INTERVAL SCALE

Purpose: To measure attitudes with an instrument which yields an approximately interval level scale.

EXHIBIT 12.6:   STEPS FOR DESIGNING A THURSTONE EQUAL APPEARING INTERVAL SCALE

1. Originate statements reflecting differing degrees of the variable to be measured.

2. Select judges who assign the statements to eleven categories from most favorable through most unfavorable with category six assigned a neutral position.

3. Assign each statement the median or mean ranking of all judges.

4. Omit all statements with large variances among the judges' ratings.

5. Make up the scale with the ten to twenty statements which have a range of assigned scores 1 through 11.

Advantages: Yields a scale which most researchers treat as interval.

Disadvantages:

1. Selection of appropriate judges is critical. As the scale values are determined by averaging judges' ratings, they reflect the judges' attitudes.

2. Time consuming process.

3. Expensive process.

CAUTION: The time and expense required for the Thurstone appear to outweigh any advantages. Other rating scales are easier to generate and use.

Recommended Reference: Thurstone [65].

THE SEMANTIC DIFFERENTIAL

Purpose: To measure the meaning of concepts by selecting a concept and then choosing a series of bipolar adjectives to which Ss respond on a seven point scale.

EXHIBIT 12.7   AN EXAMPLE OF A SEMANTIC DIFFERENTIAL

GENERAL MOTORS

1. Clean	_:	_:	_:	_:	_:	_:	_:	Dirty	E**
2. Large	_:	_:	_:	_:	_:	_:	_:	Small	P
*3. Dark	_:	_:	_:	_:	_:	_:	_:	Bright	E.
4. Active	_:	_:	_:	_:	_:	_:	_:	Passive	A
*5. Slow	_:	_:	_:	_:	_:	_:	_:	Fast	A
6. Strong	_:	_:	_:	_:	_:	_:	_:	Weak	P
*7. Bad	_:	_:	_:	_:	_:	_:	_:	Good	E
*8. Shallow	_:	_:	_:	_:	_:	_:	_:	Deep	P
9. Sharp	_:	_:	_:	_:	_:	_:	_:	Dull	A

*About half the adjective pairs (items 3,5,7,8) are reversed to reduce response bias which is a typical procedure. The asterisks do not appear on the instrument.

**The letters note adjectives which reflect evaluative, potency and activity factors. These do not appear on the instrument.

Comment: Three, five, seven and nine point scales have been studied and, although the seven point scale appears to be preferable, any of these others may be used.

Advantages:

1. Ease of response.

2. Quantity of data yielded in a short administration time.

Disadvantages:

1. Difficulty in generating true bipolar adjectives.

2. Time and expertise needed to factor analyze adjectives which have not been tested.

Comment: A great deal of research has been conducted on the Semantic Differential to ascertain the applicability of the technique and most research supports its use. It is widely used in research.

EXHIBIT 12.8   STEPS FOR DESIGNING A SEMANTIC DIFFERENTIAL

1. **Select the Concepts.** These should be chosen for their capabilities of differential responses. They should not be so similar that they measure the same variable because there would be no variance in responses. For example, if Hitler and Stalin are to be rated, Churchill and Roosevelt might also be included.

2. **Select the Bipolar Adjectives.** These should represent one or more of Osgood's factors, evaluative, potency, activity or some researcher selected factors. If using unresearched adjectives, their factor relationship should be determined through statistical analyses.

3. **Randomly Assign Adjective Placement.** The adjective pairs should be randomly assigned a position on the instrument. Also randomly assign placement of about half of the negative adjectives and about half the positive adjectives to the left side.

4. **Place Each Concept on a Separate Sheet of Paper,** using the same pairs of adjectives and the same placement.

5. **Determine and Specify from what Viewpoint Ss Should respond.** Concepts can be rated from the Ss point of view or from some other person's point of view. For example: "Please rate these concepts as you think a stockholder in Standard Oil would rate them."

Explanation: In their research Osgood et al. [51] discovered that the adjective pairs reflected three underlying factors which they named evaluative, potency and activity factors. Probably the most useful cluster of adjectives are those termed evaluative, such as good-bad and clean-dirty. Activity factors are reflected by adjectives such as sharp-dull and fast-slow while large-small and strong-weak are potency related adjectives.

Each concept is placed on a separate sheet with the same set of biploar adjectives. Concepts might be names of people, products or organizations or statements, short phrases or single words intended to elicit respondents' attitudes.

SCORING AND ANALYSIS OF THE SEMANTIC DIFFERENTIAL

For scoring the Semantic Differential, numbers one through seven are assigned with seven indicating the most favorable bipolar adjective.

Analyses can take many forms: comparing concepts, groups of Ss or even factors. Sometimes scores are summed for adjectives measuring the same factor (aggregated analysis) but, as in summated rating scales, such summations often hide valuable information which individual analysis of adjectives can yield.

Probably the most commonly used reporting of the Semantic Differential results is Profile Analysis in which the average of all Ss responses is plotted as illustrated in Exhibit 12.9.

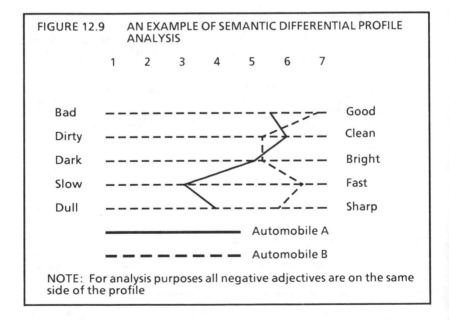

FIGURE 12.9   AN EXAMPLE OF SEMANTIC DIFFERENTIAL PROFILE
                 ANALYSIS

NOTE: For analysis purposes all negative adjectives are on the same side of the profile

Recommended Reference: Osgood, Suci & Tannenbaum [51].

THE SINGLE ANCHOR SCALE

Purpose: To measure the meaning of concepts by using an instrument similar to the Semantic Differential with a change in the number of anchors to one (unipolar). The number of scale categories varies from five to ten, depending on the researcher. Score values can vary from using all positive numbers to using +5 through -5.

Advantages:

1. Avoids generating bipolar adjectives, thus saving resources.

2. Slightly easier to administer and rate than the Semantic Differential.

Disadvantages: The major disadvantage is that the unipolar adjectives must be selected very carefully so that Ss and researchers have common meanings. For example, a researcher might contrast dull with sharp while Ss may think of bright or shiny.

Comment: It is a nuisance and time consuming to use negative numbers. Thus, many researchers use all positive numbers.

EXHIBIT 12.10   STEPS FOR CONSTRUCTING A SINGLE ANCHOR SCALE

1. **Select the Concepts.**

2. **Select the Unipolar Adjectives.** Select about half positive and about half negative adjectives.

3. **Randomly Assign Placement of theAdjectives.**

4. **Place Each Concept on a Separate Piece of Paper** using the same adjectives for each concept and the same placement.

5. **Determine from what Viewpoint Ss Should Respond.** Ss can rate the concepts from the Ss point of view or from some other persons point of view.

Analyses: Analyses of the single anchor scale are similar to those of the Semantic Differential.

MULTIDIMENSIONAL SCALING (MDS)

Purpose: To identify underlying dimensions of respondents' judgments (why people select specified objects or hold specified attitudes) by using various methods to place the judgments in multidimensional property space.

Assumptions:

1. Judgments by Ss may have more than one dimension -- Ss may be using more than one criterion (dimension) when making judgments.

2. Neither Ss nor researchers can identify these dimensions a priori (before the analysis).

EXHIBIT 12.11   STEPS FOR DESIGNING A MULTIDIMENSIONAL
                    SCALING PROCESS

NOTE: MDS methods fall into three categories:

1. **Nonmetric** uses rank order (ordinal) input data to develop geometric configurations in space. Output measures are distances between points in space (ratio level measurement).

2. **Fully Nonmetric** uses rank order (ordinal) input of distances between factors as input. Output is a rank order (ordinal) by dimensions, not configurations of points.

3. **Fully Metric** uses ratio level input of distances between factors. Output is ratio level.

THE FOLLOWING STEPS ARE FOR NONMETRIC MDS, A FREQUENTLY USED MDS IN RESEARCH

1. Select the computer program for analysis.

2. Select the criterion for judging; e.g., similarity among brands.

3. Determine the number of objects or factors to be judged; e.g., ten brands of video recorders.

4. Design the instrument (cards are useful) on which each object is paired with each other object.

5. Write instructions for responding; e.g., "Please rate each pair of video recorders on the degree of similarity to each other."

6. Determine a time limit for Ss response.

Advantages: Helps identify the number and kind of criteria (dimensions) people use when making judgments.

Disadvantages:

1. Requires computer programs and computers.

2. Difficulty in selecting the appropriate computer program because there are disagreements about the appropriateness of each program available at the time of this writing.

3. Lack of research on the validity of MDS.

4. Lack of researchers trained in MDS.

5. Difficulty in determining the number and meaning of the different dimensions.

Comments: MDS is particularly useful in marketing research when people cannot verbalize why they select specific products. Because of the potential usefulness, a body of knowledge about MDS is developing and use of this method is expected to increase.

ADMINISTRATION OF A MDS INSTRUMENT

Present the instrument and instructions to Ss and collect the completed instruments at the end of the time period.

EXHIBIT 12.12   STEPS FOR ANALYSIS OF A MULTIDIMENSIONAL
                   SCALING INSTRUMENT

1. Use the selected computer program to configure data.

2. Determine the number of dimensions.

3. Measure the distance between objects.

4. Label (name) the dimensions according to researcher knowledge of the objects.

Recommended Reference: Green and Carmone [30].

GUTTMAN SCALOGRAM ANALYSIS

Purpose: To determine if a cumulative scale is unidimensional (measures one variable).

Advantages: Assesses unidimensionality of a scale.

Disadvantages: Extremely tedious and expensive process.

CAUTION: Scalogram analysis is not recommended because of the time consumption and subsequent costs.

Process: Scalogram analysis is conducted after the instrument, which is in the form of statements or questions, is administered to a pilot group or to the group under study. For the complete process see Edwards [26].

RANK ORDER METHODS

Purpose: To yield a rank order of objects or factors by having respondents place them in order according to preselected criteria.

EXHIBIT 12.13   STEPS FOR DESIGNING A RANK ORDER
                     INSTRUMENT

1. Determine the objects or concepts to be ranked.

2. Determine the basis on which to rank: e.g., preference for or satisfaction with the object.

3. Determine the numbering system: is rank 1 positive or negative?

4. Write the instructions.

5. Place instructions and concepts on paper or cards. If using physical objects, gather the objects.

EXHIBIT 12.14   EXAMPLE OF A RANK ORDER ITEM

Please rank the following automobiles 1,2,3,4 according to WHICH YOU WOULD PREFER TO OWN. Use the number one for the automobile you would most prefer to own and the number four to indicate the one you would least prefer to own.

AUTOMOBILE	RANK
Ford Pinto	_____
Lincoln Continental	_____
Volkswagon Bus	_____
Toyota Tercel	_____

Advantages:

1. Respondents easily understand directions.

2. Similar to real world in forcing discrimination among objects.

Disadvantages:

1. Forced choice, nonindependent responses do NOT yield degree of respondent preference or attitude. Yields only information that respondent prefers one object or factor over another. Respondents compare objects selected by the researcher and may not like any object on the list but are not allowed a "dislike" response.

2. Response time is longer than for other instruments such as rating scales, which will also yield a rank ordering of objects.

3. Because of longer response time, fewer items can be used.

4. Some respondents resent the task of rank ordering.

5. Yields ordinal data.

Comment: Why use ranking when another instrument such as a rating scale will yield: (1) a range of respondent preference for each object, (2) a rank ordering of each object by using averages or percentages and (3) a scale which most researchers treat as equal interval.

Recommended Reference: Guilford [32].

THE CONSTANT SUM METHOD

Purpose: To yield a rank order of factors by respondents assigning a portion of a constant number of points (usually 100) to each of the factors according to respondents' preference for each factor.

Advantages:

1. Similar to real world in forcing discrimination.

2. Yields slightly more information than rank order techniques by essentially assigning weight to each factor.

Disadvantages:

1. Does NOT yield the individual factor information which a rating scale produces as respondents are forced to spread the 100 points among all factors. While dislike of a factor can be indicated by a small weight, even zero, the respondent cannot give all factors a low weight because weights must sum to 100.

2. Some respondents have difficulty in summing to 100.

3. Because some people have difficulty with addition, the number of factors must be severely limited -- usually not more than 10 factors and the instructions must be exceptionally clear.

4. The assumption of the constant sum method yielding equal interval data has not been sufficiently examined at this writing.

5. The time required for completion is longer than for the rank order method and other instruments such as rating scales.

CAUTION: The disadvantages of the Constant Sum Method appear to outweigh the advantages and it is not recommended.

EXHIBIT 12.15   STEPS FOR DESIGNING A CONSTANT SUM
                     INSTRUMENT

1. Determine the objects or concepts to be rated.

2. Determine the basis for rating: e.g., preference, satisfaction.

3. Write instructions.

4. Place instructions and concepts on paper or cards. If using objects,
   gather the objects.

EXHIBIT 12.16   EXAMPLE OF A CONSTANT SUM ITEM

Please assign points to each product listed below according to how
desirable each product is for you to have in your living quarters. The
total number of points must add to 100 points.

PRODUCT	POINTS
Clothes Washer	_____
Television Set	_____
Clothes Dryer	_____
Microwave Oven	_____
Telephone	_____
	100

THE Q TECHNIQUE

Purpose: To measure factors with an instrument that yields a rank
order of the factors and a normal distribution of the ratings. This is done
by having respondents rank order objects by sorting them (or their
representations such as cards) into a prespecified number of piles. These
are called Q sorts.

Advantages:

1. Yields a rank order and a normal distribution, which is advantageous
   statistically. Each pile must have a required and varying number of
   cards which make up an approximately normal distribution.

2. The process allows many objects, usually 60-120, to be ranked.

Disadvantages: A large amount of time, and consequent costs, is required to generate the cards and to conduct the personal interviews required by the sorting process.

Comment: Q sorts do not seem to offer sufficient advantages to overcome the time and cost factors.

EXHIBIT 12.17   STEPS FOR DESIGNING A Q SORT

Q sorts require respondents to rank order objects -- often cards -- by placing them in different piles according to some prespecified criteria. As it is unrealistic to expect a respondent to do a straight rank ordering of 60-120 objects, each pile has a required and varying number of cards which make up an approximate normal distribution.

1. **Select the Criterion to Which Ss Will Respond.** This is determined by the research problem and includes, but is not limited to, factors such as name of a product (Chevette), name of an organization (IBM), a concept (Ideal Boss) or an event (the Summer Olympics).

2. **Select the Two End Descriptors.** Often presented in most/least terms such as most/least pleasing, highly approve/disapprove or very important/unimportant.

3. **Generate or Select 60-120 Items or Objects.** These can be paintings, photographs, words, phrases or any object. If the object is large either use a photograph of it or describe it. If using photographs, words, phrases, etc., place them on individual cards.

4. **Divide the Total Number of Cards** into categories so that the resulting distribution approximates a normal distribution.

5. **Write Instructions for the Administrators to Give Ss.** For example: "Please place each of the 70 cards into one of the eleven piles according to how much you approve of IBM policies. The piles to the left reflect those cards most approved by you; to the right least approved by you. If you are unsure, place the card in the middle. The total number of cards to be placed in each pile is listed beneath the line."

Most approved -- -- -- -- -- -- -- -- -- -- Least Approved

No. of cards   2 3 5 8 11 12 11 8 5 3 2

SCORING THE Q SORT

Assign scores according to the group in which the objects are placed. The usual scoring is 0-10 with ten reflecting the most positive score.

For Example:

Number of cards required: 2   3   5   8   11 12 11 8   5   3   2

Value assigned to each
    card in the pile: 10 9 8   7   6   5   4   3   2   1   0

Recommended References: Stephenson [59], Kerlinger [36].

PAIRED COMPARISON METHOD

Purpose: To obtain a rank order of objects or concepts by presenting respondents with sets of two concepts (statements, words, phrases, objects) and instructions to select one of the two for each set according to some criterion (e.g., preference, value, satisfaction).

EXHIBIT 12.18   STEPS FOR DESIGNING PAIRED COMPARISON ITEMS

1. Determine the concepts or factors to be compared.

2. Determine the basis for comparison (preference, satisfaction)

3. Write instructions.

4. Place instructions and concepts on paper or cards.

EXHIBIT 12.19   EXAMPLE OF PAIRED COMPARISONS

For each pair of employees, please circle the name of the employee who was the most productive during the last quarter.

Pair #	1	2	3	4	5	6
	Smith	Wicks	Jones	Smith	Polk	Wicks
	Jones	Smith	Wicks	Polk	Jones	Polk

Advantages: Similar to real world in forcing discrimination.

Disadvantages:

1. Paired comparisons use forced choice items. Ss must choose among alternatives even when no choice is desirable (which would you prefer to find in your home, snakes or bats?). Thus, dislike of a concept cannot be demonstrated as it can in rating scales where each concept is rated independently.

2. Forced choice often creates respondent resentment which can result in lying or careless responses.

3. Forced choice items lack independence of response. Response to one concept of a pair affects response to the other. Nonindependent responses limit the types of statistical analyses.

4. Extremely time consuming for respondent, especially when each concept must be paired with each of the other concepts.

CAUTION: Paired Comparisons are not recommended because of the serious disadvantages.

Recommended Reference: Edwards [26].

CHECKLISTS

Purpose: To obtain information from respondents by having them check one or more of several alternatives listed.

Advantages:

1. Easy for respondent to answer.

2. Fast for respondent to answer.

Disadvantages: Because of the ease of response there is a tendency for researchers to use checklists when rating scales might be better and a tendency for Ss to be careless in responding.

EXHIBIT 12.20   STEPS FOR DESIGNING A CHECKLIST

1. Write stem and responses for each item.

2. Write directions

3. Place directions and items in appropriate positions on paper.

4. Conduct a pilot test.

5. Revise items, if necessary.

EXHIBIT 12.21   EXAMPLE OF A CHECKLIST ITEM

Check the state(s) in which you would prefer to work (check as many as apply).

　　　　　　 1. Maine
　　　　　　 2. Michigan
　　　　　　 3. Pennsylvania
　　　　　　 4. Texas

Comment: Note that much more information would be available if a rating scale were used for the item in Exhibit 12.21 because EACH state would be rated on respondents' preference to work there.

THE DELPHI METHOD (DELPHIC POLL)

Purpose: To gather a consensus of experts' opinions using several rounds of questionnaires or interviews (sometimes using on-line computers) and controlled feedback of results.

Assumptions:

1. Experts are the best source of opinions.

2. Expert opinion will be better if experts respond independently and anonymously.

3. Opinions will be even better if respondents are allowed to modify their responses after receiving feedback on how the rest of the group responded.

4. Several rounds of questionnaires (usually 3-5) and feedback of results will bring about a consensus of opinions.

Advantages:

1. Reflects the most up-to-date consensus of experts.

2. Avoids conflicts among respondents because of anonymity.

3. Supposedly encourages innovative thinking.

Disadvantages:

1. Lack of independent response after the first round because of feedback of results to respondents on the 2nd and later rounds.

2. Time consuming and costly because of the several rounds and the preparation of statistical summaries for feedback. With the increased use of on-line computers for the entire process, time will no longer be a major problem.

Comment: The Delphic Poll emerged in the 1940's in connection with secret war-time applications. It appears to be a fairly good method for predicting future events and is often used as a long range planning tool. It can also be used for other types of opinion gathering.

To date there has not been much research on the validity of the method and consequently there are strong opinions, both pro and con, on the appropriateness of its use. The Delphi can be viewed as simply another data collection instrument recognizing that it yields nonindependence of response after the first round and that selection of the experts is critical to the results. Experts should be selected from a complete listing using a defensible selection method. As with any other instrument, if there is a better way than the Delphi to gather the information, it probably should be used.

EXHIBIT 12.22   STEPS FOR DESIGNING A DELPHIC POLL

1. Select the events or objects to be rated.

2. Select the method of rating events -- probabilities are often requested for the occurrence of future events.

3. Select the future time period, if asking for predictions.

4. Write instructions for each round of questionnaires.

5. Write the questionnaire. Often respondents are encouraged to be creative in their responses.

6. Pilot test the questionnaire.

7. Revise the questionnaire, if necessary.

EXHIBIT 12.23   STEPS FOR ADMINISTERING A DELPHIC POLL

1. Obtain a listing of experts

2. Randomly select the number needed for the sample.

3. Contact the selected sample, explain the project and Delphi method, and ask if they are willing to participate.

4. Administer the questionnaires for round one.

5. Summarize the results of responses by using measures of central tendency and dispersion and/or frequency distributions.

6. Send the statistical summary of the results along with or included on the next round of questionnaires.

7. Ask respondents whose opinions fall outside the dispersion measure the reasons for their opinions.

8. Examine the reasons for extreme opinions and modify or add questions, if necessary.

9. Give feedback on minority opinions in next round.

10. Repeat steps 5-9 until opinions converge, usually 3-5 rounds.

Recommended Reference: Linstone and Turoff [46].

EXHIBIT 12.24   STEPS FOR DESIGNING A PROJECTIVE MEASURE

CAUTION: UNTRAINED PEOPLE SHOULD NOT ATTEMPT TO
DESIGN OR INTERPRET PROJECTIVE MEASURES SUCH AS AN
INKBLOT TEST.

1. **Determine the Stimuli**. These can range from pictures, objects, sounds and colors to written statements or role playing.

2. **Determine the Desired Responses**. Lindzey [45] classified projective measures by 5 types of responses.

   2.1 **Association**. Ss respond with the first thought that comes to mind. For example, the word "Pinto" might elicit the words: car, pony, Ford, or small. Sometimes only the first thought expressed in a word or phrase is requested. In successive word association the Ss are asked to give a series of words or phrases.

   2.2 **Construction**. Ss construct something like a drawing or a description. For example, Ss might be given a picture of a Jaguar and a Volkswagon and asked to describe the two owners.

   2.3 **Completion**. Ss complete an incomplete stimulus like a sentence or story. For example, Ss might be given the incomplete sentence: Bankers are.......

   2.4 **Choice or Ordering**. Ss choose one of several stimuli or place stimuli in order. For example, Ss place pictures of clothing in the order in which the clothing appeals to the Ss.

   2.5 **Expression**. Ss construct something but the analysis is focused on the how, when or why rather than the product as it would be in the construction response. For example, a group of managers role play a planning session and the researcher measures leadership behaviors.

3. **Write directions**.

4. **Place the stimuli and the directions together**.

PROJECTIVE TECHNIQUES

Purpose: To assess emotional states or attitudes by having Ss project their internal states by responding to relatively unstructured and ambiguous stimuli.

Advantages: Lack of structure supposedly allows Ss to project their inner feelings, attitudes or states.

Disadvantages:

1. Lack of structure can lead to extremely low validity and reliability estimates; unacceptable for many decisions.

2. Administration, often on a one-to-one basis, is time consuming.

3. Scoring is usually difficult and time consuming.

4. Many projective techniques require highly trained administrators.

5. Costs are high because of disadvantages 2, 3 and 4.

CAUTION: Projective techniques have acquired a poor reputation because of their usually low validities and reliabilities. This IS a critical problem and projective techniques are generally not recommended if there is a better way to obtain the information. However, selected techniques such as word association and sentence completion are useful, especially for exploratory work.

Recommended Reference: Lindzey [45].

CONTENT ANALYSIS

Purpose: To make inferences about variables by systematically and objectively analyzing the content and/or process of communications.

Advantages:

1. Can be used with any type of communication.

2. Widely applicable in many situations since most situations involve communications. These can include newspapers, TV and radio programs or commercials, films, books, letters, speeches and memos; income, purchasing, expense and sales records; brochures, minutes of meetings, listings on the stock exchange, job position notices and annual reports. As this is a partial list, consider the possibilities!

3. Usually free of response bias because analyses of communications is usually done without Ss awareness (e.g., analysis of existing written material).

4. Can usually be carried out at researchers' convenience because the communication is usually recorded in print, on tape or on video.

5. Can be easily checked for accuracy, if recorded.

6. Useful for predictions when direct observation is not feasible such as U.S. government agencies analyzing Russian newspapers.

7. The most appropriate method for analyzing open-ended items in questionnaires.

8. Computer programs which handle both the content analysis and the statistical analysis are available [62].

9. Can be used with existing data or with data that the researcher has Ss generate.

EXHIBIT 12.25   STEPS FOR DESIGNING A CONTENT ANALYSIS

1. List the variables to be measured.

2. Determine what specific communication content or process is an indicator (measure) of each variable.

3. Determine the unit of analysis: that is, what portion of the communication will be used as the smallest unit to analyze. Examples are words, phrases, sentences, paragraphs, pages, news articles, TV programs or commercials, films, minutes of meetings and transactions such as a banking or purchasing transaction.

4. Determine the coding categories or scales.

5. Collect or have Ss generate communications.

6. Select a random sample of these communications and pilot test the content analysis.

7. Adjust the categories or unit of analysis, if necessary.

8. Code the total sample of communications using the revised instrument.*

*Coders should be trained and interrater reliabilities computed between coders.

Comment: Content analysis can reveal information important to business and government organizations and could be conducted much more frequently than it is.

Disadvantages: Can be time consuming and thus may be more costly than some direct methods.

Comment: Content analysis is not a statistical analysis but a set of methods to analyze communications. Statistical analysis follows the content analysis.

Recommended References: Berelson [7] is the classic reference. Pool [53]. Budd, Thorp & Donohew [9].

Comment: Content analysis is widely used for data collected by observation methods and by examination of documents and materials. Examine Exhibits 12.27 and 12.28 for examples. However, these examples do not do justice to the varied applications of content analysis. If you desire additional information there are many books and articles available.

OBSERVATION INSTRUMENTS

While there are some existing instruments for observation many researchers design their own instruments. Before deciding to design an instrument examine existing ones to see if one of them would be appropriate.

For example, observation instruments are often used to examine verbal and nonverbal behaviors of subjects. One of the classic and well-known instruments for assessing interaction is the Bales Interaction Process Analysis [6]. This instrument is used to analyze verbal and nonverbal behaviors with such categories as "agrees" or "asks for opinion." This is only one example and you might find some existing instrument which meets your needs, thus saving you both time and costs.

Observation instruments are as varied as the different kind of situations in which observations take place. They might include many variables and be 4 pages long or consist of a single item. An example of a short observation instrument is given in Exhibit 12.26.

EXHIBIT 12.26 EXAMPLE OF A SHORT OBSERVATION INSTRUMENT

Store _____ Day _____ Date _____ Observer _____

Department: _____

Record the number of males and females who make at least one

purchase between 10 and 11 A.M. and 12 (noon) and 1 P.M.

	Number of MALES	Number of FEMALES
10:00 A.M. to 11:00 A.M.	_____	_____
12:00 Noon to 1:00 P.M.	_____	_____

EXHIBIT 12.27   AN EXAMPLE OF A STRUCTURED OBSERVATION INSTRUMENT WHICH
              ALLOWS RECORDING OF UNANTICIPATED BEHAVIORS AND EVENTS

1. Restaurant: _____   2. Day: _____   3. Date:_____

4. Waitress/Waiter: _____   5. Time: _____   6. Observer:_____

7. Number of Customers in party: _____

8. Elapsed time from customer seating to waitress/waiter arrival: _____

	Task	Satisfactory	Unsatisfactory	Comment
9.	Greeted customer(s):	____	____	_____
10.	Brought water:	____	____	_____
11.	Presented menus:	____	____	_____
12.	Served coffee/tea	____	____	_____

13. Elapsed time from
    order to meal: _____

14.	Served meal:	____	____	_____
15.	Refilled beverages:	____	____	_____
16.	Presented check:	____	____	_____

17. Elapsed time from
    meal completion
    to check: _____

Appearance

| 18. | Uniform | ____ | ____ | _____ |
| 19. | Neatness | ____ | ____ | _____ |

20. Record any relevant behavior or event which occurred during this time period:

_____

_____

_____

STRUCTURED AND UNSTRUCTURED OBSERVATIONS

Observation instruments can vary in their degree of structure: that is, in the specificity of the factors in the observation situation which the observer will record.

Definition: *Fully Structured Observation Instrument*: An instrument on which the observer records researcher specified behaviors or events.

Definition: *Fully Unstructured Observation Instrument*: An instrument on which the observer records any behavior or event which is relevant to the research situation.

On a structured instrument problems can arise if the categories are too rigid and consequently important behaviors might be omitted. However, unstructured instruments often allow the observer too much opportunity to make unwarranted inferences, resulting in inaccurate data.

One way to avoid both these problems is to specify the relevant categories or items before data collection but include space on the instrument for the observer to record unanticipated behaviors or events. Exhibit 12.27 illustrates this approach.

CAUTION: Fully unstructured instruments are rarely used as the final research instrument. However, they are sometimes used to discover typical behaviors or events prior to designing the final observation instrument.

REMINDERS

Remember that, in some situations, events can be recorded using audio or video recorders or cameras. You will still need an instrument to record the observations from the film. However, having permanent records means that several observers can view the same situation and interrater reliability is usually higher. Having permanent records also allows the observers to work at convenient times with less pressure and fewer distractions than occur when present at the event.

CAUTION: OBSERVERS MUST BE TRAINED IN THE APPROPRIATE USE OF THE INSTRUMENT.

INSTRUMENTS FOR EXISTING DOCUMENTS, MATERIALS AND ARTIFACTS

The type of instrument selected or designed to use with existing documents or materials depends largely on the type of information desired. The variety is enormous.

For example, when the space shuttle, CHALLENGER, exploded in January 1986, NASA immediately began research activities to try and pinpoint the cause. They had a wide variety of existing information including flight data, films of the explosion and recovered pieces of the shuttle. Each of these types of existing documents and materials would

EXHIBIT 12.28   EXAMPLES OF ITEMS FOR EXISTING DOCUMENTS AND MATERIALS*

Type of Existing Data	Instructions to Recorder	Example of Item
1. Sales/costs records	Record the dollar amount of gross sales and cost of sales for each company listed.	Company: A, B, C, D — Gross Sales $___ — Cost of Sales $___
2. Physical Materials	Record the weight of each box of cereal in the sample.	Cereal: A, B, C, D — Weight ___
3. Written Advertising	For each occurrence of the product name, record the size of the type and the location of the name.	AD: A, B, C — Typesize ___ — Location ___
4. Films/Video tapes	For each 30 minute segment, record the number of positive and negative verbal or nonverbal reactions when bankers are mentioned.	Segment: 1, 2, 3, 4 — Verbal (Pos/Neg) ___ — Nonverbal (Pos/Neg) ___
5. Magazines, Books, etc.	For each article, record the number of times phrases related to increases and decreases in power and wealth are used as descriptors of the oil industry.	Article: A, B, C, D — Power (Inc/Dec) ___ — Wealth (Inc/Dec) ___

*These few examples cannot sufficiently illustrate the wide variety of possible items. For example, rating scales are sometimes used. Variables can range from color, size, verbal or nonverbal behaviors to types or values of words used. See the recommended references for additional information.

require some sort of instrument for recording, measuring or summarizing the data.

The most important factors in designing an instrument for existing data are to provide: (1) a format and categories which prompt the data collector to record the most appropriate information in the desired form and (2) instructions to encourage (and a place to record) unanticipated findings.

Exhibit 12.28 gives examples of a variety of items which might be used on instruments for existing documents and materials. These are, of course, a small sample of the many and varied items possible.

WHERE YOU ARE NOW

At this point you should have:

1. Determined the types of instruments which will best measure your variables,

2. Either selected or designed the instruments,

3. Pilot tested the instruments if you designed them or modified existing ones,

and recognized that:

4. Each type of instrument has advantages and disadvantages,

5. The researcher must weigh these advantages and disadvantages considering the nature of the variables and the constraints of the research project and

6. Nonindependent responses create serious disadvantages and should be used cautiously.

13

SELECT THE STATISTICAL TEST

TERMS DEFINED IN CHAPTER THIRTEEN

CHAPTER THIRTEEN

SELECT THE STATISTICAL TEST

STEPS TO TAKE AFTER READING THIS CHAPTER

1. List the level of measurement for each variable.

2. Determine the statistical purpose:

   2.1   Examining the significance of group differences.

   2.2   Examining the relationship among variables.

3. Determine the number of dependent and independent variables, or predictor and criterion variables, if appropriate.

4. Determine if the observations are independent or related.

5. Refer to the decision trees at the beginning of this chapter.

6. Select the appropriate statistical procedure, using the information gathered in steps 1-4 with the decision trees.

7. Review the information presented on statistical concepts.

8. Review the selected statistical procedures for later use.

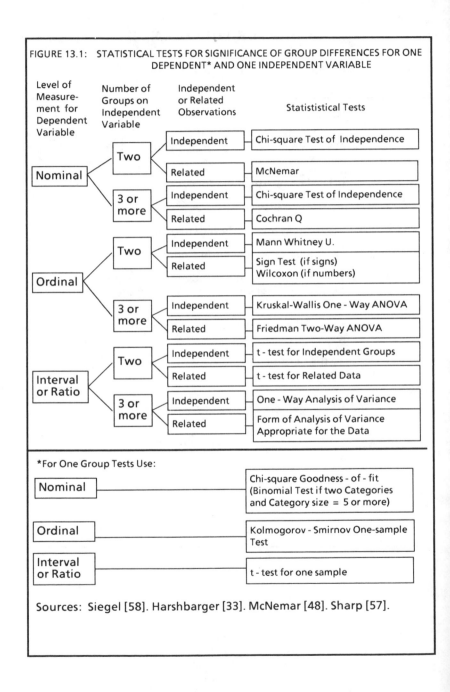

FIGURE 13.1:   STATISTICAL TESTS FOR SIGNIFICANCE OF GROUP DIFFERENCES FOR ONE DEPENDENT* AND ONE INDEPENDENT VARIABLE

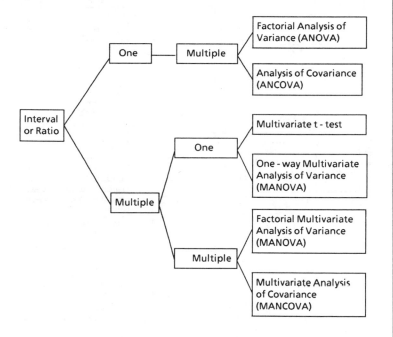

FIGURE 13.2   STATISTICAL TESTS FOR SIGNIFICANCE OF GROUP
              DIFFERENCES FOR MULTIPLE MEASURES

Sources: Yaremko et al. [71]. Davis and Cosenza [22].
Kerlinger [36] [37].

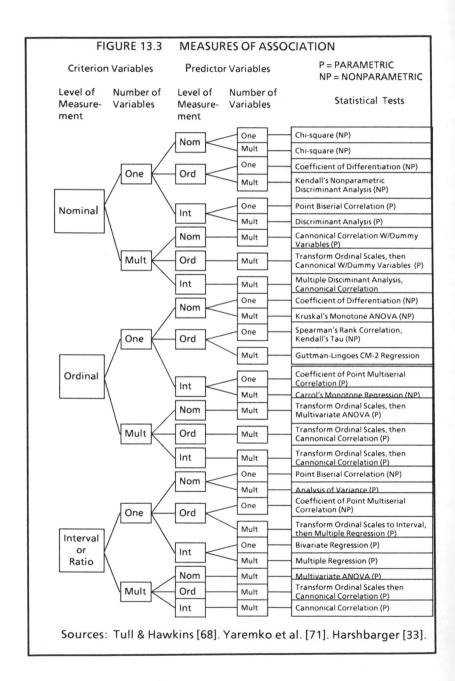

FIGURE 13.3   MEASURES OF ASSOCIATION

Sources: Tull & Hawkins [68]. Yaremko et al. [71]. Harshbarger [33].

Many novice researchers become quite uncomfortable when reaching the point where the appropriate statistical analysis must be selected. In addition, the thought of computing the analysis and then interpreting the results is intimidating to some people.

The best way to overcome these feelings is to acquire a good reference on statistical procedures which includes how to select, compute and interpret statistical tests appropriate for various types of data. Fortunately there are many of these references available [33] [34] [35] [47] [49] [57]. Computation is usually not a major problem because of the widespread availability of computer programs which carry out the necessary computations very quickly.

To help you in the selection of the appropriate statistical tests, 3 decision trees are given at the beginning of this chapter. Information on how to use these is included in this chapter. In addition, examples of the computation and interpretation of the most commonly used statistical tests are included.

STATISTICAL CONCEPTS

The following section is included for researchers who may wish to review some basic statistical concepts and definitions before proceeding to the selection of the statistical test.

DESCRIPTIVE AND INFERENTIAL STATISTICS

Definition: *Descriptive Statistics*: Measures used to describe and summarize data such as measures of central tendency, variability and relationship.

Definition: *Inferential Statistics*: Statistical procedures used to draw inferences about a population by using sample data from that population. Examples of statistical tests used for inferences are t-tests, chi-square tests and analysis of variance tests. Two types of statistical inference are: (1) estimation and (2) hypothesis testing.

Definition: *Statistical Estimation*: Estimation of an unknown population value (point estimate) or range of values (interval estimate) from a known sample value.

Examples of point and interval estimates are given in Chapter 7.

Hypothesis testing was discussed in Chapter 4. For convenience the same hypothesis testing flow chart given in Chapter 4 is repeated in Figure 13.4.

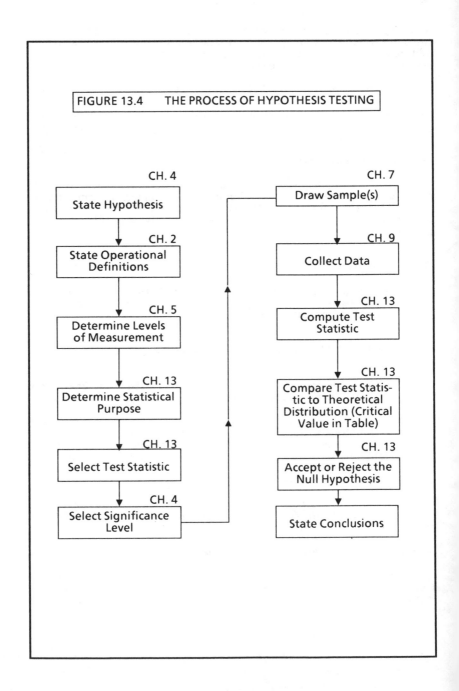

FIGURE 13.4   THE PROCESS OF HYPOTHESIS TESTING

STATISTICS AND PARAMETERS

Remember that statistical characteristics of the population are termed parameters and those of the sample are called statistics. Commonly used symbols for statistics and parameters are given in Exhibit 13.1.

EXHIBIT 13.1	COMMONLY USED SYMBOLS FOR SAMPLE AND POPULATION CHARACTERISTICS	
Characteristic	**Sample Statistic**	**Population Parameter**
Mean	$\bar{X}$	μ
Standard deviation	S	σ
Variance	S^2	σ^2
Pearson product-moment correlation	r	P

Hypotheses are always stated in terms of the POPULATION characteristics being examined. For example:

Ha: Annual sales of pain relievers will be higher in states which have experienced no product tampering than in states which have experienced product tampering.

Symbolic hypothesis: Ha: $\mu_{npt} > \mu_{pt}$

After data collection the computations are carried out on the SAMPLE data. Thus the SAMPLE means, $\bar{X}_{npt}$, $\bar{X}_{pt}$ are used to estimate the POPULATION means, μ_{npt}, μ_{pt}.

Remember that hypotheses are always stated in terms of the POPULATION characteristics to be estimated. Thus, symbolic forms of hypotheses use the symbols for parameters.

PARAMETRIC AND NONPARAMETRIC TESTS

CAUTION: You will see the terms "parametric" and "nonparametric" tests used frequently. It is natural to associate these with the term parameter and indeed the original meaning of parametric test was one in which the hypothesis concerned parameters. However, common usage has led to the definitions given here. These indicate that a parametric test requires at least interval level of measurement. Thus a test to compare medians (parameters) would be called a nonparametric test because the level of measurement is ordinal, not interval.

Definition: *Parametric Test*: A statistical test for which the hypothesis concerns parameters (e.g., means, correlations), the required level of measurement is usually at least interval and there are several assumptions of the statistical model, usually concerning the shape of the distribution and the spread of scores.

Comment: According to Yaremko et al. [71, p. 169], the term parametric test "refers primarily to tests based on assumed sampling from binomally or normally distributed populations." Siegel [58, p. 19] includes independent observations drawn from normally distributed populations and equal population variances in his list of the elements of the parametric statistical model.

Examples: *t-test, Analysis of Variance, Pearson product-moment correlation.*

Definition: *Nonparametric Test*: A statistical test for which the statistical model usually does not require the assumptions about the population parameters and does not require interval level of measurement. The assumptions are few and usually concern independent observations and/or continuity of the variables.

According to Yaremko et al. [71, p. 155] "in common usage, the term also includes distribution-free tests." The chi-square goodness-of-fit test is an example.

Definition: *Distribution-free Test*: A statistical test which does NOT require assumptions about aspects of the population distribution such as "a normal distribution of scores in the population" or "equal variances" which are assumptions of the parametric t-test. Distribution-free tests are often called nonparametric tests. Examples are the sign test and the Mann-Whitney test.

THE NORMAL DISTRIBUTION

There are several theoretical distributions of scores which are commonly used in statistical analyses. Some of these are the normal distribution, the binomial distribution and the t distribution. However, one distribution, the normal distribution, is emphasized because it is the distribution for random error of continuous scores and is used widely in data analysis and interpretation.

Definition: *Normal Distribution*: A probability distribution used to interpret many variables. The distribution is unimodal and symmetric, thus the mean, median and mode are identical. It is bell-shaped and the most frequent score is at its peak. A normal distribution can be completely specified by its mean and standard deviation.

In a normal distribution 68.3% of the scores lie within $\pm$ one standard deviation of the mean, 95.4% within $\pm$ two standard deviations of the mean and 99.7% within $\pm$ three standard deviations of the mean. The remaining .3% of scores lie outside of $\pm$ three standard deviations of the mean since maximum and minimum scores are considered infinite.

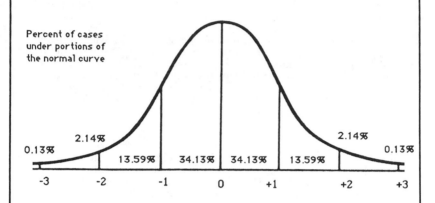

FIGURE 13.5   CHARACTERISTICS OF THE NORMAL DISTRIBUTION

Percent of cases
under portions of
the normal curve

2.14%

0.13%   0.13%

13.59%   34.13%   34.13%   13.59%

2.14%

-3   -2   -1   0   +1   +2   +3

Standard deviation units

- 68.3% of the scores lie within ± one standard deviation of the mean.

- 95.4% of the scores lie within ± two standard deviations of the mean.

- 99.7% of the scores lie within ± three standard deviations of the mean.

- Unimodal and symmetric. Thus mean, median and mode are identical

Symbols: $N(\bar{X}, S), N(\mu, \sigma), ND(\bar{X}, S), ND(\mu, \sigma)$

Synonyms: *Normal Curve, Error Curve, Gaussian Curve, DeMoivre Curve.*

Comment: The normal distribution includes approximately six standard deviations with a specified percent of scores lying within each standard deviation. These percentages always remain the same, making the normal distribution easy to interpret.

Given a set of scores which is normally distributed, the distribution can be completely specified by indicating the mean and standard deviation. Thus, given the information that a set of scores is ND (50,10), one knows that the scores are approximately normally distributed, the mean is 50 and the standard deviation is 10. Then the distribution of scores can be specified by using the unvarying percentages associated with the normal distribution given in Figure 13.5.

For example, knowing that the mean is 50 and the standard deviation is 10 and using the normal distribution illustrated in Figure 13.5, place the number 50 at the center of the distribution where 0 standard deviation is indicated. This is the mean. Now add the standard deviation of 10 to the mean of 50, which equals 60. This is the score at one standard deviation above the mean. Continue this process and the results will be:

Number of Standard Deviations	Score
3 standard deviations below the mean	20
2 standard deviations below the mean	30
1 standard deviation below the mean	40
The mean	50
1 standard deviation above the mean	60
2 standard deviations above the mean	70
3 standard deviations above the mean	80

Because the distribution of scores is always the same for any normally distributed set of scores, the percentages given in Figure 13.5 can be used to interpret these scores. Thus, referring to the data above and using the percentages given in Figure 13.5, you can see that approximately 34% of the scores will be between the scores of 50 and 60 and approximately 95% of the scores will be between 30 and 70.

THE CRITICAL VALUE

After a test statistic such as t test is computed the result is compared with figures given in a table for that statistic. These figures are called critical values. If the computed value equals or exceeds the critical value given in the table, the results are significant and the null hypothesis is rejected. If the computed value is less than the critical value, the results are not significant and the null hypothesis is not rejected.

These tables of critical values represent various theoretical distributions of scores such as the normal distribution discussed previously, the chi-square distribution, the F distribution and the t distribution. In essence the tables indicate that at a given significance level, for example the .05 level, the critical value given is so extreme that it could not have occurred by chance. In other words, it is at that point that the results of the test are statistically significant.

Definition: *Critical Value*: A value appearing in tables for specified statistical tests indicating at what computed value the null hypothesis can be rejected (the computed statistic falls in the rejection region).

Comment: In order to locate the appropriate critical value, many tables require a priori information on: (1) the selected level of significance, (2) one or two tailed test and (3) the degrees of freedom associated with the specific statistical test.

Example: It is hypothesized that males and females will differ in their preference for red or green cars. A significance level of .05 is selected. After data collection and recording of preferences a chi-square statistic is computed.

The computed chi-square = 4.75. Reference to the chi-square table of critical values in the Appendix indicated that at the .05 level with one degree of freedom a chi-square value of 3.84 is significant. Since the computed chi-square value of 4.75 equals or exceeds the critical value of 3.84, the null hypothesis is rejected. Thus, the research hypothesis that males and females will differ in their preference for red or green cars is supported.

DEGREES OF FREEDOM

Many statistical tests use the concept of degrees of freedom both in the computation of the formulas and when locating critical values in the various tables.

Definition: *Degrees of Freedom*: Generally, the number of values which are free to vary, computed by the number of values used with a certain statistic minus the number of restrictions placed on the data. The formulae for computing degrees of freedom for each of the major statistical tests are given in statistics books.

Symbol: df

Example: If there are 10 numbers which must sum to 100 (a restriction) then 9 of these numbers are free to vary but the 10th number must be the value required by the difference of the sum of the 9 numbers and the total of 100.

For example, given the numbers 9,7,10,14,11,9,20 and 15 with the restriction that 10 numbers must sum to 100, the 10th number is not free to vary but must be 5. Thus there would be 9 df.

Comment: Fortunately you do not have to figure out the number of restrictions. Each statistical test has the degrees of freedom associated with it specified. The method for computing degrees of freedom is usually found near the formula for the statistic in most statistics books.

For example, the degrees of freedom for a t test for two independent groups are computed by: $(n_1 - 1) + (n_2 - 1)$ where n_1 is the number of scores for group one and n_2 is the number of scores for group two.

TERMINOLOGY

Three terms which occur frequently in discussion of statistical analyses are defined here because there tends to be some confusion about what they mean.

Definition: *Univariate Techniques:* Statistical techniques involving one dependent variable.

Definition: *Bivariate Techniques:* Statistical techniques involving two dependent variables.

Definition: *Multivariate Techniques:* Statistical techniques involving two or more dependent variables or, in some cases, one dependent variable and two or more independent variables.

CONCEPTS TO REVIEW

Before selecting the appropriate statistical test for your data, it may be advisable to review the following concepts which were presented in other chapters.

Concept	Chapter
1. Probability	4
2. Level of significance	4
3. Type I and Type II errors	4
4. Hypothesis testing	4
5. Levels of measurement	5
6. Sampling	7

DETERMINE THE STATISTICAL PURPOSE

In order to select the statistical test which is appropriate for your data, it is helpful to consider what the statistical purpose is. One way to view this is to determine if the purpose is to examine: (1) the significance of group differences or (2) associations between or among variables.

These are the two most commonly used statistical purposes. If your research requires some other purpose, refer to an advanced book on statistics.

To determine the statistical purpose, examine the hypotheses or research questions. Is your intent to compare groups to see if they are significantly different from one another or to see if there is an association between variables? Some examples are given to help you with this decision.

SIGNIFICANCE OF GROUP DIFFERENCES

Examining the significance of group differences is used when the researcher wishes to know if one group has more or less of some variable. Typical hypotheses or research questions which lead to testing group differences are:

1. There will be less vandalism in plants located in the Southwest than in those located in the East.

Two groups of plants, Southwestern and Eastern, are compared to discover if one group has a significantly lower incidence of vandalism.

2. Do a higher proportion of women than men invest in bonds?

Two groups, women and men, are compared to discover if a higher proportion of one group invests in bonds.

3. Does number of products purchased differ among four different product brands?

Four groups, different brands, are compared to discover if the number of products purchased is significantly different.

As indicated in Figures 13.1 and 13.2 there are a variety of statistical tests available for testing significance of group differences.

DEGREE OF ASSOCIATION AMONG VARIABLES

Examining the degree of association among variables is used when the researcher wishes to assess the magnitude of the relationship between two or more variables. Examination of associations (relationships) is widely used in research, particularly when several items of information are collected on the same people. Illustrative hypotheses or research questions are:

1. There will be a positive relationship between level of absenteeism and level of obesity of employees.

2. Is family income related to the number of video cassettes purchased?

3. The fewer the number of children in the family, the more likely it is that the parents invest in stocks and bonds.

CAUTION: Remember that measures of relationship (association) indicate only the degree to which variables are related and not that one variable causes another.

Comment: Note that often the choice of the statistical purpose depends on what will best answer your research needs. For example, in #1 above, in examining the degree of relationship of absenteeism and obesity, obesity might be measured by recording the number of pounds each employees exceeds recommended weights. These same variables could be used to examine the significance of group differences by categorizing employees as obese or not obese with obese defined as 20# over recommended weights. Then the two groups, obese and not obese would be compared on level of absenteeism to assess group differences. Note that conclusions still can NOT be that obesity causes absenteeism because there is no experimental treatment.

DEPENDENT AND INDEPENDENT VARIABLES

The discussion of dependent and independent variables in Chapter Two indicated that these two terms are usually reserved for experimental research. However, it is common practice to describe statistical tests in terms of dependent and independent variables. One reason for this is that the dependent variable is usually the variable that is analyzed while the independent variables are often used to form groups.

For example, if an hypothesis stated that level of absenteeism depended on amount of weight loss, the independent variable could be used to form two or more groups, such as loss over 20#, loss 10-20#, and loss less than 10#. Then the dependent variable, level of absenteeism, would be recorded and analyzed.

PREDICTOR AND CRITERION VARIABLES

The terms predictor and criterion variables are used in the decision tree for selecting measures of association. These terms are used for convenience because often the researcher is trying to find a variable which is a good predictor of another variable which is called the criterion variable.

For example, what variables might be used to predict next year's sales (the criterion variable)? Are last year's resignations a good predictor of this year's resignations?

Also, associations are discussed in statistical references in terms of predictor and criterion variables so it is advisable to become accustomed to the terms.

INDEPENDENT OR RELATED OBSERVATIONS

As indicated in the decision trees in Figures 13.1 and 13.2, whether the observations gathered in the research are considered independent or related makes a difference in which statistical test is selected.

Definition: *Independent Observations:* Observations which are not related to one another and thus cannot affect one another. For example, a questionnaire is given to 100 randomly selected consumers. There is no reason to believe that the responses of one consumer will have any effect on the responses of the other consumers.

Definition: *Related Observations*: Observations which are NOT independent but related in some way and thus one observation might affect another. For example, parents and their children are selected for a study of consumer food preferences. It is highly likely that food preferences of children are related to their parents' food preferences. A commonly used set of related data occurs when people are studied before and after some experiment or event.

SELECT THE STATISTICAL PROCEDURE

At this point you have determined the level of measurement for each variable, the statistical purpose, the number of dependent and independent or predictor and criterion variables and whether the variables are independent or related. You are now ready to use the decision trees to select the appropriate statistical procedure.

There are three decision trees given at the beginning of the chapter. They are set up as follows:

FIGURE	STATISTICAL PURPOSES	Level of Measurement
13.1	Significance of group differences for one dependent and one independent variable	All levels
13.2	Significance of group differences for multiple dependent and independent variables	Interval or ratio
13.3	Measures of association	All levels

First, decide which decision tree lists procedures for your statistical purpose. Figures 13.1 and 13.2 are used if you are examining the significance of group differences. Figure 13.3 is used if you are examining the degree of association among variables.

Second, simply enter the decision tree with the appropriate level of measurement and follow the branches to the recommended statistical test.

For example, level of measurement for the dependent variable absenteeism (number of days absent) is ratio. There are two groups of people, obese and not obese, and your purpose is to examine the significance of differences in absenteeism between these two groups. The observations are independent.

You can then use Figure 13.1, statistical procedures for the significance of group differences for one dependent and one independent variable. Find interval (and ratio) level of measurement, independent observations and discover that the t test for independent groups is the appropriate statistical test.

When you have selected the appropriate statistical test, find the formulas and related information for the test and proceed with the computations.

Examples of the most commonly used statistical tests are given here. These include: (1) the chi-square test of independence, (2) the t test for means of independent groups, (3) one-way analysis of variance and (4) the Pearson product-moment correlation. In addition an example is given for using linear regression and a conceptual illustration of two-way analysis of variance is presented. For information on other statistical tests, refer to any standard statistical reference.

THE CHI-SQUARE TEST OF INDEPENDENCE

The most frequently used chi-square statistics are the chi-square goodness-of-fit test, used for one sample which is divided into categories, and the chi-square test of independence, used for two or more samples. Chi-square is widely used in research because of the large amount of data collected at the nominal level of measurement. The chi-square test of independence is discussed here.

Definition: *Chi-Square Test of Independence*: A statistical test for two or more groups when data is at the nominal level. The null hypothesis is that the variables are independent of each other and the research hypothesis is that the variables are related (not independent).

Symbol: X^2

Purpose: To test if two or more groups differ significantly on a selected characteristic. If they do then the variables are related and the research hypothesis is supported. If they do not differ significantly then the variables are considered independent and the null hypothesis is not rejected.

Another way of stating this is: do the number of frequencies in each category for one group differ from the number of frequencies in each category for another group?

Chi square is based on the difference between OBSERVED and EXPECTED frequencies. For example, if there were no relationship between religious affiliation and union membership the expected frequencies for membership and nonmembership should be about the same for both Protestants and Catholics.

If a research study indicated that a significantly higher proportion of Catholics than Protestants were union members or a significantly higher proportion of Protestants were union members then the observed frequencies would differ significantly from the expected frequencies and the variables religious affiliation and union membership would be considered related.

Definition: *Expected Frequencies:* The frequencies of observations expected to occur. Expecteds are obtained in one of four ways: (1) all are assumed to be equal, (2) they are obtained by prior knowledge (e.g., last year's sales figures), (3) theory indicates the figures or (4) they are computed from the frequencies in the margins of the contingency table.

For the chi-square test of independence the expecteds are computed from the marginal frequencies.

EXHIBIT 13.2   USE CHI-SQUARE TEST OF INDEPENDENCE WHEN YOU HAVE:

1.   Nominal level of measurement.

2.   Independent observations.

*3.   At least 80% of the expected frequencies are more than five. No expected is less than one.

**4.   A two tailed test.

5.   Ho: Two or more groups do not differ significantly on the observed characteristic (or the two variables are independent).

*Use the Fisher Exact Probability Test or combine categories if these requirements are not met.

**Chi square is considered a two tailed statistic. However, a one-tailed test may be used with a 2x2 contingency table [48] [15]. For a one-tailed test, simply double the selected significance level when entering the table, e.g., if the selected significance level is .05 for a one-tailed test, use the tabled figures under the column head .10 for a critical value of 2.71 for 1 df.

Chi Square Formula:

$$X^2 = \Sigma \ \frac{(O-E)^2}{E}$$

where Σ = sum of, 0 = observed frequency, E = expected frequency degrees of freedom (df) = (number of rows-1) (number of columns -1)

Computation for Expected Frequency for Each Cell

$$E = \frac{(horizontal \ marginal \ frequency)(vertical \ marginal \ frequency)}{Total \ frequency}$$

EXHIBIT 13.3:   EXAMPLE OF A CHI-SQUARE APPLICATION

Ha: Department Heads, Comptrollers and Chief Executive Officers (CEO's) will not
        be equally favorable about increasing the amount of liability insurance for
        executives in their companies.

Ho: Department Heads, Comptrollers and Chief Executive Officers (CEO's) will be
        equally favorable about increasing the amount of liability insurance for
        executives in their companies (or favorableness toward increasing liability
        insurance is independent of position held).

Level of Significance Selected: .05

Data: The three groups were given a questionnaire concerning their attitude
        toward increasing companies' liability insurance.

                    STEPS FOR COMPUTATION AND INTERPRETATION

1.   Record the observed frequencies in a contingency table.

     Table 1:   Observed Frequencies

	Favorable	Unfavorable	Total
CEO's	12	01	13
Comptrollers	10	11	21
Dept. Heads	09	07	16
	31	19	50

2.   Compute Expecteds: (marginal) (marginal)/total

	Favorable		Unfavorable		Total
CEO's	(31*13)/50	= 8.06	(19*13)/50	= 4.94	13.00
Comptrollers	(31*21)/50	= 13.02	(19*21)/50	= 7.98	21.00
Dept. Heads	(31*16)/50	= 9.92	(19*16)/50	= 6.08	16.00
		31.00		19.00	50.00

     * = multiply

     Expecteds indicate that given 13 CEO's and 31 people who are favorable about
     increased insurance one would expect 8 CEO's to be favorable.

3.   Check that 80% of the expecteds are greater than 5 and no expected is less than 1.

     80% of the 6 expected frequencies = 4.8 or 5 expecteds. Of the 6 expecteds
     computed 5 (83%) have values greater than 5 and no expected value is less than
     one. Thus, the general chi-square formula may be used.

EXHIBIT 13.3 (cont.)   EXAMPLE OF A CHI-SQUARE APPLICATION

4. Compute the chi-square value:

$$X^2 = \Sigma \frac{(O-E)^2}{E}$$

O	E	O-E	$(O-E)^2$	$(O-E)^2/E$
12	8.06	3.94	15.52	1.93
10	13.02	3.02	9.12	.70
9	9.92	.92	.85	.09
1	4.94	3.94	15.52	3.14
11	7.98	3.02	9.12	1.14
7	6.08	.92	.85	.14
			$X^2 =$	7.14

5. Compute the degrees of freedom: (rows-1) (columns-1).

    df = 2   (3 rows - 1) (2 columns - 1) = 2

6. Find the critical value in the chi-square table in the Appendices

    CV = 5.99 for 2df, .05 significance level, two tailed test.

7. Reject the null hypothesis if computed X^2 equals or exceeds the critical value.

    Decision: Ho rejected. Computed X^2 of 7.14 exceeds critical value of 5.99.

8. Conclusion: The research hypothesis, that the three groups of employees will
    not equally favor increased liability insurance, is supported. There
    is a 95% probability that this conclusion is correct.

EXHIBIT 13.4   THE PROCESS FOR COMPUTING A CHI-SQUARE TEST
OF INDEPENDENCE

1. Record the observed frequencies in a contingency table.

2. Compute and record the expected frequencies for each cell.

3. Check that 80% of the expected frequencies are greater than 5
   and no frequency is less than 1 before using the general chi-
   square formula.

4. Compute the chi-square formula.

5. Compute the degrees of freedom.

6. Find the critical value in the chi-square table in the Appendices
   using the appropriate degrees of freedom and the pre-selected
   level of significance.

7. Reject the Ho if the computed X^2 is equal to or exceeds the critical
   value.

8. Draw conclusions about supporting or not supporting the null
   hypothesis.

CAUTION: Several cautions should be observed when considering use
of the chi square test of independence.

1. When using a 2x2 contingency table the computed chi-square is not a
   good approximation of the chi-square distribution. Thus a different
   formula is used because it incorporates a correction factor. This is
   called Yates correction for continuity and always yields a more
   conservative value. The formula is:

$$X^2 = \frac{N(|AD - BC| - \frac{N}{2})^2}{(A+B)(C+D)(A+C)(B+D)}$$

where: N = the total number of frequencies
   and A,B,C,D = frequencies within the cells as illustrated.

A	B	A + B
C	D	C + D
A + C	B + D	N

2. Use of the chi-square test requires sufficiently large expected frequencies:

   2.1   For a 2x2 table, all expected frequencies must be 5 or more. If they are not, use the Fisher test.

   2.2   For tables larger than 2x2, such as 2x3 or 4x5, 80% of the expected frequencies must be 5 or more and no expected may be less than 1. If these conditions are not met you may wish to combine adjacent cells or draw a larger sample.

3. Chi-square is essentially a nondirectional statistic. Thus, the table of critical values is set up for nondirectional tests.

However, for a 2x2 contingency table where degrees of freedom = 1, a directional hypothesis may be tested. Simply compare the computed X^2 to the critical value in the table at double the alpha (significance) level you selected for a directional test.

For example, an alpha of .05 for a directional test would correspond to an alpha of .10 for a nondirectional test and the tabled critical value indicated is 2.706.

Directional tests for contingency tables larger than 2x2 are not recommended. See Cochran [15] for additional information.

Recommended Readings: One classic reference is Cochran [15]. Siegel [58] is excellent, as is McNemar [48]. Most statistics references cover these points.

t-TEST FOR COMPARING MEANS OF TWO INDEPENDENT GROUPS

There are several t-tests used for the purpose of comparing means, as indicated in the decision trees. One formula is used for comparing a sample mean with a population mean (a one sample t formula) and another formula is used for comparing related data such as two observations for each subject.

A third category of t-tests is used to compare means of two independent groups and includes several formulas. The formula given below assumes that the variances of the two groups' scores are homogeneous (approximately equal).

Definition: *t-test*: One of several statistical tests used with interval or ratio level data when the hypothesis concerns comparison of means, the scores are normally distributed and the population variances are unknown.

EXHIBIT 13.5   USE THE t-TEST FOR TWO INDEPENDENT GROUPS
                WHEN YOU HAVE:

     1. Interval or ratio level of measurement.

     2. Two groups and want to test the difference in means.

     3. Random sampling from the population(s).

     4. Normally distributed scores.

   * 5. Unknown population variances.

  ** 6. Scores of the two groups are independent.

 *** 7. Variances of the two groups are approximately equal.

     8. Ho = the means of the two groups are equal.

  * If the population variances are known, use a Z test.

 ** If the two groups are related (matched or the same people on
two separate observations) use the t formula for related data.

*** Some statisticians recommend using a variance test to test the
homogeneity of the two variances prior to using a t-test.
Others feel this is not essential if the sample sizes are equal [34].
However, when there are unequal samples sizes and small
samples, unequal variances will affect the t value. If you have
these conditions either use equal sample sizes or change to a
nonparametric test.

    Statisticians do not agree among themselves if normally
distributed scores are required or not in every circumstance. Refer to
any of the recommended texts if you have scores which are not
normally distributed.

EXHIBIT 13.6:   EXAMPLE OF A t TEST APPLICATION

Hm: Of newly hired people who sell video recorders, more video recorders will be sold by salespeople who have previous experience in selling electronic equipment than by salespeople who do not have such experience.

$$Hm: \mu_e > \mu_{ne}$$

Ho: Salespeople with previous experience in selling electronic equipment will sell the same number or fewer video recorders than those who do not have such experience.

$$Ho: \mu_e \leq \mu_{ne}$$

Level of Significance selected: $\alpha = .01$

Data: The number of video recorders sold by each of 17 newly hired people over a six month period and whether or not the person has previous experience is recorded.

STEPS FOR COMPUTATION AND INTERPRETATION

1.   Record the scores for each of the two groups.

EXPERIENCED		NOT EXPERIENCED
		57
	55	53
	81	44
	76	62
	52	55
	87	68
	62	37
	67	48
	71	39
$\Sigma X =$	551	463
$n =$	8	9
$\overline{X} =$	68.88	51.44
$S^2 =$	151.27	107.78

Where: ΣX = sum of the scores n = number of scores

$$\overline{X} = \frac{\Sigma X}{n} = mean \qquad S^2 = \frac{\Sigma(X - \overline{X})^2}{n-1} = variance$$

EXHIBIT 13.6 (cont.)   EXAMPLE OF t TEST APPLICATION

2. Compute the t formula for two independent groups:

$$t = \frac{\overline{X}_1 - \overline{X}_2}{\sqrt{\left[\frac{(n_1 - 1)S_1^2 + (n_2 - 1)S_2^2}{n_1 + n_2 - 2}\right]\left(\frac{1}{n_1} + \frac{1}{n_2}\right)}}$$

$$t = \frac{68.88 - 51.44}{\sqrt{\left[\frac{(8 - 1)(151.27) + (9 - 1)(107.78)}{8 + 9 - 2}\right]\left(\frac{1}{8} + \frac{1}{9}\right)}}$$

$$t = \frac{17.44}{\sqrt{\left[\frac{1058.89 + 862.24}{15}\right](.125 + .111)}} = \frac{17.44}{\sqrt{(128.08)(.236)}}$$

$$t = \frac{17.44}{5.50} = 3.17$$

3. Compute the degrees of freedom   df = n_1 + n_2 - 2

$$df = 8 + 9 - 2 = 15$$

4. Find the critical value in the t table

CV = 2.602 for 15 df, .01 significance level, one-tailed test.

5. Reject the null hypothesis if the computed value equals or exceeds the critical value.

Decision: reject the Ho. Computed value of 3.17 exceeds the critical value of 2.602

6. Draw a conclusion about the research hypothesis:

Conclusion: The research hypothesis, that salespeople with previous experience in selling electronic equipment will sell more video recorders than salespeople without such experience, is supported. There is a 99% probability that this conclusion is correct.

FORMULA FOR THE t-TEST FOR INDEPENDENT GROUPS

$$t = \frac{\overline{X}_1 - \overline{X}_2}{\sqrt{\left[\dfrac{(n_1 - 1)(S_1^2) + (n_2 - 1)(S_2^2)}{n_1 + n_2 - 2}\right]\left[\dfrac{1}{n_1} + \dfrac{1}{n_2}\right]}}$$

where:

$\overline{X}_1$, $\overline{X}_2$ = means of groups 1 and 2

s_1^2, s_2^2 = variances of groups 1 and 2

n_1, n_2 = sample sizes of groups 1 and 2

Ho: $\mu_1 = \mu_2$

$df = n_1 + n_2 - 2$

EXHIBIT 13.7   PROCESS FOR COMPUTING A t-TEST FOR TWO INDEPENDENT GROUPS

1. Record the scores for each group.

2. Compute the t formula.

3. Compute the degrees of freedom.

4. Find the critical value in the table using the degrees of freedom, the prespecified significance level and whether the hypothesis leads to a one or two tailed test.

5. Reject the null hypothesis if the computed value equals or exceeds the critical value.

6. Draw conclusions about supporting or not supporting the research hypothesis.

ANALYSIS OF VARIANCE

Definition: *Analysis of Variance*: A variety of statistical techniques used to assess the significance of differences among means using methods which partition the total variance into several components.

Abbreviation: *ANOVA*

There are a variety of analyses of variance. The most frequently used are the one-way ANOVA and the two-way ANOVA.

Definition: *One-way Analysis of Variance*: An analysis of variance with one dependent and one independent variable.

Synonym: *One Factor Analysis of Variance.*

Definition: *Two-way Analysis of Variance*: An analysis of variance with one dependent and two independent variables.

Synonym: *Two Factor Analysis of Variance.*

EXHIBIT 13.8   USE ONE-WAY ANALYSIS OF VARIANCE WHEN
YOU HAVE:

1. Interval or ratio level of measurement.

2. One independent variable.

* 3. Test concerning means for three or more groups.

4. Random sampling from the population(s).

5. Normally distributed scores.

6. Scores of the groups are independent.

** 7. Variances are homogeneous.

   * One-way ANOVA can also be used with two groups but it is more common to use the t-test. Conclusions are the same.

   ** Unequal variances are not considered a problem if the sample sizes are equal, according to some statisticians [34].

Statisticians do not agree among themselves that normally distributed scores are always required. See Hays [34].

EXHIBIT 13.9   FORMULAS FOR ONE-WAY ANALYSIS OF VARIANCE

Sources of Variation	Sum of Squares (SS)			Degrees of Freedom (df)	Mean Square (MS)	F
Between groups	$\dfrac{(\Sigma X_1)^2}{n_1} + \dfrac{(\Sigma X_2)^2}{n_2} + \dfrac{(\Sigma X_3)^2}{n_3}$ $+ ... + \dfrac{(\Sigma X_k)^2}{n_k} - \dfrac{(\Sigma X_t)^2}{N_t}$			$k-1$	$\dfrac{SS_{bet}}{df_{bet}}$	$\dfrac{MS_{bet}}{MS_{with}}$
Within groups	$SS_{total} - SS_{bet}$			$df_t - df_b$	$\dfrac{SS_{with}}{df_{with}}$	
Total	$\Sigma X^2_t - \dfrac{(\Sigma X_t)^2}{N_t}$			$N-1$		

Where:

ΣX = sum of scores ΣX^2 = each score squared and summed

n = number of scores

ΣX_t = total sum of scores ΣX_t^2 = each score squared and summed over total number of scores

$(\Sigma X)^2$ = sum of scores squared $(\Sigma X_t)^2$ = total sum of scores squared

k = number of groups

Note that SSbet + SSwith = Total SS and df bet + df with = Total df

Hr: All of the means are not equal   Ho: $\mu_1 = \mu_2 = ... \mu_k$

EXHIBIT 13.10   A ONE-WAY ANALYSIS OF VARIANCE APPLICATION

Ha: There will be a difference in the number of computers sold by salespeople given four types of bonuses.

$$\mu_a \neq \mu_b \neq \mu_c \neq \mu_d$$

Ho: There will be no difference in the number of computers sold by sales people given four different types of bonuses.

$$\mu_a = \mu_b = \mu_c = \mu_d$$

Significance level selected: $\alpha = .05$

Data: Sixteen salespeople were randomly assigned to one of four types of plans: (1) extra 2% commission, (2) one year athletic club membership, (3) extra 1% commission plus 6 months club membership and (4) a stock bonus plan. The number of computers sold by each of the sixteen people was then recorded.

STEPS FOR COMPUTATION AND INTERPRETATION

1.   Record and summarize the scores for each of the groups.

Table 1:   Number of Computers Sold under Different Bonus Plans

One	Two	Three	Four			
6	0	2	3			
4	3	0	2			
5	1	1	2			
5	2	1	3			
$\Sigma X_1 = 20$	$\Sigma X_2 = 6$	$\Sigma X_3 = 4$	$\Sigma X_4 = 10$	$= 40$	$=$	ΣX_T
$\Sigma X^2_1 = 102$	$\Sigma X^2_2 = 14$	$\Sigma X^2_3 = 6$	$\Sigma X^2_4 = 26$	$= 148$	$=$	ΣX^2_T
$n_1 = 4$	$n_2 = 4$	$n_3 = 4$	$n_4 = 4$	$= 16$	$=$	N_T
$\bar{X}_1 = 5$	$\bar{X}_2 = 1.5$	$\bar{X}_3 = 1$	$\bar{X}_4 = 2.5$			

Where: $\Sigma X =$ sum of scores $\Sigma X^2 =$ each score squared and summed

   $\Sigma X_T =$ total sum of scores $\Sigma X^2_T =$ each score squared and summed over total number of scores

   $n =$ number of scores   N = total number of scores

   $(\Sigma X)^2 =$ sum of scores squared $(\Sigma X_T)^2 =$ total sum of scores squared

   $k =$ number of groups

EXHIBIT 13.10 (cont.)   A ONE-WAY ANALYSIS OF VARIANCE APPLICATION

2. Compute the sum of squares for Between groups, Within groups and Total.

$$SS_B = \frac{(\Sigma X_1)^2}{n_1} + \frac{(\Sigma X_2)^2}{n_2} + ... + \frac{(\Sigma X_k)^2}{n_k} - \frac{(\Sigma X_T)^2}{N_T}$$

$$SS_B = \frac{(20)^2}{4} + \frac{(6)^2}{4} + \frac{(4)^2}{4} + \frac{(10)^2}{4} - \frac{(40)^2}{16} = 138 - 100 = 38$$

$$SS_T = \Sigma X_T^2 - \frac{(\Sigma X_T)^2}{N_T}$$

$$SS_T = 148 - \frac{(40)^2}{16} = 148 - 100 = 48$$

$$SS_W = SS_T - SS_B$$

$$SS_W = 48 - 38 = 10$$

3. Compute the degrees of freedom for Between groups, Within groups and Total.

   df Bet   =   K-1 = 4-1 = 3

   df Total   = N_T-1 = 16-1 = 15

   df With   =   df Total - df Bet = 15-3 = 12

4. Find the Mean Square Between and Within groups.

$$MS_B = \frac{SS_B}{df_B} = \frac{38}{3} = 12.6667$$

$$MS_W = \frac{SS_W}{df_W} = \frac{10}{12} = .8333$$

EXHIBIT 13.10 (cont.)   A ONE-WAY ANALYSIS OF VARIANCE APPLICATION

5. Find the F ratio

$$F = \frac{MS_B}{MS_W} = \frac{12.67}{.83} = 15.27$$

6. Place computed information in ANOVA table

Source of Variance	Sum of Squares	Degrees of Freedom	Mean Square	F
Between groups	38	3	12.67	15.27
Within groups	10	12	.83	
Total	48	15		

7. Find the critical value in the F table

    CV = 3.49 α = .05,   df = 3 for numerator and 12 for denominator

8. Reject the null hypothesis if the computed value equals or exceeds the critical value.

    Ho: rejected. Computed value of 15.20 exceeds critical value of 3.49

9. Draw conclusions about the research hypothesis.

    The research hypothesis, that there will be a difference in number of computers sold by salespeople given four different bonus plans, is supported.

EXHIBIT 13.11   THE PROCESS FOR COMPUTING A ONE-WAY ANALYSIS OF VARIANCE

1. Record and summarize the scores for each of the groups.

2. Compute the sum of squares (SS) for Between groups, Within groups and Total. SS Within can be found by subtracting the Between SS from the Total SS.

3. Compute the degrees of freedom for Between groups, Within groups and Total. Within df can be found by subtracting the Between df from the Total df.

4. Find the Mean Square (MS) Between by dividing SS Between by df Between.

5. Find the Mean Square Within by dividing the SS Within by the df Within.

6. Find the F by dividing the MS Between by the MS Within.

7. Place the information in an ANOVA table.

8. Find the critical value in the F table using the df for Between and Within and the prespecified probability level.

9. Reject the Ho if the computed value equals or exceeds the critical value.

10. Draw conclusions about supporting or not supporting the research hypothesis.

CAUTION: While a significant F indicates that the means are not equal, it does not indicate which means are different from each other. Thus, if a significant F is found, ANOVA is usually followed by another procedure to determine differences among the various means.

The procedures used to test for significant differences among the means are called multiple comparisons. These fall into two general categories: (1) a priori planned comparisons and (2) post hoc comparisons.

A priori planned comparisons are used when the researcher determines, prior to data collection, the specific hypotheses to be tested. For example, using the data in Exhibit 13.4, the researcher may wish to test the research hypothesis that the means of the extreme groups, groups 1 and 4, will be higher than the means of the middle groups, groups 2 and 3.

Post hoc comparisons are used after a significant F ratio is found in ANOVA. If a nonsignificant F ratio is found, none of the means will differ from one another and there is no need for any further tests.

All possible comparisons among the means may be made with post hoc multiple comparisons. There are several post hoc multiple comparison tests. Selection of the appropriate test requires reference to a statistics book or expert.

Comment: An example of the Scheffé test for post hoc multiple comparisons is given here. The Scheffé is a conservative method and thus "safe" to use. However, its use may yield fewer statistically significant differences among means than a less conservative test. Refer to statistics sources if you wish to find out the requirements, advantages and disadvantages of less conservative post hoc multiple comparison methods.

THE SCHEFFÉ TEST FOR POST HOC MULTIPLE
COMPARISONS AFTER AN ANOVA

Definition: *Scheffé Test*: A test for post hoc multiple comparisons which uses the F distribution and allows all possible comparisons between means to be tested.

EXHIBIT 13.12   **Scheffé Formula**: For comparison of Group 1 and Group 2 means

$$F = \frac{(\overline{X}_1 - \overline{X}_2)^2}{MS_W \left(\dfrac{n_1 + n_2}{n_1 n_2} \right)(k-1)}$$

where:

$$\overline{X}_1, \overline{X}_2 = means\ of\ groups\ 1\ and\ 2$$

$$n_1, n_2 = sample\ sizes\ of\ groups\ 1\ and\ 2$$

$$k = number\ of\ groups$$

$$MS_W = mean\ square\ within$$

Compute a separate F for every comparison

EXHIBIT 13.13   THE PROCESS FOR COMPUTING A SCHEFFÉ TEST

1. Compute the Scheffé test for the first comparison.

2. Compare the computed F to the critical value already found for the ANOVA.

3. If the computed value equals or exceeds the critical value, the two means are significantly different.

4. Repeat steps 1 through 3 for each comparison.

5. Draw conclusions about the significance of differences among the various comparisons.

EXHIBIT 13.14:   EXAMPLE OF A SCHEFFÉ TEST APPLICATION

Using the example of ANOVA given in Exhibit 13.10, there would be 6 comparisons to discover which group means are significantly different.

1. $\bar{X}_1$ and $\bar{X}_2$

2. $\bar{X}_1$ and $\bar{X}_3$

3. $\bar{X}_1$ and $\bar{X}_4$

4. $\bar{X}_2$ and $\bar{X}_3$

5. $\bar{X}_2$ and $\bar{X}_4$

6. $\bar{X}_3$ and $\bar{X}_4$

1. Compute the Scheffé test for the first comparison.

$$F = \frac{(\bar{X}_1 - \bar{X}_2)^2}{MS_W \left(\dfrac{n_1 + n_2}{n_1 n_2} \right)(k-1)}$$

Where $\bar{X}_1 = 5$ $\bar{X}_2 = 1.5$ $MS_W = .83$ $n_1 = 4$ $n_2 = 4$ $k = 4$ (figures from Exhibit 13.10)

$$F = \frac{(5-1.5)^2}{.83 \left(\dfrac{4+4}{16} \right)(3)} = \frac{(3.5)^2}{1.245} = \frac{12.25}{1.245} = 9.84$$

2. Compare the computed F to the critical value already found for the ANOVA in Exhibit 13.10.

CV for ANOVA problem in Exhibit 13.10 = 3.49

3. If the computed value equals or exceeds the critical value, the two means are significantly different.

The computed F of 9.84 exceeds the critical value of 3.43. Thus there was a significantly greater number of computers sold under Bonus Plan one than under Bonus Plan two.

EXHIBIT 13.14 (cont.)   EXAMPLE OF A SCHEFFÉ TEST APPLICATION

4.   Repeat steps 1 through 3 for each comparison substituting the appropriate subscripts for each comparison.

For comparison $\bar{X}_1$ and $\bar{X}_3$

$$F = \frac{(\overline{X}_1 - \overline{X}_3)^2}{MS_W \left(\dfrac{n_1 + n_3}{n_1 n_3} \right) k - 1}$$

Comparison 2: $\overline{X}_1 and\ \overline{X}_3$: $F = \dfrac{(5-1)^2}{.83 \left(\dfrac{8}{16} \right)(3)} = \dfrac{16}{1.245} = 12.85$

Significant

Comparison 3: $\overline{X}_1\ and\ \overline{X}_4$: $F = \dfrac{(5-2.5)^2}{1.245} = \dfrac{6.25}{1.245} = 5.02$

Significant

Comparison 4: $\overline{X}_2 and\ \overline{X}_3$: $F = \dfrac{(1.5 - 1.0)^2}{1.245} = \dfrac{.25}{1.245} = .20$

Not Significant

Comparison 5: $\overline{X}_2 and\ \overline{X}_4$: $F = \dfrac{(1.5 - 2.5)^2}{1.245} = \dfrac{1.0}{1.245} = .80$

Not Significant

Comparison 6: $\overline{X}_3\ and\ \overline{X}_4$: $F = \dfrac{(1 - 2.5)^2}{1.245} = \dfrac{2.25}{1.245} = 1.81$

Not Significant

5.   Draw Conclusions:

A significantly greater number of computers were sold under Bonus Plan One (extra 2% commission) than any of the other 3 Bonus Plans.

There were no significant differences in number of computers sold under Bonus Plans Two, Three and Four.

TWO-WAY ANALYSIS OF VARIANCE

Two-way analysis of variance is used when there are one dependent and two independent variables. It is also called factorial analysis and is usually used in conjunction with a factorial experimental design.

A major advantage of two-way ANOVA is that it provides a test of what is termed the interaction between the two independent variables on the dependent variable, as well as testing the effects of each factor.

Thus, there are three separate hypotheses for two-way ANOVA as follows:

Ho: The means of the A variable are equal.
Ho: The means of the B variable are equal.
Ho: The interaction of A and B for each cell are equal.

The purpose here is to give you a conceptual understanding of the results of two-way ANOVA. The following ANOVA table indicates that the sources of variance include variance associated with the: (1) first independent variable A, (2) second independent variable B, (3) interaction of the A and B variables, (4) within groups -- also called the error term and (5) total group.

Note that the two-way ANOVA table is similar to but not the same as the one-way table in that there are more sources of variance.

EXHIBIT 13.15   TWO-WAY ANALYSIS OF VARIANCE TABLE

Source of Variance	Sum of Squares	df	Mean Square	F
A	SS_A	a-1	$\dfrac{SS_A}{df_A}$	$\dfrac{MS_A}{MS_W}$
B	SS_B	b-1	$\dfrac{SS_B}{df_B}$	$\dfrac{MS_B}{MS_W}$
AB	SS_{AB}	(a-1) (b-1)	$\dfrac{SS_{AB}}{df_{AB}}$	$\dfrac{MS_{AB}}{MS_W}$
Within (error)	SS_W	N-ab		
Total	SS_T	N-1		

where: a = the number of conditions of variable A

         b = the number of conditions of variable B

EXHIBIT 13.16   CONCEPTUAL EXAMPLE OF TWO-WAY ANALYSIS OF VARIANCE

1. Hypotheses to be tested:

    H_1: The average amount invested in stocks and bonds will differ.

    H_2: The average amount invested by men and women will differ.

    H_3: Men and women will invest different amounts in stocks and bonds.

2. Results of the analysis:

    After computing a two-way ANOVA, the results indicated:

Source of Variance	F
A (type of investment, stocks/bonds)	Not significant
B (sex of investor, male/female)	Not significant
AB (interaction of type of investment and sex of investor	Significant

3. The researcher concludes:

    3.1   There is no significant difference in amount invested in stocks and bonds.

    3.2   There is no significant difference in amount invested by males and females.

    3.3   Males and females invest differentially in stocks and bonds.

4. The researcher examines the means in order to interpret the significant interaction.

    Average Amount Invested in Stocks
    and Bonds by Males and Females

	Stocks	Bonds	
Males	$\bar{X} = \$2000$	$\bar{X} = \$1000$	$\bar{X}_M = \$1500$
Females	$\bar{X} = \$1000$	$\bar{X} = \$2000$	$\bar{X}_F = \$1500$
	$\bar{X}_S = \$1500$	$\bar{X}_B = \$1500$	

5. Examination of the mean amount invested in stocks and bonds by males and females indicates that females invested a significantly higher amount in bonds than did males, while males invested a greater amount in stocks.

6. This exaggerated example illustrates the usefulness of two-way ANOVA. In this example, one analysis provided information on possible significant differences in amounts invested by: (1) type of investment, (2) sex of investor and (3) the interaction of type of investment and sex of investor.

Note that three F ratios are tested for significance to correspond with the three hypotheses. These are: (1) the F ratio to test if the A means are equal, (2) the F ratio to test if the B means are equal and (3) the F ratio to test if the AB interaction is significant. One, two, all or none of these ratios might be significant. Exhibit 13.16 gives an example to help your conceptual understanding of two-way ANOVA. If you wish additional information refer to the recommended readings.

Recommended References: Edwards [25]. Kerlinger [36].

BIVARIATE REGRESSION: THE PEARSON PRODUCT-MOMENT CORRELATION

Regression techniques are often used to examine the association between or among variables. They are called regression techniques because of the phenomenon that, when there is less than a perfect relationship, the predicted score will be closer to the mean of its group of scores than will the predictor score to its group mean.

> Unless there is a perfect relationship between variables, there is a tendency for groups which score at a specific level above or below the mean on the predictor variable to be closer to the mean on the criterion variable.

For example, assume that applicant screening test scores and job performance scores are correlated but not perfectly correlated. Because of the regression phenomenon job applicants who score high on the screening test will tend to score closer to the mean on the job performance evaluation than they did on the screening test. Exhibit 13.19 illustrates this phenomenon.

EXHIBIT 13.17   USE THE PEARSON PRODUCT-MOMENT CORRELATION WHEN YOU HAVE:

1. Interval or ratio level of measurement for both variables.

2. Normally distributed scores.

* 3. A linear relationship between the two variables.

*Linear relationship: The points on the scattergram representing each XY observation fall about a straight line rather than a curved line. To determine, plot the points on a scattergram.

Statisticians do not agree on the requirement of normally distributed scores.

An assumption when using the Pearson is that the variance of the Y scores is the same for every X value. This is known as homoscedasticity and is discussed in most statistics references.

Multiple regression involves a set of predictor variables and a criterion variable. The multiple correlation coefficient, R, represents the degree of association between the predictors and the criterion.

Bivariate regression involves one predictor variable and one criterion variable. The Pearson product-moment correlation coefficient, r, represents the degree of relationship between the predictor and the criterion variable and is discussed here.

Definition: *Pearson Product-moment Correlation Coefficient:* A measure of the relationship between two variables which are at the interval or ratio level of measurement and are linearly related. The coefficient can range from -1.00, indicating a perfect negative relationship, through zero, indicating no relationship, to +1.00, indicating a perfect positive relationship.

Symbols: ρ, r.

EXHIBIT 13.18   FORMULA FOR THE PEARSON PRODUCT-MOMENT
                       CORRELATION

$$r = \frac{N\Sigma XY - (\Sigma X)(\Sigma Y)}{\sqrt{\left[N\Sigma X^2 - (\Sigma X)^2\right]\left[N\Sigma Y^2 - (\Sigma Y)^2\right]}}$$

where:

N   = number of paired scores

ΣXY = Each X multiplied by its corresponding Y, then summed

ΣX = sum of X scores ΣX^2 = each X squared, then summed

ΣY = sum of Y scores ΣY^2 = each Y squared, then summed

$(\Sigma X)^2$ = sum of X scores, $(\Sigma Y)^2$ = sum of Y scores, squared
             squared

df = n-2

EXHIBIT 13.19: PEARSON PRODUCT-MOMENT CORRELATION APPLICATION

Hi: The correlation between level of employee absenteeism and the number of times they receive supervisor reprimands will be significantly different from zero.

Hi: $p \neq 0$

Ho: There will be no relationship between level of absenteeism and the number of supervisor reprimands.

Ho: $p = 0$

Significance level selected: $\alpha = .05$

Data: The number of days absent and the number of supervisor reprimands are recorded for ten employees.

STEPS FOR COMPUTATION AND INTERPRETATION

1. Record and summarize the scores.

Name	Days Absent X	Supervisor Reprimands Y	XY	X^2	Y^2
Smith	16	17	272	256	289
Dunn	14	15	210	196	225
Lock	12	15	180	144	225
Mayo	12	10	120	144	100
Knod	10	11	110	100	121
Kent	10	9	90	100	81
Jones	9	11	99	81	121
Topp	8	9	72	64	81
Gray	7	8	56	49	64
Dean	2	5	10	4	25

$\Sigma X = 100$ $\Sigma Y = 110$ $\Sigma XY = 1219$ $\Sigma X^2 = 1138$ $\Sigma Y^2 = 1332$

EXHIBIT 13.19 (cont.)   PEARSON PRODUCT-MOMENT CORRELATION APPLICATION

2. Compute the correlation coefficient r:

$$r = \frac{N\Sigma XY - (\Sigma X)(\Sigma Y)}{\sqrt{\left[N\Sigma X^2 - (\Sigma X)^2\right]\left[N\Sigma Y^2 - (\Sigma Y)^2\right]}}$$

$$r = \frac{10(1219) - (100)(110)}{\sqrt{\left[10(1138) - (100)^2\right]\left[10(1332) - (110)^2\right]}}$$

$$r = \frac{12190 - 11000}{\sqrt{(11380 - 10000)(13320 - 12100)}} = \frac{1190}{\sqrt{(1380)(1220)}}$$

$$\frac{1190}{\sqrt{1683600}} = \frac{1190}{1297.54} = .917$$

3. Compute the degrees of freedom: N-2   Where N = number of pairs.

    df = 10 - 2 = 8

4. Find the critical values in the r table

    CV = .632   α = .05   df = 8

5. Reject the null hypothesis if the computed value equals or exceeds the critical value.

    Ho: rejected.
              Computed value of .917 exceeds critical value of .632.

6. Draw conclusion about the research hypothesis.

    The correlation between level of absenteeism and supervisor reprimands is significantly different from zero. (Stated differently, the correlation is statistically significant.)

INTERPRETATION OF THE PEARSON PRODUCT-MOMENT CORRELATION

1. The Pearson product-moment correlation tests the Ho that the correlation is zero. There are three possible alternative hypotheses: the population correlation (p) is significantly different from zero (two tailed test), is greater than zero (one tailed test) or is less than zero (one tailed test).

2. When examining a correlation coefficient, look at the size and the sign. The size indicates the magnitude or strength of the relationship and the sign indicates direction of the relationship, whether it is positive or negative.

3. A positive correlation indicates that the variables are varying together. A negative correlation indicates that as one variable is increasing the other variable is decreasing. A correlation of .85 between typing speed and number of errors indicates that as typing speed increases the number of errors also increases (positive correlation). A correlation of -.85 between typing speed and number of words correct indicates that as typing speed increases the number of correct words decreases (negative correlation). BOTH CORRELATIONS ARE THE SAME SIZE.

4. A rough interpretation of correlation is: high = .85 to 1.00, moderate = .50 to .84, low = 0 to .49.

5. CORRELATION DOES NOT IMPLY CAUSE AND EFFECT.

6. The correlation coefficient does NOT indicate a percentage. However, one type of interpretation is to find the percent of variance the two variables have in common. This is done by squaring the r. In the typing speed/number of errors example, r squared = .72 $(.85^2)$ indicating that 72% of the variance in the number of errors is accounted for by the typing speed.

An example of an application of the Pearson product-moment correlation is given in Exhibit 13.19.

EXHIBIT 13.20   THE PROCESS FOR COMPUTING A PEARSON CORRELATION

1.   Record the two sets of scores.

2.   Compute the formula for r.

3.   Compute the degrees of freedom.

4.   If N is less than 30*, use the r table to find the critical value.

5.   Reject the Ho if the computed value equals or exceeds the critical value.

6.   Draw conclusions about supporting or not supporting the research hypothesis.

*   If N is 30 or over, use the following:

   1.   Compute $z = r \sqrt{N-1}$

   2.   Find the probability of occurrence in the z table.

   3.   Reject the Ho if the probability found in the z table is equal to or less than the prespecified significance level.

EXHIBIT 13.21   EXAMPLE OF USING THE REGRESSION EQUATION FOR PREDICTION

Purpose: To compute predicted scores for each predictor score listed in Exhibit 13.19.

Data: From Exhibit 13.19

STEPS FOR COMPUTATION

1. Compute beta* using the raw score formula:

$$b = \frac{N\Sigma XY - (\Sigma X)(\Sigma Y)}{N\Sigma X^2 - (\Sigma X)^2}$$

Where:

N   = the number of paired observations

ΣXY = the sum of each predictor score multiplied by its criterion score.

ΣX = the sum of the predictor scores ΣY = the sum of the criterion scores

ΣX^2 = the sum of each squared X $(\Sigma X)^2$ = the sum of all the X's, squared.

Refer to Exhibit 13.19 for these figures and substitute in the formula.

$$b = \frac{10(1219) - (100)(110)}{10(1138) - (100)^2} = \frac{12190 - 11000}{11380 - 10000} = \frac{1190}{1380} = .8623$$

*Note the similarities in the beta formula and the Pearson product-moment correlation formula.

2. Compute alpha using the raw score formula.

$$a = \bar{Y} - b\bar{X}$$

Where:

$\bar{X}$ = the mean of the predictor variable. $\bar{Y}$ = the mean of the criterion variable.

b = the beta coefficient computed in Step 1.

$$a = 11 - .8623(10) = 2.38$$

EXHIBIT 13.21 (cont.)   EXAMPLE OF USING THE REGRESSION EQUATION FOR PREDICTION

3. Compute a predicted score, $\hat{Y}$, for each predictor score, X, listed in Exhibit 13.19, using the regression equation:

$\hat{Y}$ = bX + a

Where: $\hat{Y}$ = the predicted score   X =   the predictor score

        b = the slope of the regression line or the average amount that Y varies with an increase of one unit of X.

        a = the Y intercept or the amount of Y when X = 0.

Predictor Scores X (Number of days absent)	Criterion Scores Y (Supervisor reprimands)	Predicted Scores $\hat{Y}$ (Prediction for number of reprimands)
16	17	16.18
14	15	14.45
12	15	12.73
12	10	12.73
10	11	11.00
10	9	11.00
9	11	10.14
8	9	9.28
7	8	8.42
2	5	4.10

$\hat{Y}$ for score (X) of 16 = $\hat{Y}$ = .8623(16) + 2.38 = 16.18
$\hat{Y}$ for score (X) of 14 = $\hat{Y}$ = .8623(14) + 2.38 = 14.45
$\hat{Y}$ for score (X) of 12 = $\hat{Y}$ = .8623(12) + 2.38 = 12.73
$\hat{Y}$ for score (X) of 10 = $\hat{Y}$ = .8623(10) + 2.38 = 11.00
$\hat{Y}$ for score (X) of 9 = $\hat{Y}$ = .8623(09) + 2.38 = 10.14
$\hat{Y}$ for score (X) of 8 = $\hat{Y}$ = .8623(08) + 2.38 = 9.28
$\hat{Y}$ for score (X) of 7 = $\hat{Y}$ = .8623(07) + 2.38 = 8.42
$\hat{Y}$ for score (X) of 2 = $\hat{Y}$ = .8623(02) + 2.38 = 4.10

Conclusion: If an employee is absent 16 days, the predicted number of supervisor reprimands is 16.18. If an employee is absent 8 days, predicted reprimands is 9.28.

PREDICTION: THE REGRESSION COEFFICIENT

Sometimes researchers wish to use specific predictor scores to predict criterion scores. That is, using the data in Exhibit 13.19, if John is absent 8 days how many supervisor reprimands might be expected? (Remember just because two variables are related does not imply cause and effect. That is, there is no implication that number of days absent causes reprimands.)

If the correlation between absenteeism and supervisor reprimands were perfect (1.00), then all that would have to be done to predict the number of reprimands is examine the data on which the correlation is computed. However, few variables are perfectly related and other steps must be carried out to account for the imperfect relationship.

The regression equation is used for this type of prediction to correct for imperfect correlations between variables. This equation produces the least amount of error in fitting a line through the various plotted points. The line is called the least squares solution. An example of a regression equation application is given in Exhibit 13.21.

WHERE YOU ARE NOW

At this point you should have:

1. Selected the appropriate statistical test for your hypotheses or research questions by using the decision trees,

2. Reviewed the procedure you selected either by using the formulas in this book or in another reference,

3. Reviewed statistical concepts,

and you should be able to:

4. Find critical values in the tables in the Appendices and

5. Compare computed values with critical values to accept/reject null hypotheses and support/not support research hypotheses.

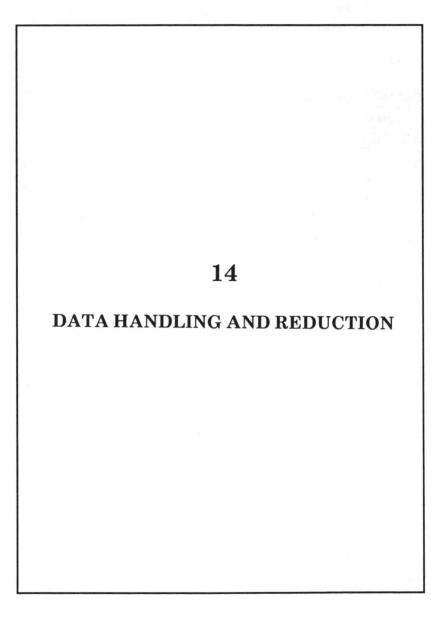

14

DATA HANDLING AND REDUCTION

TERMS DEFINED IN CHAPTER FOURTEEN

CHAPTER FOURTEEN

DATA HANDLING AND REDUCTION

STEPS TO TAKE AFTER READING THIS CHAPTER

1. Plan for assigning a unique identification to each subject.

2. Check that each item on the instrument is at the appropriate and desired level of measurement.

3. Check that, for structured items, each item form is set up to avoid coding after data collection.

4. Check that the statistical analysis is appropriate for each research question or hypothesis.

5. Plan sufficient time for editing data and examining it for unanticipated findings and possible generation of new variables by combining variables.

6. Plan for reducing and summarizing the data by sketching out the procedures for summarizing.

7. Select the desired statistical package for computer use, if necessary.

8. Try out the summarization and statistical analyses by using fictitious or pilot data.

PREPARATION FOR DATA HANDLING

ASSIGN IDENTIFICATION NUMBERS

Every element in the sample should have a unique identification number by which to identify it. This is particularly important to maintain anonymity if the sample consists of people.

The procedure is simple. If the Ss have been randomly selected or randomly assigned, the numbers used for the random procedure can be used. Make a master list of names with corresponding identification numbers and keep it in a secure file in case further reference is needed.

ASSURE APPROPRIATE AND DESIRED LEVEL OF MEASUREMENT

To ensure using the selected statistical analysis it is important that the item representing each variable be at the appropriate and desired level of measurement. The researcher will know if the level of measurement is appropriate by reviewing the requirements for each level and using that information accordingly.

For example, the researcher may wish to use a t-test, but have ordinal data. In such a case the level of measurement is neither appropriate for the t-test nor desired by the researcher.

ESTABLISH AND BUILD IN CODING PROCEDURES

It saves resources to include as many coding devices as feasible with the instrument. This can be done in a number of ways including the following.

1. **Assign Numbers to Categories.** By assigning numbers the data can be recorded quickly on data sheets or by entering directly in a computer. If not numbered, someone must code the categories after data collection which is very time consuming.

2. **Include Computer or Spreadsheet Column Numbers on the Instrument.** It saves time if the appropriate column number corresponding to the item is placed adjacent to the item directly on the instrument. It is easier and faster to enter data directly from the instrument if the column number is provided.

3. **Use Pilot Study Results for Establishing Categories for Open Ended Items.** If there are open-ended items they will need to be content analyzed in order to set up categories. While this is sometimes done after data collection, if a pilot study is used the categories can be set up prior to data collection. Then, after the data is collected a sample of responses can be selected to see if the categories will be inclusive. If there are some responses which do not fit into these categories, add categories BEFORE starting to code the data.

USING OPTICAL MARK READING ANSWER SHEETS

Occasionally researchers use optical mark reading sheets to record responses. These are sheets of paper on which answers are shaded in using a pencil. A mark reader then "reads" the sheets and can be programmed to generate information such as frequency distributions and measures of central tendency.

Optical mark reading sheets are usually not recommended for questionnaires because often respondents become confused about how to fill them out appropriately.

CHECK THAT THE ANALYSIS IS APPROPRIATE

Check that each type of statistical analysis and summary of data yields data in the form you desire. Actually lay out the tables, charts, graphs and figures using fictitious (or pilot) data. This allows a thorough examination to ascertain that the final information will be in the desired form and that the statistical analysis is appropriate to answer the research questions or hypotheses.

Remember, at this point the data are not collected and there is still time to change to more appropriate procedures. AFTER DATA COLLECTION IT IS TOO LATE TO CHANGE!

PLAN FOR EDITING THE DATA

After data collection, the instruments will have to be edited for errors and inconsistencies. Plan before data collection how to carry out the editing and the approximate time to allow for this process.

You can expect to find any or all of the following.

1. **Nonresponse (Missing Data)**. Respondents sometimes omit items either deliberately or inadvertently. Interviewers sometimes become confused or pressured and omit items. Occasionally interviewers and respondents omit a whole page of items -- frequently the last page if it is on the reverse side of a page. The latter can be avoided by adding "go to the next page" or "over" at the bottom of the pages.

   Decide how to handle possible missing data. Some choices are to reinterview, telephone the respondent, discard the entire instrument or simply accept the omission and have a smaller number of respondents for that particular item. Your choice will largely depend on the time and cost required to pick up the missing data and the importance of the missing response to the research project.

2. **Incorrect Responses**. Despite clear instructions some respondents do not understand them or tend to be careless. This leads to responses checked in the wrong places, questions incorrectly answered and a variety of other possibilities which make the responses unusable.

   While these possible occurrences can be considered missing data, occasionally researchers use some sort of decision rule for these responses. For example, a mark or a check between two numbers rather than directly at the number is relatively common. Some researchers use the 1/2 point for such cases. That is, if the mark is between responses 2 and 3 but is closer to #2 they consider it a #2 response. Whatever the decision rules are, they should be made clear to the people who edit, code and enter data.

   Recommendation: The author recommends omitting such responses on the basis that no one can really know what the respondent's intentions really were.

3. **Illegible Handwriting**. Decisions must be made on how to handle illegible handwriting. Many people's handwriting can be deciphered over time but do you have the time?

4. **Invective or Strong Language**. Occasionally a respondent resents a request to complete a questionnaire or interview schedule, is angry at the sponsor of the project or is just plain feeling ornery. The results can be the return of a mutilated instrument, written invective or the use of so-called "foul language."

Although these occurrences are rare a decision must be made about the handling of them. The choices usually are either to use whatever data is there or to discard the entire instrument. The question is: can the responses be valid when given by people who are demonstrating anti-social behavior?

Regardless of the decision, attention should be given to whatever the respondent says or writes because there may be a legitimate complaint couched in the unfortunate selection of words.

Recommendation: The author recommends discarding such instruments on the basis that people who exhibit such behaviors may also be likely to deliberately respond falsely.

However, the instruments should be kept and a summary of the responses and written comment should be prepared for the sponsor: e.g., "the analysis does not include responses from 3 people because their responses may not be valid. A brief summary of their responses and comments is enclosed."

5. **Inconsistent Responses**. A decision must be made about inconsistent data. For example, a respondent might check the age group "15-18" and then check the educational level "doctoral degree." In fact, some researchers use items like these as "lie" scales to determine if a respondent may be lying and thus invalidate the entire instrument.

PLAN TIME TO EXAMINE DATA

Plan for time in which the data can be examined thoroughly for unanticipated results beyond answering your research questions or hypotheses. This step cannot be overemphasized. Time and time again this author has seen researchers ignore or simply not be aware of what the data are screaming out.

Many times these researchers fail to examine the data because they become so engrossed in the hypotheses or research questions that they tend to forget the other information WHICH WAS ASKED TO PROVIDE A COMPREHENSIVE PICTURE. Consider the examples in Exhibit 14.1.

Recommendation: Place a large sign above the desk with the words: "LOOK AT YOUR DATA."

EXHIBIT 14.1   EXAMPLES OF NOT EXAMINING OR IGNORING THE
                DATA

THE STATEMENT GIVEN	WHAT WAS OMITTED AND SHOULD HAVE BEEN INCLUDED
1. Significantly more respondents use Brand X than Brand Y.	97% of the respondents did not use either brand.
2. The hypothesis that the Texas plant had a higher rate of absenteeism was supported at the .05 significance level.	No employeee in either plant was absent more than two days per month.
3. A larger proportion of people preferred viewing TV during the daytime rather than prime time or late evening hours.	75% of the respondents were females who did not work outside the home.
4. The correlation of .09 was significant at the .05 level.	There were 10,000 respondents and large N's can lead to significant but meaningless correlations. An r of .09 indicates very little relationship between variables.

UNANTICIPATED FINDINGS

One of the major reasons for examining the data is to discover unanticipated findings. These are data which the researcher did not expect to find. In the above example the researcher did not anticipate that 97% of the respondents did not use either Brand X or Brand Y (although perhaps he should have).

Unanticipated findings cover a broad range from the example given above to some very startling findings. Useful new products and processes have evolved from unanticipated findings and perhaps would not have come about otherwise.

UNANTICIPATED CONSEQUENCES

Unanticipated consequences is a term which some researchers use interchangeably with unanticipated findings. However, unanticipated consequences, through common useage, has come to mean consequences to subjects, to larger populations or to the environment which were not anticipated.

An extreme example of unanticipated consequences is the effect of the atomic bomb on Hiroshima, Japan and the world. The researchers at Los Alamos did not anticipate all the long term physical effects on the people of

Hiroshima, the psychological effects on the Japanese people and other populations nor all the environmental effects.

In experimental research Ss are often administered some type of treatment from which specific effects are expected. However, the treatment may also result in unanticipated consequences.

Any type of research study may lead to unanticipated consequences. People who complete a survey on movie attendance may begin to attend more movies or people given certain diets may begin to crave sugar. Since researchers often cannot anticipate such outcomes, it is wise to be alert to their possible occurrence and monitor the research carefully. Often follow-up studies are conducted to assess any unanticipated consequences.

GENERATE NEW VARIABLES FROM EXISTING ONES

One way to provide additional information without adding to the instrument is to use combinations of variables to generate new variables. While this should be planned when generating the instrument, it can also be done after the data collection.

For example, questionnaire items include measures of the variables: (1) frequency of attendance of concerts or ballets, (2) frequency of attendance of the legitimate theatre, and (3) frequency of dining in restaurants. These variables can be combined to form another variable termed "type of lifestyle" with the categories "high attenders, medium attenders and low attenders."

In order to combine different items they must have something in common. For example, the variables "number of laser disks purchased, number of eight-track tapes purchased and number of cassette tapes purchased" can all be combined into a variable termed "number of audio tapes and disks purchased."

PLAN FOR DATA REDUCTION AND SUMMARIES

Planning is necessary to yield the appropriate time and format for reducing and summarizing the data so that it will be in a form from which meaning can be derived clearly and easily.

Many research projects yield enormous amounts of data. It doesn't take much to do so. If there are 20 variables under study and the sample is 200 people, there will be 4000 individual observations. Some studies include several hundred variables!

FREQUENCY DISTRIBUTIONS

The first step in data reduction for almost all research projects is to produce a frequency distribution of responses for each variable.

Definition: *Frequency Distribution*: An arrangement of scores or categories with the frequency of occurrence (f) of each score or category indicated.

EXHIBIT 14.2 EXAMPLES OF FREQUENCY DISTRIBUTIONS

1. **Number of Thursday Sales**

Number of Sales Each	f	Total Sales
5	12	60
4	21	84
3	36	108
2	23	46
1	18	18
0	14	0
Total	124	316

12 People made 5 sales each on Thursday

2. **Preferred Travel Mode**

Mode	f
Airplane	120
Auto (driver)	110
Train	85
Auto (passenger)	46
Bus	22
Total	383

Of 383 people, 120 preferred flying.

3. Example of Frequency Distribution with Class Intervals

Score on Screening Test	f
95-99	3
90-94	5
85-89	12
80-84	18
75-79	23
70-74	20
65-69	19
60-64	15
55-59	7
50-54	5
Total Applicants	127

Of 127 applicants, 3 scored between 95 and 99 on the screening test.

4. Frequency Distribution with Percentage of Total Responses

Number of TV Sets Owned	Number of Respondents	Percent of Total Response
0	20	8
1	80	32
2	60	24
3	50	20
4	40	16
Total	250	100%

The table indicates that 60 respondents, 24% of the total number of respondents, owned 2 TV sets.

Frequency distributions are usually reported with the absolute frequency, which is the number of responses for each score or category. The percent of total responses for each score of category is often added for easier interpretation as illustrated in Exhibit 14.2.

CAUTION: To avoid a long list of scores when the range of scores is large, researchers usually place the scores into intervals called class intervals. The size of the interval is usually determined by selection of the size which produces no more than twenty and no fewer than ten intervals.

The next step is usually to use some statistics which summarize the data. The most frequently used statistics are measures of central tendency and measures of variability.

Measures of central tendency indicate the average or most frequently appearing score. Measures of variability indicate to what degree the scores are dispersed or spread out.

Comment: Most computer programs for frequency distributions will also give measures of central tendency and variability.

MEASURES OF CENTRAL TENDENCY

One of the first summary or descriptive statistics examined is usually a measure of central tendency.

Definition: *Measure of Central Tendency:* A measure of the average or typical score in a distribution of scores. The three most frequently used measures of central tendency are: (1) the mean, which requires at least interval level of measurement, (2) the median, which requires at least ordinal level of measurement and (3) the mode, which requires at least nominal level of measurement.

CAUTION: Note that this definition indicates that a mode, median or mean may be used with interval level data, a mode or median with ordinal level data but with nominal data only a mode may be used.

THE MEAN

Means are very familiar to all of us because they are used so frequently throughout our lives to report average scores. For example, businesses frequently report their average gross sales, expenses, number of people hired and number of units sold.

Definition: *Mean:* A measure of central tendency which usually refers to the arithmetic average computed on scores which are interval or ratio level of measurement. Reference to other types of means usually includes their descriptors, e.g., the harmonic mean or geometric mean.

Symbols: $\bar{X}, \mu, M$

EXHIBIT 14.3   THE PROCESS FOR COMPUTING A MEAN

1. Record the scores.

2. Add all the scores.

3. Divide by the total number of scores.

FORMULA:

$$\overline{X} = \frac{\Sigma X}{N}$$

Where:

$\overline{X}$ = the mean of a sample: ΣX = sum of the scores: N = number of scores

EXAMPLE: The number of microwave ovens sold over 5 days was:

10, 9, 15, 6, 10.

$\Sigma X = 50$ $\overline{X} = 50/5 = 10$ (the average number of microwave ovens sold per day)

CAUTIONS ABOUT USING THE MEAN

1. The mean reflects and is affected by every score in the distribution, because every score is used in the summation.

2. Thus, extreme scores affect the mean. For example: 5 salespeople sold the following number of dishwashers: 40, 6, 6, 5, 3. If a mean were computed the conclusion would be that the average sales of the 5 people was 12 dishwashers. Yet, four of the five people sold less than 7 and one sold 40! The mean is not a representative measure of central tendency in such cases.

3. When there are extreme scores either use the median or, in the case of a set of very dissimilar scores, describe the scores. For example, in #2 above one might report that the median number of dishwashers sold was 6 but that one person sold 40. If there are few scores submit the complete set of scores for better understanding.

4. The mean is appropriate only for data at the interval or ratio level of measurement.

5. Thus, the mean cannot be used when ratio or interval level data has been changed to ordinal. For example, response formats often do not include lower or upper limits, which changes the level of measurement from ratio to ordinal as illustrated below.

"How many working TV sets do you have in your home?"

_____ None

_____ One

_____ Two or more

Because there is no upper limit (two or more could be 10 TV sets) the level of measurement is changed from ratio to ordinal and means cannot be computed.

> Despite these cautions the mean is considered the most stable measure of central tendency. The basis for this conclusion is that when several samples are drawn from a population the means of these samples will be quite similar and will differ less than will sample medians or modes.

THE MEDIAN

Definition: *Median*: A measure of central tendency which is the middle score in an ordered set of scores which are at the ordinal or higher level of measurement. With an odd number of scores the median is the middle score. For an even number of scores the median is halfway between the two middle scores.

Abbreviation: Med.

EXHIBIT 14.4   THE PROCESS FOR COMPUTING A MEDIAN

1. Record the scores in order from highest to lowest.

2. Select the middle score, if there is an odd number of scores.

3. If there is an even number of scores, add the two middle scores together and divide by 2.

EXHIBIT 14.5   EXAMPLES OF COMPUTING MEDIANS

Odd Number of Scores	Even Number of Scores
10	15
7	12
5	10
3	8
2	5
	4
Median = 5	
	Median = 9
	(10 + 8) /2

THE MODE

Definition: *Mode*: A measure of central tendency which is the most frequently appearing score in a distribution of scores which are at the nominal or higher level of measurement.

EXHIBIT 14.6   THE PROCESS FOR SELECTING A MODE

1. Record the scores in order from highest to lowest.

2. Select the most frequently occurring score as the mode.

Example: 15,15,15,9,8,8,1,1,1,1.

   The mode   = 1   the most frequently occurring score

CAUTION: Note that the mode is very unstable. If the two lowest scores were omitted the mode would be 15 instead of 1.

MEASURES OF VARIABILITY

Measures of variability are used to assess the spread or dispersion of a set of scores. They are most frequently used in: (1) statistical analyses and (2) in research projects when it is desirable to know if the scores are close together or widely spread.

Definition: *Variability*: The degree to which scores within a distribution of scores differ from each other. The most frequently used measures of variability are the standard deviation and its square, the variance. Both require at least interval level of measurement.

Definition: *Variance*: A measure of variability which is the mean of the squared deviations from the mean in a distribution of scores which are at the interval or ratio level of measurement. The variance is the standard deviation squared.

Symbols: s^2, σ^2

Definition: *Standard Deviation*: A measure of variability which is the square root of the variance. It indicates the average of the scores' deviations from the mean of a distribution of scores which are at the interval or ratio level of measurement.

Symbols: s, σ

Comment: There are several formulas for the standard deviation but they yield the same result as illustrated in Exhibit 14.8. Note that the standard deviation is usually used in discussion of scores because the score units are the same as the original scores from which the standard deviation was computed. The variance reflects squared score units and it is difficult to remember in discussions that squared units are being considered.

EXHIBIT 14.7   CHARACTERISTICS OF THE THREE MEASURES
                 OF CENTRAL TENDENCY

	Mean	Median	Mode
1. Level of Measurement Required	Interval or Ratio	Ordinal	Nominal
2. How to Find	Sum of the scores divided by number of scores	Find the middle score	Count the most frequently occurring score
3. Stability	Very Stable	Less Stable	Least Stable
4. Other	Affected by extreme scores because uses every score in distribution	Can use with extreme scores because concentrates on middle score	Can fluctuate widely with change in one score

Example of Computation

$$\underline{X}$$

$$
\begin{array}{l}
8 \\
8 \\
6 \\
6 \\
5 \\
4 \\
4 \\
\underline{4}
\end{array}
$$

$\Sigma X = \overline{45}$ $\bar{X}$ $= 5.63$
$N = 8$ Med $= 5.5$
        Mode $= 4$

EXHIBIT 14.8:   COMPUTATION OF THE STANDARD DEVIATION AND THE VARIANCE

FORMULAS FOR STANDARD DEVIATION

$$\sigma = \sqrt{\frac{\Sigma(X - \overline{X})^2}{N}} = \sqrt{\frac{\Sigma x^2}{N}} = \sqrt{\frac{N\Sigma X^2 - (\Sigma X)^2}{N^{2*}}}$$

Where:

$\Sigma X = the\ sum\ of\ scores$ $\Sigma X^2 = each\ score\ squared\ and\ summed$

$(\Sigma X)^2 = the\ sum\ of\ scores,\ squared$ $N = number\ of\ scores$

$\overline{X} = the\ mean$ $x = X - \overline{X}\ or\ deviation\ score$

*Note that N(N-1) is used in place of N^2 when computing s, the sample standard deviation.

1.   Record and summarize the scores

If using deviation formula			If using computational formula
X	X - X̄ or x	x^2	X^2
7	3	9	49
6	2	4	36
5	1	1	25
4	0	0	16
3	-1	1	9
2	-2	4	4
1	-3	9	1
$\Sigma X = 28$	$\Sigma x = 0$	$\Sigma x^2 = 28$	$\Sigma X^2 = 140$

N = 7
X̄ = 4

2.   Compute the standard deviation

Deviation Formula   Computational Formula

$$\sigma = \sqrt{\frac{28}{7}} = \sqrt{4} = 2 \qquad\qquad \sigma = \sqrt{\frac{7(140)\ \ 28^2}{7^2}} =$$

$$\sqrt{\frac{980 - 784}{49}} = \sqrt{\frac{196}{49}} = \sqrt{4} = 2$$

3.   If the variance is desired simply square the standard deviation.

$$\sigma^2 = 2^2 = 4$$

THE RANGE

The range is a simple measure of variability often used for a quick look at the data.

Definition: *Range*: A measure of variability which is usually computed by subtracting the smallest score from the largest score. The range is sometimes defined as the largest minus the smallest score plus one, but this should be used "for a discrete distribution in which scores must take on whole-number values" [33, p. 96].

Example: The set of scores: 36, 18, 12, 5 has a range of 31.

CONTINGENCY TABLES AND CROSS TABULATIONS

Another useful method to summarize and examine data is by using a contingency table in which observations are cross tabulated.

Definition: *Contingency Table*: A table which shows joint classifications of two or more variables, indicating the number of observations in each of the joint classifications (cells).

Definition: *Cross Tabulation*: The tabulation of the total number of observations into joint classifications of two or more variables.

Abbreviation: Crosstabs.

Synonym: Crossbreaks.

It is much easier to interpret contingency tables if percentages are included. Note in Exhibit 14.9 how much clearer it would be to state that 67% of the females and 40% of the males preferred money for a bonus.

Contingency tables are easier to interpret if percentages are added. Three sets of percentages can be computed: (1) the percentage each cell is of the total number of observations, (2) the percentage of the column totals and (3) the percentage of the row totals.

Usually the percentage of the row or column totals is used. The percentage of the total is rarely required. The choice of using the row of column percentage is made by the researcher. However, it is more common to use the row percentages which usually indicate the independent variable.

For example, in Exhibit 14.9 the row percentages would indicate that 67% of the females preferred money while 60% of the males preferred vacations. If column percentages were used, the interpretation would be that 50% of the people who preferred money were female while 75% of those who preferred vacations were male.

Comment: Cross tabulations in contingency tables are especially useful because: (1) associations between variables can be easily assessed, (2) the process can be used with any level of measurement since only frequencies are used, (3) the process allows a quick examination of the data and (4) a statistical test (chi-square) can be computed using the layout of the contingency table. An example of a contingency table is given in Exhibit 14.9.

EXHIBIT 14.9   EXAMPLE OF A CONTINGENCY TABLE

Bonus Preferences

	Money	Vacation	Total
Females	20	10	30
Males	20	30	50
	40	40	80

20 of the 30 females and 20 of the 50 males preferred money as a bonus.

USING PERCENTAGES

The addition of percentages to frequency distributions or contingency tables often aids with interpretation of the data. However, care must be taken in how percentages are used.

1. Do not use percentages with small numbers. They will be misleading.

For example:

NUMBER AND PERCENT OF PEOPLE
PURCHASING TYPES OF BEANS

Type	Number	Percent
Green Beans	4	50
Pinto Beans	2	25
Kidney Beans	1	12.5
Wax Beans	1	12.5
Total	8	100%

A reader sees that 25% of the people purchased pinto beans, certainly misleading when considering only 2 people purchased them.

2. Do not interpret data using large percentages. Readers have difficulty interpreting figures such as "costs increased by 2,000 percent." Instead use a statement such as "costs were 20 times greater than the 1985 figures." Exhibit 14.10 illustrates the use of percentages with a contingency table.

EXHIBIT 14.10   EXAMPLE OF A CONTINGENCY TABLE AND CROSS TABULATION WITH PERCENTAGES

Satisfaction with Investments by Employment Status

Satisfied with Investments

Employment Status	Yes % (n)	No % (n)	Total % (n)
Self-Employed	40% (16)	60% (24)	100% (40)
Employed by others	57% (30)	43% (23)	100% (53)
Temporarily Unemployed	26% (7)	74% (20)	100% (27)
Total	44% (53)	56% (67)	100% (120)

56% (n = 67) of the total respondents were not satisfied with their investments.

Over half (57%) of the respondents who were employed by others were satisfied with their investments.

Almost three-fourths (74%) of respondents temporarily unemployed were not satisfied while 60% of self-employed were not satisfied with their investments.

USING A COMPUTER

Data from most research projects will be inputted directly into a computer. Data handled by hand rarely occurs since the availability of computers is now widespread.

There are many existing statistical programs which provide frequency distributions, measures of central tendency and variability and a variety of statistical analyses. Programs can even be written for computer editing of your specific data.

Selection of computer programs for a specific research project depends on the type and capacity of available computers and the form of the output desired. Greater computer capabilities and new statistical packages are continually being developed.

STATISTICAL PACKAGES

One of the benefits of the computer revolution is that researchers no longer have to contend with hours and hours of statistical analysis using hand-held or desk calculators. Indeed, the rapid advances over the past few years have even led to the almost total demise of key punch cards and card readers. Data is now usually entered directly into a computer.

In order to compute statistical analyses of the data, the computer must be programmed to provide the various calculations. Fortunately, there are software packages available which compute a wide variety of statistical analyses [50].

Some of these programs are called multifunction statistical packages and provide several different statistical procedures. Frequency distributions, means, standard deviations, cross tabulations, chi square tests, t-tests and analysis of variance tests are examples.

Two frequently used multifunction packages are the Statistical Package for Social Sciences (SPSS) and Statistical Software (BMDP). Both are relatively easy to use and create appropriate and useful output. These are just two examples of several packages available.

The choice among the various statistical packages available is often a matter of which is available in a researcher accessible computer facility. If you have a choice among several packages examine the manuals (documentation) to determine which is preferable for your purposes.

To use multifunction statistical packages acquire the program manuals and follow the directions. The manuals for the major packages give explicit directions and require very little experience. An alternative is to have a person knowledgeable in the use of the particular package conduct the analysis.

CAUTION: One of the least desirable but prevalent outcomes of the use of statistical packages is that, because they are easy to use, many people inexperienced in statistical procedures run statistical analyses but do not know how to interpret the output.

The result is often misinterpretation, sometimes completely erroneous, of the output of the statistical tests. This is turn leads to errors in the decisions based on these statistical tests.

EXHIBIT 14.11   EXAMPLE OF HOW INSTRUMENT RESULTS ARE
ENTERED INTO A COMPUTER

(1-2)   Store Name: _____   (4-5)   Number of Employees: _____
(6-7)   Manager's years of experience: _____
(8-9)   Number of Vendors used last calendar year: _____
(10-11) Number of Vendors used previous calendar year: _____

CODED RESULTS OF INSTRUMENT

Store I.D.#	Number of Employees	Manager Experience	N of Vendors Last Year	N of Vendors Previous Year
01	23	10	27	35
02	36	12	32	27
03	18	19	12	15
04	29	17	21	18
05	11	04	07	10
06	48	14	35	32
07	52	18	28	25
08	24	16	18	19
09	39	15	42	40
10	19	08	26	20
11	15	07	17	19
12	41	22	30	28

COMPUTER   INPUT
Column: 12345678901
Spread Sheet: ABCDEFGHIJK

Data input: 01 23102735
                 02 36123227
                 03 18191215
                 04 29172118
                 05 11040710
                 06 48143532
                 07 52182825
                 08 24161819
                 09 39154240
                 10 19082620
                 11 15071719
                 12 41223028

Row 1 indicates that store #01 had 23 employees, the manager had 10 years of
experience, there were 27 vendors used last year and 35 vendors the previous
year.

The problem is becoming so widespread that it is advisable to have an expert in statistical analysis examine the actual computer output to aid with interpretation of the data.

Remember that a statistical package for computers is simply a marvelous tool for saving enormous amounts of time by producing, reducing, summarizing and analyzing large quantities of data in a short time period. The important aspects remain the same as they were prior to the widespread use of statistical packages; using the appropriate input and being able to interpret the output appropriately.

We all know computers are fun to play with when time permits. Some researchers pay more attention to the process than the results.

USING A SPREAD SHEET

If a computer facility or statistical packages are not available and if there is a small amount of data, the spread sheet capabilities of a personal computer might be used for analysis of the data. It is an easy process.

Simply enter the data using the spread sheet program and then use the arithmetic functions to compute the selected statistical procedures and analyses. While statistical packages are preferable for sophisticated and extensive analyses, the spread sheet is useful for small quantities of data which require minimal analyses.

Exhibit 14.11 indicates how data is coded and entered into a computer using either a statistical package or a spread sheet.

WHERE YOU ARE NOW

At this point you should have planned for the time, personnel and processes for:

1. Coding of the data, if necessary,

2. Editing the data, if necessary,

3. Examining the data for unanticipated findings,

4. Entering the data into the computer,

5. Summarizing the data and

6. Computing the statistical analyses.

15

CONDUCT THE PILOT STUDY AND COMPLETE THE PROPOSAL

TERMS DEFINED IN CHAPTER FIFTEEN

CHAPTER FIFTEEN

CONDUCT THE PILOT STUDY AND COMPLETE THE PROPOSAL

STEPS TO TAKE AFTER READING THIS CHAPTER

1. Conduct a pilot study, if feasible.

2. Modify, eliminate or add research procedures, if necessary.

3. Complete the proposal.

4. Submit the proposal to the sponsors, if necessary.

CONDUCT THE PILOT STUDY

A pilot study is often conducted as a trial run prior to investing substantial time and money in the actual project. The pilot study serves many purposes which may include tests of the: (1) sampling method, (2) research design, (3) data collection method, (4) instrument (validity, reliability, ease of use and results yielded) and (5) data analyses. Sometimes data from pilot studies are used to provide estimates for computing sample sizes.

Definition: *Pilot Study:* A preliminary micro-research study which uses the same research procedures as the major study and Ss drawn from the same population but who will not be used in the major study. The purpose of this trial run is to assess the various research procedures prior to the major study so that modifications or estimations can be made, if necessary.

Synonyms: Pilot Test, Pilot Run

IS A PILOT STUDY NECESSARY?

Pilot studies require time and money. Thus, they are carried out only when the investment is worth the return. If the researchers are using familiar research techniques and standardized instruments, a pilot study is often not conducted.

However, if using an untried instrument or the research procedures are not familiar or are new, a pilot study is highly recommended.

Recommendation: A pilot study is highly recommended even if it is indeed a small one because of time or money constraints. Most people cannot imagine the number of unanticipated events which can occur throughout a research study until they start to conduct research. Any experienced researcher can tell "horror" stories about subjects who suddenly refuse to participate, move to another country or quit their jobs; instruments which do not yield the appropriate data to answer the research questions; interviewers who become ill or miss work; and computers which spit out the wrong information because of poor programming.

Many of these disasters or annoyances can be avoided by thorough planning and a pilot study. Unanticipated events may still occur but you will be better prepared.

HOW TO CONDUCT A PILOT STUDY

The pilot study is conducted just like the major study but with a smaller sample which will NOT be included in the actual study. Thus all the steps of the research process are followed. At this point the hypotheses or research questions are stated, and the operational definitions, design, data collection methods and instruments determined. The next steps are given in Exhibit 15.1.

EXHIBIT 15.1   HOW TO CONDUCT A PILOT STUDY

1. Select a sample from the specified population according to the selected sampling procedures. These Ss will not be used in the actual study.

2. Administer the experiment, if experimental design is used.

3. Administer the selected instruments with the specified data collection methods.

4. Analyze the data with the selected statistical analyses.

5. Check that each procedure yielded the appropriate information.

    5.1   Did the sampling yield appropriate Ss?

    5.2   Did the data collection methods and interviewers or observers yield appropriate information?

    5.3   Did results of the instruments answer the research hypotheses or questions? Were the instruments sufficiently valid and reliable. Could Ss respond easily?

    5.4   Were the statistical analyses appropriate for the data and the research hypotheses or questions?

6. Make any changes necessary in the research procedures before conducting the actual study.

ADVANTAGES OF THE PILOT STUDY

There are many advantages to conducting a pilot study. A list of some of the most useful ones is given below.

1. Provides information on possible ethical problems overlooked previously.

2. Helps determine if the selected variables are the appropriate ones to study.

3. Helps determine if the research questions or hypotheses are appropriate.

4. Provides information which may help with the interpretation of the review of literature and related information.

5. Helps determine if the operational definitions are adequate or need modification.

6. Helps determine if the levels of measurement are appropriate for the selected variables.

7. Provides a check that the population is appropriately defined.

8. Provides information on the feasibility and appropriateness of the sampling method.

9. Helps determine sample size by allowing estimation of variance from the pilot sample.

10. Provides information on the appropriateness of the research design to accomplish the objectives.

11. Provides a check on all aspects of the data collection method.

12. Provides additional training for interviewers, instrument administrators, experimenters, coders and data editors.

13. Provides a check on the validity and reliability of the instruments.

14. Provides a check on the ease and time required for Ss to respond to the instrument.

15. Provides data on which to base modifications of the instrument.

16. Provides a check on the appropriateness of the statistical tests and procedures.

17. Provides data to examine for unanticipated findings.

18. Provides information to help discover unanticipated consequences, if they exist.

19.   Provides information at low cost on which to base a decision to continue or abandon the project.

20.   Provides information for modification of all procedures prior to conducting the actual study.

21.   Enhances the probability of the proposal being accepted because actions based on pilot study results almost always improve the project.

22.   Enhances the researcher's reputation for thoroughness because sponsors are likely to be impressed with the professional implications of conducting a pilot study.

COMPLETE THE PROPOSAL

As suggested in Chapter One, the proposal can be written throughout the planning stages for the different research processes. If the proposal has been worked on over the planning time there is little left to do.

If you still have not written the proposal you can delay no longer. The first step is to refer to Chapter One which gives suggestions for writing each section.

Before writing anything be sure to find out if the proposal must be in a sponsor specified format. If so, use that format regardless of your own inclinations. Some sponsors will not even read a proposal unless it is in the requested format.

After you have completed the proposal, use the check list in Exhibit 15.2 to make sure that: (1) all important aspects of the proposed research are included in the proposal, (2) the format is appropriate, (3) the project is feasible, (4) the reasons for conducting the research are sufficiently important for allocation of resources and (5) the budget is realistic.

Remember that the proposal often serves as a contract between the researcher and the sponsor. This carries with it an obligation for the researcher to conduct the study as specified in the proposal and to provide the information and/or products designated, within the specified time frame.

The obligation of the sponsor is to provide the budget, materials, personnel, etc. specified in the proposal at the time periods designated.

EXHIBIT 15.2   CHECKLIST FOR THE RESEARCH PROPOSAL

1. **The Beginning**

____   1.1   Does the title page indicate the title, the name of the prospective sponsor, researchers' names, phone numbers, addresses and date of transmittal?

____   1.2   Is the title a succinct explanation of the proposed project?

____   1.3   Does the abstract indicate clearly what is to be done, how it will be carried out and what the expected products will be?

____   1.4   Is the importance of the research mentioned in the abstract so a reader who skims will note it?

____   1.5   If using a letter of transmittal, are the highlights of the abstract pointed out?

____   1.6   Is the expected output of the project, such as reports or products, clearly specified in the abstract, the letter of transmittal or in the introduction to the proposal?

2. **The Research Problem**

____   2.1   Is the importance of the problem conveyed to the reader without exaggeration?

____   2.2   Does the level of importance of the problem warrant the requested budget and/or other resources?

____   2.3   If the research findings for the problem have implications for larger than local application, is this pointed out?

____   2.4   Is the purpose of the research stated in clear and simple terms?

3. **Review of Related Information and Literature**

____   3.1   Are prior research findings and their relationship to the problem indicated?

____   3.2   Is prior information about the organization itself and the relationship of this information to the project indicated, if this is relevant to the research?

____   3.3   If using a theory, is it clear to the reader how the theory applies to the problem and the hypotheses?

____   3.4   Is it clear what the study will add to what is already known?

____   3.5   Are references cited where appropriate?

____   3.6   Is the literature review related to the population, the variables or theories?

EXHIBIT 15.2 (cont.)   CHECKLIST FOR THE RESEARCH PROPOSAL

4. **The Hypotheses or Research Questions**

____   4.1   Are hypotheses stated when there is sufficient information to make predictions?

____   4.2   Are research questions stated when there is insufficient information for prediction or when exploration of information peripheral to the major problem is desired?

____   4.3   Are the variables within the hypotheses or research questions sufficiently clear for the reader to pick out quickly?

____   4.4   Are the relationships to be tested in the hypotheses or examined in research questions appropriately stated?

____   4.5   Are the hypotheses or research questions presented as a logical outcome, flowing from the research problem and the review of related information and literature?

____   4.6   Are research hypotheses stated rather than null hypotheses?

____   4.7   Are the hypotheses or research questions stated in the form they will be tested or examined?

____   4.8   Is each variable operationally defined in measureable terms?

5. **The Population and Sample**

____   5.1   Is the population clearly defined in the description of it?

____   5.2   Is the population size given?

____   5.3   Is the sampling method completely specified?

____   5.4   If stratification will be used, is there a statement about what the strata will be and why stratification will be used?

____   5.5   If the sampling does not include random procedures is there a statement justifying the procedure used?

____   5.6   Are the intended sample size and the rationale for selecting that number indicated?

6. **Research Design**

____   6.1   Is it clear which type of research design will be used?

____   6.2   If using experimental or quasi-experimental design, is the specific design given and explained?

____   6.3   If using experimental design, are the different levels of the treatment specified and explained?

EXHIBIT 15.2 (cont.)   CHECKLIST FOR THE RESEARCH PROPOSAL

___ 6.4   If using experimental design, was it stated that the subjects will be randomly assigned to treatments?

___ 6.5   If using quasi-experimental design, is there an explanation why true experimental design could not be used?

___ 6.6   Have procedures been used to lessen the threats to internal and external validity?

___ 6.7   Has as much control as feasible been imposed on the design?

___ 6.8   If using historical design, is sufficient information given about the representativeness and possible distortions or omissions in the data gathered from primary and secondary sources?

7. Data Collection Methods

___ 7.1   Is the data collection method the most appropriate and feasible for assessing the hypotheses or research questions?

___ 7.2   Would a less expensive data collection method provide equally good information?

___ 7.3   If interviewing, administering instruments or observing, are time and resources planned for training?

___ 7.4   If examining documents, materials or artifacts, will the data be sufficiently representative and reliable for conclusions to be drawn?

___ 7.5   If using observations or examination of documents or materials, will time or event sampling be used or will entire segments be observed or examined?

___ 7.6   Will the data collection method affect subjects' responses? If so, would the effect be sufficiently serious to change data collection methods?

8. Instrumentation

___ 8.1   Does the instrument measure the variables appropriately?

___ 8.2   Are the levels of measurement yielded the same as the researcher planned?

___ 8.3   Does the instrument have evidence of the appropriate types and magnitudes of validity estimates?

___ 8.4   Does the instrument have evidence of the appropriate types and magnitudes of reliability estimates?

___ 8.5   Can subjects respond to the instrument in a reasonable time period?

___ 8.6   Is it sufficiently easy for subjects to respond to the instrument?

EXHIBIT 15.2 (cont.)   CHECKLIST FOR THE RESEARCH PROPOSAL

____   8.7   Is the instrument easy to administer in a reasonable time period?

____   8.8   Will the results of the instrument be easy to interpret?

____   8.9   Are the costs of the instrument within the allocated budget?

____   8.10   Will the instrument have any social or psychological effects on the subjects? If so, are there measures incorporated to deal with these effects?

____   8.11   If the instrument is new or a modified version, was the instrument pilot tested?

____   8.12   Is there a copy of each instrument in the appendices?

9. Statistical Tests and Analyses

____   9.1   Are the selected statistical tests appropriate to test the hypotheses or answer the research questions?

____   9.2   Do the levels of measurement of the variables coincide with the levels required for the statistical procedures?

____   9.3   If the observations will be "related" to each other, is the statistical test appropriate for nonindependent responses?

____   9.4   Is there provision for the examination of data to determine any unanticipated findings?

____   9.5   Will descriptive and data reduction measures, such as frequency distributions, measures of central tendency, measures of variability or cross tabulations, be included to enhance the interpretation of the data?

10. Time Schedule

____   10.1   Is the time schedule presented in an easy-to-read form such as a PERT chart?

____   10.2   Is the method used to compute the time estimates specified?

____   10.3   Are the time estimates consistent with the personnel resources requested in the budget?

____   10.4   Are the time estimates realistic given the specific procedures required by the project?

____   10.5   Are the time estimates given in minimum/maximum time periods?

____   10.6   Do the time estimates coincide with the time periods requested by the sponsor?

EXHIBIT 15.2 (cont.)   CHECKLIST FOR THE RESEARCH PROPOSAL

11. **Budget**

____ 11.1 Is the total amount of the budget consistent with the importance of the project?

____ 11.2 Have personnel salaries and fringe benefits, including those for the project directors, been included?

____ 11.3 Do the personnel costs include increases anticipated at the time the project is conducted?

____ 11.4 Have costs for supplies, equipment, facilities, etc., been checked for accuracy by knowledgeable people?

____ 11.5 Do those costs include anticipated increases or decreases?

____ 11.6 Are overhead or indirect costs included?

12. **Personnel**

____ 12.1 Have the project directors and major associates been mentioned by name and area of expertise?

____ 12.2 Are resumés for each major researcher or associate included in the appendices?

____ 12.3 Are sufficient personnel available for all the research procedures should the proposal be funded?

13. **References**

____ 13.1 Are references given for each citation in the proposal?

____ 13.2 Are the references appropriate for the concepts described?

____ 13.3 Are the references balanced between the classic authors and the more recent ones?

____ 13.4 Are references cited distinguished from bibliographic information?

____ 13.5 Are the references appropriately placed in the text and at the end of the proposal or in the appendices?

14. **Appendices**

____ 14.1 Do extensive charts, graphs, tabulations or other lengthy materials appear in the appendices so that proposal reading is not interrupted?

____ 14.2 Are appendices clearly delineated by titles and letters or numbers?

EXHIBIT 15.2 (cont.)   CHECKLIST FOR THE RESEARCH PROPOSAL

15. General

____   15.1   If there are any ethical considerations is there an explanation of how they will be handled?

____   15.2   Will subjects be available for the proposed research?

____   15.3   If cooperative organizations will be involved, is there hard evidence, such as letters of commitment, that they will participate?

____   15.4   Has the proposal been edited for grammatical and numerical errors?

____   15.5   Can a nonspecialist read the proposal and understand the objectives?

____   15.6   Have other proposals submitted to the sponsor been examined to determine the concerns of the proposal reviewers?

____   15.7   Are the format and the wording of the proposal sufficiently succinct so that it can be read easily and quickly while grasping the major points?

SUBMIT THE PROPOSAL TO THE SPONSOR

Whether the proposal is intended for internal or external sponsors, there are a few additional cautions to consider prior to submission.

1. Submit the proposal in time to meet the specified deadline. Many sponsors will refuse to accept a proposal received after the deadline.

2. If mailing the proposal, ensure that first class postage is attached. It is amazing how often this detail is overlooked, resulting in late submission.

3. Be sure the proposal is addressed to the required person and address to avoid delays; another common error.

4. Do not allow the physical appearance of the proposal to reflect extravagance. Some researchers attempt to "dress up" the physical appearance to impress the sponsor. This usually has an effect opposite of what was intended.

   While the proposal should reflect care in preparation of the physical appearance, the sponsors are more impressed with a professional approach to solving a problem than with unnecessary frills.

5. If presenting the proposal personally in front of a group, prepare visual aids to help keep the presentation brief and concise.

6. Be prepared to negotiate the budget.

Remember that proposal reviewers are usually busy people who may only read the abstract and examine the budget and skim the rest of the proposal. Grab their attention with a clear and concise layout of the research objectives and procedures. Provide sufficient detail for the careful reader to thoroughly understand exactly what is being proposed, how much time it will take and what it will cost.

WHERE YOU ARE NOW

At this point you should have:

1. Conducted the pilot study, if necessary,

2. Modified, added or omitted procedures based on pilot study results,

3. Completed the proposal,

4. Used the check list to help catch any omissions,

5. Submitted the proposal to the sponsor, if necessary

and you should be aware of:

6. The many advantages of conducting a pilot study and

7. The tremendous number of details involved in proposal writing and submission.

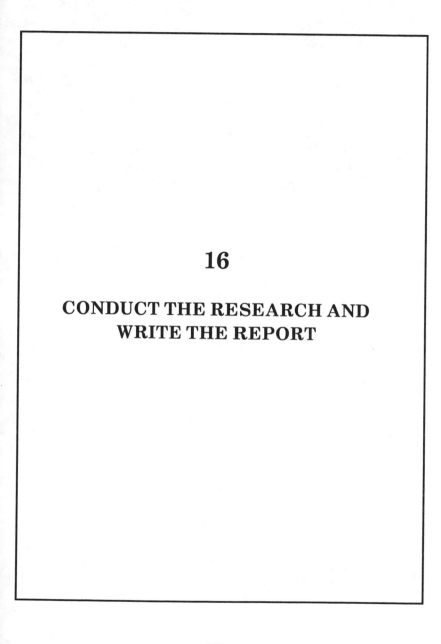

16

CONDUCT THE RESEARCH AND WRITE THE REPORT

TERMS DEFINED IN CHAPTER SIXTEEN

CHAPTER SIXTEEN

CONDUCT THE RESEARCH AND WRITE THE REPORT

STEPS TO TAKE AFTER READING THIS CHAPTER

1. Select the sample.

2. Make arrangements for contact with the sample, if necessary.

3. Conduct the experiment(s), if using an experimental design.

4. Collect the data.

5. Conduct data handling and reduction procedures.

6. Analyze the data.

7. Test the hypotheses and/or answer the research questions.

8. Examine the data for unanticipated findings.

9. Write the research report and submit it.

10. GO OUT AND CELEBRATE A JOB WELL DONE!

CONDUCT THE RESEARCH

Now is the time when the value of all that planning time and effort is demonstrated. The payoff is in terms of the smooth implementation of all the selected and planned procedures. Remember though, that unexpected events do occur during most research projects.

During the conduct of the research decisions are minimal because the researcher is following the steps specified in the proposal.

SELECT THE SAMPLE

There are no decisions at this point as the sampling plan is specified. Remember to oversample in case of loss of Ss.

MAKE ARRANGEMENTS FOR CONTACT WITH SUBJECTS

After the sample is selected arrangements must be made for bringing the Ss and the researchers together. Much of this work has been done in the planning stage but for some projects there needs to be implementation of such plans.

Examples are: (1) contacting Ss to arrange times and dates for interviews or experiments, (2) obtaining completed consent forms, (3) arranging to use equipment or materials selected as samples, and (4) arranging to use sites selected as samples.

In short, this is the time to carry out those procedures which could not be done until the sample was selected.

CONDUCT THE EXPERIMENT, IF USING EXPERIMENTAL DESIGN

If using an experimental design requiring a pretest, remember to administer the pretest prior to the experiment.

If the research involves experimental design, there are no decisions at this stage since the design is specified in the proposal.

COLLECT THE DATA

Regardless of the type of research data will be collected using some form of instrument. Again there are no decisions at this stage because the data collection method has been determined and the instrument designed or selected.

Interviewers, observers or instrument administrators should be trained and reliability estimates obtained before conducting the research.

CONDUCT DATA HANDLING AND REDUCTION PROCEDURES

It is extremely helpful to review data handling and data reduction procedures prior to analyzing the data. Although most of the decisions in this area are already made, there may be points which have been neglected.

If you have not conducted a pilot study, take a sample of the completed instruments and try out any coding or editing procedures to assure the results are in the form desired.

ANALYZE THE DATA

While the statistical analyses have been determined in the proposal, there is a possibility of making modifications at this stage. For example, you may wish to generate new variables by combining variables or compute analyses of variables you had not considered before.

It is common practice to obtain a matrix of correlations between all variables to obtain insights into relationships which may not have been hypothesized. Correlations often aid in understanding the data and are not difficult to generate with the use of a computer.

TEST THE HYPOTHESES AND/OR ANSWER THE RESEARCH QUESTIONS

Your primary task is to test the stated hypotheses or answer the research questions. This is why all that time and money were spent on conducting the research.

Were the above statements necessary? Yes! You would be surprised at the number of research reports in which no answers are given about the hypotheses or research questions.

EXAMINE THE DATA FOR UNANTICIPATED FINDINGS

Researchers should always be alert to findings which were unexpected or unplanned. A review of the section on data handling may be helpful at this stage.

In addition to testing hypotheses and answering research questions, frequency distributions, measures of central tendency and variability and a correlation matrix are all useful in examining the data. After these are examined, LOOK AT YOUR DATA in every way you can think of. You will sometimes be amazed at the number of relationships or interpretations which have been missed.

WRITE THE RESEARCH REPORT

Definition: *Research Report:* A report, usually submitted to the sponsor(s) of the project or professional journals, which includes concise but inclusive descriptions of the research objectives, methodology and findings. Research reports vary considerably because of the variety of purposes for which they are prepared.

The last step of the research process is to write the report and submit it to the sponsors of the project. This is not as time consuming as it might be because much of the report has been written as the proposal. Whole sections of the proposal can often be used just as they are written with the exception of changing from the future tense of the proposal to the past tense of the report.

The section titles and content which should be included in the research report vary considerably with the type of sponsor. For example, the report for a study conducted for your own organization will differ considerably from the report required by an outside funding agency or a professional journal.

Sections which are generally included in almost all research reports are given here. Sections of the proposal which can usually be used for the report are noted.

SECTIONS WHICH ARE INCLUDED IN MOST RESEARCH REPORTS

1. **Title Page.** This should include the title of the report, the researchers' names, date and the organization to whom the report is submitted. If the report is confidential it should be noted on the title page with bold letters.

2. **Table of Contents.** The table of contents usually lists the major topics or chapters, subtopics, tables, figures, and appendices. A table of contents is not usually included in articles submitted to professional journals.

3. **Summary of the Findings.** While this is not common practice, the author has found it very useful to include a summary of the findings in the first pages of the report. This particularly appeals to busy business executives. However, for a journal article a summary of the findings is included in the abstract.

4. **Abstract or Summary of the Study.** This section includes brief statements on each of the following sections. It should include why the study was done, the specific hypotheses or research questions, the research methodology and the major findings.

5. **Problem.** The need for the study is explained in terms of the problems which initiated the study. A review of literature or related information is usually included. This section can usually be taken from the proposal.

6. **Purpose.** This section includes the hypotheses or research questions or specific objectives of the research and can usually be taken from the proposal.

7. **Research Methodology.** This section includes all the information concerned with how the research was carried out. The following should be included.

   7.1   Operational definitions.

   7.2   Description of the population, the sampling procedures and the number in the sample.

   7.3   Description of the data collection methods, the instruments and their validities and reliabilities.

   7.4   Description of the experiment(s), if experimental design was used.

   7.5   A brief description of any unexpected events or problems which may have occurred during the conduct of the research which may have affected the results.

   7.6   Statements indicating the type of analyses conducted.

Comment: The information in this section can usually be stated with a few sentences per point. Make it sufficiently explicit so that the reader knows exactly what was done and how it was done but keep it short. Any lengthy explanations, particularly those which require extensive charts, graphs or figures, should probably be placed in the appendices.

Much of this section can be taken from the proposal.

8. **Findings.** This is the most important section of the report and should be presented as such. In this section the sponsor discovers what the payoff is for the investment of resources. The findings should be presented with precision and clarity. A discussion of the findings should be presented with summary statistics and results of the analyses. Extensive statistical tables should be placed in the appendices with appropriate reference in the test. Charts, graphs and tables should be used to help the reader quickly grasp the information.

   Remember that the primary findings are those which test the hypotheses or answer the research questions of the study and should be presented first. Secondary analyses and unanticipated findings should follow.

9. **Conclusions.** In this section the researcher draws conclusions from the findings as they relate to the hypotheses, research questions or objectives of the study. This consists of interpreting the results of the study according to acceptable research knowledge and practice. Not all readers will be knowledgeable about the technical aspects of research and it is the responsibility of the researcher to point out those conclusions which are acceptable and those which are not.

   For example, if there are significant but very small correlations, the researcher should point out that the small size of the correlations indicates very little relationship. If the sampling was not random, the researcher should point out the limitations of the conclusions because of the sampling. If some event occurred during the administration of the instrument or the experiment which might have affected the results, it is important to discuss the possible consequences on the findings.

10. **Recommendations.** This is a controversial section which is included in some reports and not in others. The decision whether to include it or not depends on the sponsors and the audience of the report. Many organizations feel that researchers do not have sufficient information about the total organization and its goals to make recommendations. Other organizations expect the researcher to make recommendations. If you are writing a report for publication in your professional field, recommendations are usually expected. If you are writing the report for a business firm, discuss this point with the sponsor.

11. **References.** Few research studies can be conducted without reference to information gathered from the organization itself or from other sources such as books, journals or census data. Appropriate citations should be made in the text regarding the reference and a list of references should be included [1]. The form of this list varies depending on what publishing style is used.

12. **Appendices.** The appendices might include copies of the instruments, instructions to interviewers, statistical information which is too lengthy to place in the text or drawings of physical layouts. Any information which is extensive or which will be read by only a small number of people should be included.

Appendices are NOT usually used in articles published in journals.

SUGGESTIONS FOR WRITING THE REPORT

1. **Review the Section on Writing Proposals.** Much of the proposal goes in the research report almost directly as written. One difference is that the proposal includes sentences using the future tense (since it is proposing) and the report uses the past tense (the research is done). Also the proposal does not include the findings and conclusions.

2. **Follow the Proposal as the Report is Written.** The proposal states what you contracted with the sponsor. If there were procedures proposed which were not carried out or were modified, explain the reasons in the report.

3. **Use as Few Words as Possible.** The report should be brief and concise while giving a complete description of the processes and findings.

4. **Avoid Value Laden or Imprecise Words.** Be precise and specific. Instead of saying, "The local savings and loan is in terrible shape," say something like, "The number of people with passbook savings in Cin City Savings and Loan Association decreased from 25,000 to 15,000 from 1974 to 1984."

5. **Make Smooth Transitions Between Sections.** A report sounds "chopped up" if there are no sentences to connect the different sections. In addition, it is sometimes difficult to understand how one section relates to another unless there are some sentences or paragraphs which relate them.

6. **Use Visual Presentations.** Present tables, graphs, figures or charts instead of lists of figures in sentence form. These aids enhance the readers' understanding of the procedures and findings quickly.

Examples of charts and graphs are given in Exhibits 16.1 through 16.5.

7. **Avoid Technical Terminology.** The audience for the report may not be familiar with technical terminology, making the report difficult to read. For easy and quick understanding, simple language is better than long words and complex language.

When use of technical terms is unavoidable, explain them in simple language.

8. **Check Spelling and Grammar.** Frequently misspelled words include *questionnaire* (2 n's). *Phenomenon* and *stratum* are singular while *phenomena* and *strata* are plural. *Data* is sometimes used in the

singular, though plural usage is more common. Check any words about which you are unsure -- or better yet, have a person experienced in editing check them.

9. **Emphasize the Objectives and the Findings.** The purpose of conducting the research was to find out information about the hypotheses, research questions or objectives. Make it clear that this was done. This is especially important because so much research is conducted for decision making purposes and the decision makers must have their questions answered appropriately prior to making those decisions.

GRAPHS AND CHARTS

Today all executives are deluged with information. Because of this it is even more important to use graphic information in place of words.

Diagrams, charts and graphs are all good ways of presenting important information. With the availability of graphics software for computers, the task of generating graphics is much simpler than it was previously. Some computer software provides graphics capabilities for presenting graphs in color.

Some of the most frequently used graphs and charts are described here and illustrated in Exhibits 16.1 through 16.5.

BAR GRAPHS AND PIE CHARTS

Bar graphs are frequently used when the data is at the nominal or ordinal level of measurement. They usually appear with frequencies of response shown and often percentages are added. Spaces are left between bars to indicate that the data is not continuous.

The usual characteristics of bar graphs are:

1. They represent nominal and ordinal data.

2. Frequencies appear along one axis.

3. Categories appear along the other axis.

4. The bars can be horizontal or vertical.

5. Percentages are often added and usually placed at the top of the bars.

6. Bars are the same width.

7. Frequencies are indicated by the length of the bars.

8. Bars are not connected in order to indicate that the data are at the nominal or ordinal level of measurement.

Exhibit 16.1 illustrates a bar graph.

PIE CHARTS

Pie charts are sometimes used in place of bar graphs. They usually indicate the percentages and/or frequencies of responses. Exhibit 16.1 illustrates a pie chart.

HISTOGRAMS

The difference between a bar graph and a histogram is that in the histogram the bars are connected rather than spaced apart. The purpose of connecting the bars is to illustrate the continuous nature of the interval or ratio level data used.

The histogram has all the characteristics of the bar graph except:

1. Data at the interval or ratio level of measurement is required, and

2. The bars are connected to each other.

Exhibit 16.2 illustrates an histogram.

POLYGONS

A polygon can be used for the same type of data a histogram represents. Polygons are generated by placing points on the chart to indicate the frequencies or percentages taken from a frequency distribution. All the points are then connected with lines.

Polygons are used when the data are at the interval or ratio level of measurement. Exhibit 16.2 illustrates a polygon.

CUMULATIVE HISTOGRAMS

A cumulative histogram is used when it is desirable to present cumulative frequencies or cumulative percentages rather than the frequency or percentage of each score. Cumulative histograms are formed like noncumulative histograms except the information is taken from data which have been transformed into cumulative frequencies and cumulative percentages, as illustrated in Exhibit 16.3.

Note that the cumulative histogram in Exhibit 16.3 indicates both the cumulative frequencies and the cumulative percentages. Cumulative histograms can also present either one of these instead of both.

BIVARIATE PLOTS

In many instances it is helpful to show the relationship of two variables by using bivariate plots. This is done by placing a point to represent the scores on two variables simultaneously.

Exhibit 16.4 illustrates a bivariate plot and shows the data which the plot represents. Note that broken lines are used to indicate that the scores do not begin at zero.

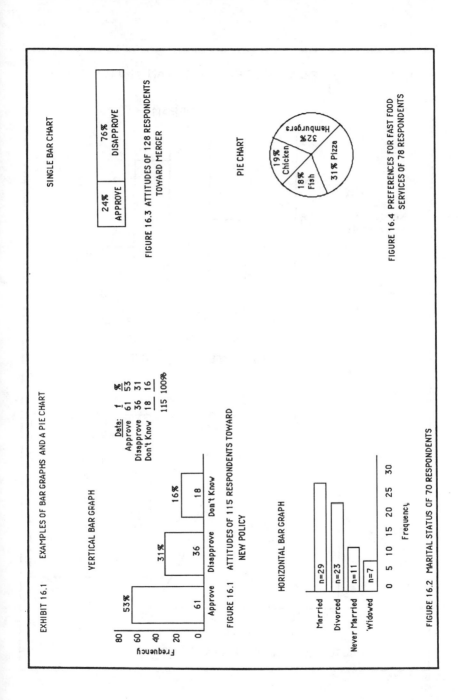

EXHIBIT 16.1   EXAMPLES OF BAR GRAPHS AND A PIE CHART

SINGLE BAR CHART

24%	76%
APPROVE	DISAPPROVE

FIGURE 16.3 ATTITUDES OF 128 RESPONDENTS
TOWARD MERGER

PIE CHART

FIGURE 16.4 PREFERENCES FOR FAST FOOD
SERVICES OF 78 RESPONDENTS

VERTICAL BAR GRAPH

Data:
	f	%
Approve	61	53
Disapprove	36	31
Don't Know	18	16
	115	100%

FIGURE 16.1 ATTITUDES OF 115 RESPONDENTS TOWARD
NEW POLICY

HORIZONTAL BAR GRAPH

FIGURE 16.2 MARITAL STATUS OF 70 RESPONDENTS

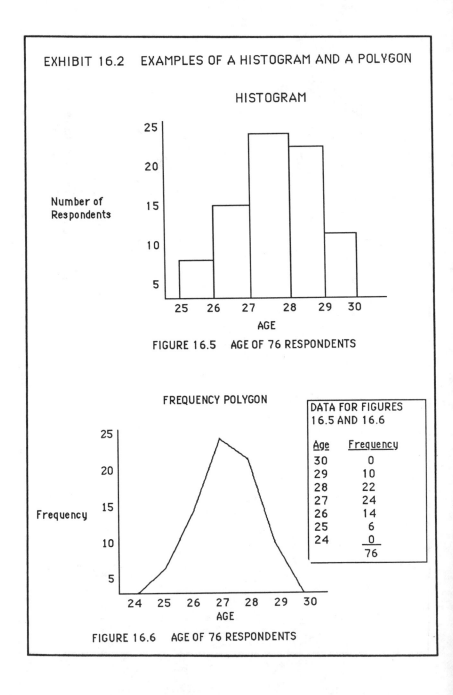

EXHIBIT 16.2   EXAMPLES OF A HISTOGRAM AND A POLYGON

HISTOGRAM

Number of Respondents

AGE

FIGURE 16.5   AGE OF 76 RESPONDENTS

FREQUENCY POLYGON

Frequency

AGE

FIGURE 16.6   AGE OF 76 RESPONDENTS

DATA FOR FIGURES 16.5 AND 16.6

Age	Frequency
30	0
29	10
28	22
27	24
26	14
25	6
24	0
	76

EXHIBIT 16.3   EXAMPLE OF A CUMULATIVE HISTOGRAM

Data:

Age	Frequency	Cumulative Frequency	Cumulative Proportion
30	0	76	1.00
29	10	76	1.00
28	22	66	.87
27	24	44	.58
26	14	20	.26
25	6	6	.08
24	0	0	.00

CUMULATIVE HISTOGRAM

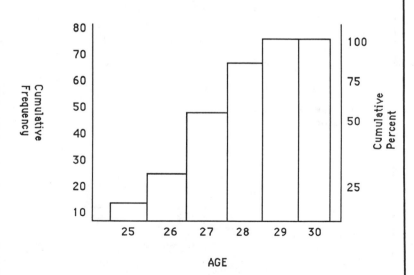

FIGURE 16.7   AGE OF 76 RESPONDENTS

EXHIBIT 16.4   EXAMPLE OF A BIVARIATE PLOT

Data:

Scores on Employment Tests and Performance Evaluations

Employee Number	Employment Test Score	Performance Evaluation
01	87	32
02	73	27
03	73	18
04	68	30
05	65	25
06	65	29
07	56	21
08	54	17
09	52	17
10	52	11

THE BIVARIATE PLOT

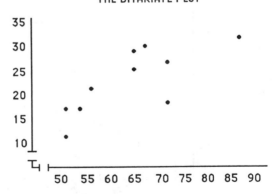

EMPLOYMENT TEST SCORE

FIGURE 16.8   PLOT OF EMPLOYMENT TEST SCORES AND
PERFORMANCE EVALUATION

EXHIBIT 16.5   EXAMPLE OF A MULTIPLE POLYGON
          Data:

Age of Female and Male Managers

| | Frequency | |
Age	Females	Males
65-69	0	0
60-64	0	5
55-59	0	3
50-54	1	4
45-49	3	2
40-44	2	3
35-39	3	4
30-34	2	5
25-29	1	3
20-24	0	0

THE MULTIPLE POLYGON

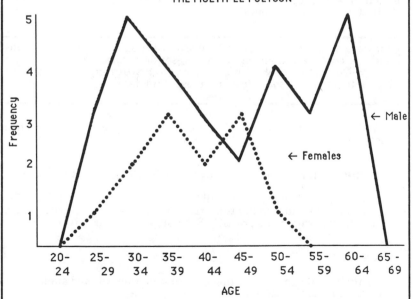

FIGURE 16.9   AGE DISTRIBUTION OF FEMALE AND MALE MANAGERS

Data at the interval or ratio level of measurement are required for bivariate plots.

MULTIPLE POLYGONS
When the same information is available for different groups, multiple polygons are useful. The major advantage is that the multiple polygon gives a visual comparison of the same data gathered from two or more groups.

As with any polygon, data at the interval or ratio level is required. Polygons, like bar graphs and histograms, can be presented horizontally or vertically.

A multiple polygon is illustrated Exhibit 16.5.

OTHER CHARTS AND GRAPHS

The charts and graphs presented here are those most frequently used to represent data. However, there are many other types of charts and graphs. For example, news magazines tend to present visually interesting charts and graphs using such devices as figures of people or animals, piled up boxes and outlines of countries. While these types of charts are not usually used in research reports, they are a good source for acquiring new ideas on the best way to present your data.

For data at the nominal or ordinal level of measurement, bar graphs and pie charts are appropriate for presenting data. For data at the interval or ratio level of measurement, histograms, polygons or bivariate plots are usually used for presenting data.

With the graphics capabilities of computer programs becoming more widely available, the use of charts and graphs is expected to increase.

PERSONAL PRESENTATION OF THE RESEARCH REPORT

Occasionally, the researcher will be asked to present the results of the research orally in addition to the written report. An oral report requires planning, preparation and practice. Some suggestions are given below.

PLANNING

1. Verify the date and time of the presentation, the expected audience and the amount of time allocated.

2. Obtain or prepare a summary of the research project. This could be the summary of the research or the summary of the findings from the written report.

3. Determine which portions of the summary can be included as a handout for the audience. Handouts are usually appreciated by the participants as they can follow the most important aspects during the presentation and take the handouts back to their desks for further perusal. Do not include the whole presentation in the handout.

4. Determine which portions of the summary you will present. Outline the form of the presentation.

5. Determine which charts, diagrams or figures you will use for visual presentation.

6. Determine which modes of visual presentations you will use. Some choices are: slide projector, chalkboard, overhead projector, magnetic or felt boards, or flip charts. Audio or video recorders may be appropriate for some reports. For other reports it may be helpful to bring in the actual research materials; for example, when testing differences among microcomputers.

PREPARATION

1. Prepare the handout for the audience. Make sufficient copies for the number of people expected to be present plus additional copies for requests and your file.

2. Prepare your presentation. Write out the whole presentation noting where visual aids will be used. Large index cards with bold type are frequently used.

3. Prepare the visual aids.

4. Check the room in which the presentation will be made for placement of the visual aids.

PRACTICE

1. Practice the presentation and use of the visual aids. If possible, have someone listen to and critique the presentation.

2. Time the presentation to ensure it will be completed within the allotted time period. Allow time for a question and answer period.

3. Add, delete or modify the presentation to keep it concise and interesting. A touch of humor is very helpful with presentations of research. A bored audience will not listen.

4. Practice several more times. You want to present the information, not read it. The more relaxed you appear, the better the presentation usually goes.

5. Practice in the room in which the presentation will be given, if possible. If you feel more comfortable with a podium on which to place your notes, see if one will be available.

6. Keep the presentation as brief as possible. People appreciate clarity but they value brevity.

7. Anticipate questions which might be asked to ensure that you have the appropriate information with you to answer adequately.

POST RESEARCH BLUES

Now the research project is completed, the results submitted to the sponsor and you are separated from an activity which has held your attention for quite some time. Not surprisingly, many researchers experience a letdown after a research project is completed.

The antidote is simple. Go out and celebrate a job well done. It wouldn't surprise me if, after a few hours of celebration, your mind begins focusing on a few concepts and another research project is in the offing.

WHERE YOU ARE NOW

FINISHED!

APPENDICES

APPENDIX A

GLOSSARY OF DEFINITIONS

A

Absolute Zero: See: Nonarbitrary Zero Point

Accidental Sampling: See: Convenience Sampling.

Alpha Error: See: Significance Level.

Alpha Level: See: Significance Level.

Alternative Forms Reliability: See : Equivalent Forms Reliability.

Alternative Hypothesis: See: Research Hypothesis.

Analysis of Covariance: A statistical analysis which eliminates the effects of an extraneous variable known to be related to the dependent variable so that causality can be attributed to the independent variable(s). For example, I Q scores are related to several performance variables and the effects of intelligence are often removed by covariance in order to attribute differences in performance to the specific independent variables under study.

Analysis of Variance: A variety of statistical techniques used to assess the significance of differences among means using methods which partition the total variance into several components.

Applied Research: Research conducted for the purpose of practical application, usually in response to a specific problem and the need for decision making.

Arbitrary Zero Point: A zero point which is set for convenience and does not mean absence of the variable.

Association Design: See: Nonexperimental Design.

Attitude Measure: An instrument which purports to measure a person's predisposition to perceive, feel and behave toward someone or something.

B

Basic Research: Research conducted for the purpose of adding to general knowledge, usually not prompted by a specific problem.

Beliefs Measures: An instrument which purports to measure a person's closely held opinion about someone or something.

Beta: See: Type II Error.

Beta Error: See: Type II Error.

Beta Level: See: Type II Error.

Bias: Nonrepresentativeness; differences between the real phenomena and the research phenomena, created by systematic errors. Bias can occur with many aspects of the research process, e.g., respondents, experimenters, test administrators, scorers, judges and sampling procedures.

Bivariate Techniques: Statistical techniques involving two dependent variables.

Blind Studies: Research in which the subjects and/or experimenters do not know what the treatment and/or the purpose of the study is. **Single-blind** indicates that the subjects are not aware and **double-blind** indicates that both subjects and experimenters are not aware of the treatment/purpose.

Blocking: Using levels of a variable to form groups (blocks) of subjects, in blocking designs such as the Randomized -Blocks Design. Frequently used variables for blocking are sex, social class, age and income.

C

Categorical Responses: Response categories which are different from one another but have no assumption of order (that one is better than or larger than another).

Category Rating Scale: A rating scale in which the rater assigns the factor to one of two or more unnumbered categories which have verbal descriptions.

Central Limit Theorem: An assumption underlying several statistical analyses [33] that given a population mean (μ_x), variance (σ_x^2) and random samples of size N, as sample sizes increase the distribution of sample means ($\bar{x}$) will approach a normal distribution with mean $\mu_x = \mu_x$ and variance $\sigma_x^2 = \sigma_x^2/N$.

Chi-Square Test of Independence: A statistical test for two or more groups when data is at the nominal level. The null hypothesis is that the variables are independent of each other and the research hypothesis is that the variables are related (not independent).

Chunk Sampling: See: Convenience Sampling.

Cluster Sampling: A sampling method in which the sampling unit is a GROUP of population elements rather than a single element. Often sampling is carried out in two (or more) stages. In the first stage the clusters are sampled, in the following stages the elements are sampled. Sometimes all the elements in each cluster are used.

Coefficient Alpha: A reliability estimate similar to the Kuder-Richardson Formula 20 for items which are not scored dichotomously.

Concurrent Validity: The degree to which a measure correlates with another measure of the same variable which has already been validated.

Condition: See: Treatment.

Confidence Interval: A range of values which have a specified probability of including the parameter estimated and are computed from values gathered from a sample of the population.

Confidence Level: The specified probability that the confidence interval will include the true value of the parameter estimated. In interval estimation this is often specified when using the term "confidence interval," e.g., "the 95% confidence interval."

Confidence Limits: The upper and lower boundaries of the confidence interval.

Confounding: The effect of an extraneous variable on the dependent variable which confuses the findings so that causality cannot be attributed solely to the independent variable(s) under study.

Construct Validity: The degree to which a measure relates to expectations formed from theory for hypothetical constructs.

Content Validity: The representativeness of the content of the instrument to the objectives of using the instrument.

Contingency Table: A table which shows joint classifications of two or more variables, indicating the number of observations in each of the joint classifications (cells).

Control Group: A group of subjects which, usually through random assignment, is equated to -- and thus assumed comparable to -- the experimental group but which does NOT receive an experimental treatment. In experimental design a control group is not necessary unless the researcher is interested in a "no treatment condition" because a second (third, fourth, etc.) experimental group can serve as the comparison group instead of a control group.

Control Variable: A variable which may affect the relationship between the independent and dependent variables which is "controlled" (effects canceled out) by eliminating the variable, holding the variable constant or using statistical methods.

Convenience Sampling: A nonrandom sampling method in which the researcher uses some convenient group or individuals as the sample.

Correlational Design: See: Nonexperimental Design.

Criterion Variable: The variable which is predicted (or, in some situations, used as a standard).

Critical Path Method: A procedure in which the estimated times for activities in a PERT chart are summed for each path in the network. The critical path is the sequence of activities which takes the longest total time to complete. A delay in the critical path will create a delay in the project. A delay in the noncritical path is called slack time.

Critical Value: A value appearing in tables for specified statistical tests indicating at what computed value the null hypothesis can be rejected (the computed statistic falls in the rejection region).

Crossectional Research: Research which examines characteristics of samples from different populations during the same time period. Usually used as an alternative to longitudinal research.

Cross Tabulation: The tabulation of the total number of observations into joint classifications of two or more variables.

D

Database: A collection of information assembled in computer accessible form.

Data Collection Method: The means by which information about variables is collected.

Degrees of Freedom: Generally, the number of values which are free to vary, computed by the number of values used with a certain statistic minus the number of restrictions placed on the data. The formulae for computing degrees of freedom for each of the major statistical tests are given in statistics books.

Demographic Measure: An instrument which purports to measure demographic characteristics such as age, national origin, sex of respondent or family size.

DeMoivre Curve: See: Normal Distribution.

Dependent Variable: The phenomenon or characteristic hypothesized to be the OUTCOME, EFFECT, CONSEQUENT or OUTPUT of some input variable. Its occurrence depends on some other variable which (usually) has preceded it in time.

Descriptive Statistics: Measures used to describe and summarize data such as measures of central tendency, variability and relationship

Dichotomous Response Item: A question or statement for which only two mutually exclusive responses are given.

Directional Hypothesis: An hypothesis in which the direction of the outcome is predicted rather than predicting inequality only. Examples: A will be better than B, X will be less than Y, A will be positively related to B.

Distribution-free Test: A statistical test which does NOT require assumptions about aspects of the population distribution such as "a normal distribution of scores in the population" or "equal variances" which are assumptions of the parametric t-test. Distribution-free tests are often called nonparametric tests. Examples are the sign test and the Mann-Whitney test.

E

Environmental Monitoring: See: Environmental Scanning.

Environmental Scanning: A process in which specific indicators critical to an organization's survival are recorded and monitored for changes. Indicators from both the internal and external environment are included. For example, an oil company might monitor gross sales (internal) and competitors' actions (external). A clothing manufacturer might monitor cotton prices (external) and their absenteeism rate (internal).

Equal Interval Scale: See: Interval Level of Measurement.

Equivalent Forms Reliability: A reliability estimate, usually indicated by a correlation, computed between scores from one form of an instrument and scores from a second form of the instrument administered to the same sample at approximately the same time.

Error Curve: See: Normal Distribution.

Ethical Research Practices: Those practices and procedures which lead to: (1) protection of human and non-human subjects, (2) appropriate methodology, (3) inferences, conclusions and recommendations based on the actual findings and (4) complete and accurate research reports.

Event: An occurrence of a specific phenomenon such as a verbal expression, two-way communication, conference, or television commercial. Events are those situations which include the variable(s) to be observed.

Event Sampling: The process of selecting a subgroup of events from a population of events specified by the researcher.

Ex Post Facto Design: See: Nonexperimental Design.

Examination of Documents, Materials and Artifacts: A data collection method in which a person (often trained) examines and records characteristics of phenomena which already exist.

Exhaustive Categories: Sufficient categories so that every event can be classified in one of the categories. For example, categories of more than 12 years of education and less than 12 years of education would not have a place to classify people with 12 years of education.

Expected Frequencies: The frequencies of observations expected to occur. Expecteds are obtained in one of four ways: (1) all are assumed to be equal, (2) they are obtained by prior knowledge (e.g., last year's sales figures), (3) theory indicates the figures or (4) they are computed from the frequencies in the margins of the contingency table.

Experimental Design: A specific plan for a research study which includes: (1) methods of selecting and assigning subjects and (2) number and types of treatment variables. Experimental designs must include at least two comparison groups with at least one group receiving a treatment (some amount of the independent variable.)

Experimental Group: A group of subjects which is administered some form of the experimental variable. There may be more than one experimental group in an experimental design, each receiving differing amounts or kinds of the treatment variable(s).

Experimental Treatment: See: Treatment.

Experimental Variable: See: Treatment Variable.

External Validity: The ability to generalize the results of the research to populations, settings, treatment variables and measurement variables; representativeness.

F

Face Validity: The appearance that an instrument measures what it purports to measure; that items appear to be related to the purpose of the instrument. For example, in an instrument supposed to measure sales ability, items such as "do you like snakes?" or "do you prefer chocolate or vanilla ice cream?" would not have face validity, which might affect subjects' responses.

Factorial Design: An extension of the true experimental designs which has more than one independent variable.

Forced-choice Item: An item which forces subjects to choose one alternative from a set of alternatives so that the subject is NOT given the opportunity to: (1) express individual opinions on each alternative or (2) select none of the alternatives. Thus, the responses are nonindependent; the response to one alternative depends on how the subject responded to the others.

Frequency Distribution: An arrangement of scores or categories with the frequency of occurrence (f) of each score or category indicated.

Fully Structured Observation Instrument: An instrument on which the observer records researcher specified behaviors or events.

Fully Unstructured Observation Instrument: An instrument on which the observer records any behavior or event which is relevant to the research situation.

G

Gaussian Curve: See: Normal Distribution.

Grab Sampling: See: Convenience Sampling.

Graphic Rating Scale: A rating scale in which lines and/or bars are added to the categories in order to give the rater a clearer idea of how to respond. The lines tend to remind the rater of a continuum and the bars tend to suggest equal intervals. A variety of forms may be used.

H

Haphazard Sampling: See: Convenience Sampling.

Historical Design: A research design for which the data or physical artifacts already exist and thus cannot be changed or manipulated. The researcher had no control over how or when or with what instruments the original data were collected.

Hypothesis: A declarative statement indicating a conjectured relationship between two or more variables which can be tested

Hypothesis Testing: The process of making statistical inferences about population characteristics by using data obtained from samples of that population.

Hypothetical Construct: A variable which is not directly observable but is inferred from other behaviors. Anxiety, self-concept and intelligence are hypothetical constructs because they cannot be observed directly but are inferred from other behaviors. Addition and subtraction ability, gross sales and net worth are observable variables.

I

Incidental Sampling: See: Convenience Sampling.

Independent Observations: Observations which are not related to one another and thus cannot affect one another. For example, a questionnaire is given to 100 randomly selected consumers. There is no reason to believe that the responses of one consumer will have any effect on the responses of the other consumers.

Independent Variable: The phenomenon or characteristic hypothesized to be the INPUT or ANTECEDENT variable. It is presumed to CAUSE the dependent variable and is manipulated, measured or selected prior to measuring the outcome or dependent variable.

Inferential Statistics: Statistical procedures used to draw inferences about a population by using sample data from that population. Examples of statistical tests used for inferences are t-tests, chi-square tests and analysis of variance tests. Two types of statistical inference are: (1) estimation and (2) hypothesis testing.

Instrument: Any type of written or physical device which is purported to measure variables.

Instrument Administration: A data collection method in which Ss respond to questionnaires, tasks, scales, tests or other devices used to measure variables. The instruments are administered by a variety of means including mail, telephone, on-line computer or in face-to-face situations to all Ss in a group or to individual Ss.

Instrumentation Effects: Effects created by subjects' responses to an instrument, the administration of the instrument or the environment in which the instrument is administered. These effects can cause major or minor distortions of the data.

Intelligence Measure: An instrument which purports to measure general factors which are related to a person's capability to learn, adapt, integrate and deal with complex and abstract activities.

Interaction Effect: In designs with two or more independent variables, the effect created when different combinations of the independent variables result in differences in the dependent variable. For example, given an experiment with two independent variables, color of numbers (green or white) and shape of dials (round or square), accuracy of reading dial numbers (dependent variable) might be higher for round dials with green numbers and square dials with white numbers than for the other combinations (round, white and square, green).

Interest Inventory: See: Interest Measure.

Interest Measure: An instrument which purports to measure vocational or occupational interests of people.

Internal Validity: The ability to conclude that the experimental (independent) variable did indeed create changes in the dependent variable. (In a measurement context internal validity refers to how well an instrument measures what it should measure.)

Interrater Reliability: The degree to which two or more judges (raters) rate the same variables in the same way.

Interval Estimate: See: Confidence Interval.

Interval Level of Measurement: Numbers assigned to objects or events which can be categorized, ordered and assumed to have an equal distance between scale values. The zero point is set arbitrarily.

Interval Scale: See: Interval Level of Measurement.

Intervening Variable: A variable which is hypothesized to exist but cannot be observed and is presumed to occur to explain the relationship between the independent and dependent variables.

Interviewer Training: Giving instruction and practice to questionnaire administrators or interviewers on exactly what to say and do during administration of the questionnaire or interview schedule.

Interviewing Method: A data collection method in which an interviewer questions people to elicit self-reports of their opinions, attitudes, values, beliefs or behaviors. Interviews are usually carried out in face-to-face situations although interactive television and on-line computers are also used.

K-L

Kuder-Richardson Reliability: A reliability estimate computed by using one of several formulas which measure the internal consistency of an instrument which is administered one time.

Longitudinal Research: Research which examines characteristics of the same subjects over an extended period of time in order to assess changes.

M

Main Effect: The effect of one independent variable on the dependent variable computed by averaging over all other independent variables. In a factorial design there is one main effect for each independent variable.

Management Information System: Methods of organizing, classifying and relating information, using computers, to provide managers with appropriate information to aid decision making.

Manipulated Variable: See: Treatment Variable.

Mean: A measure of central tendency which usually refers to the arithmetic average computed on scores which are interval or ratio level of measurement. Reference to other types of means usually includes their descriptors, e.g., harmonic mean or geometric mean.

Meaningful Zero: See: Nonarbitrary Zero Point.

Measure of Central Tendency: A measure of the average or typical score in a distribution of scores. The three most frequently used measures of central tendency are: (1) the mean, which requires at least interval level of measurement, (2) the median, which requires at least ordinal level of measurement and (3) the mode, which requires at least nominal level of measurement.

Measurement: Assigning numbers to objects or events according to rules [60].

Median: A measure of central tendency which is the middle score in an ordered set of scores which are at the ordinal or higher level of measurement. With an odd number of scores the median is the middle score. For an even number of scores the median is halfway between the two middle scores.

Mode: A measure of central tendency which is the most frequently appearing score in a distribution of scores which are at the nominal or higher level of measurement.

Moderator Variable: Another independent variable which is hypothesized to modify the relationship between the dependent and independent variable.

Motivated Hypothesis: See: Research Hypothesis.

Multiple Choice Response Item: A question or statement comprised of: (1) a stem, which is the question or statement itself and (2) the possible responses, sometimes called foils. The responses may form a scale or be categories only. Usually the respondent is instructed to select one response only but, in some situations, is allowed to choose more than one.

Multivariate Techniques: Statistical techniques involving two or more dependent variables or, in some cases, one dependent variable and two or more independent variables.

Mutually Exclusive Categories: Events which cannot occur at the same time. Thus a customer can be classified as having 12 or more years of education but cannot be classified as having less than 12 years of education at the same time.

N

Nominal Level of Measurement: Numbers assigned to objects or events which can be placed into mutually exclusive and exhaustive categories.

Nominal Scale: See: Nominal Level of Measurement.

Nonarbitrary Zero Point: A zero point which is not set arbitrarily but is a real part of the numbering system, indicating absence of the variable being measured.

Nondirectional Hypothesis: An hypothesis in which the direction of the outcome is not predicted and the stated relationship between the variables is one of inequality. Examples: A will be unequal to B; A will be related to B.

Nonexperimental Design: A research design in which an experimental variable is NOT introduced by the researcher but measures can be taken. Sometimes random selection is feasible. The researcher usually has control over who or what to measure, when the measurement takes place and what to ask or observe. Sometimes the researcher is interested in reactions to a specific event, such as a business merger, a tornado, hostage taking, etc., which occurred PRIOR to the current study (Ex Post Facto research).

Nonmanipulative Design: Nonexperimental Design.

Nonparametric Test: A statistical test for which the statistical model usually does not require the assumptions about the population parameters and does not require interval level of measurement. The assumptions are few and usually concern independent observations and/or continuity of the variables.

Nonreactive Measures: See: Unobtrusive Measures.

Normal Curve: See: Normal Distribution.

Normal Distribution: A probability distribution used to interpret many variables. The distribution is unimodal and symmetric, thus the mean, median and mode are identical. It is bell-shaped and the most frequent score is at its peak. A normal distribution can be completely specified by its mean and standard deviation.

Null Hypothesis: A declarative statement indicating that the relationship specified in the research hypothesis will NOT exist. To indicate this the symbolic form includes an equal sign. For example, Ho: $\mu_a = \mu_b$ or Ho: $\mu_a \geq \mu_b$ or Ho: $\mu_a \leq \mu_b$.

Numerical Rating Scale: A rating scale in which the rater assigns the factor to one of two or more numbered categories. The numbered categories may or may not include verbal descriptions.

O

Objective Research: Research in which the procedures and findings are not influenced or changed by the researcher's feelings, values or beliefs after the research has begun.

Observation Method: A data collection method in which a person (usually trained) observes Ss or phenomena and records information about characteristics of the phenomena.

One-factor Analysis of Variance: See: One-way Analysis of Variance.

One-way Analysis of Variance: An analysis of variance with one dependent and one independent variable.

Open-Ended Response Item: A question or statement with no fixed responses, requiring the respondent to generate a written or oral response or create something such as a drawing.

Operational Definition: A statement which defines a variable by specifying the operations used to measure or manipulate it.

Ordinal Level of Measurement: Numbers assigned to objects or events which can be placed into mutually exclusive categories and be ordered into a greater or less than scale.

Ordinal Scale: See: Ordinal Level of Measurement.

P-Q

Parallel Forms Reliability: See: Equivalent Forms Reliability.

Parameter: A population characteristic or value such as a mean, variance, proportion, etc. For example, average gross sales might be the population characteristic of interest.

Parametric Test: A statistical test for which the hypothesis concerns parameters (e.g., means, correlations), the required level of measurement is usually at least interval and there are several assumptions of the statistical model, usually concerning the shape of the distribution and the spread of scores.

Pearson Product-moment Correlation Coefficient: A measure of the relationship between two variables which are at the interval or ratio level of measurement and are linearly related. The coefficient can range from -1.00, indicating a perfect negative relationship, through zero, indicating no relationship, to +1.00, indicating a perfect positive relationship.

Performance Measure: A measure which assesses the degree to which Ss (e.g., people, animals) demonstrate mastery of knowledge or skills, or physical devices (e.g., spacecraft) demonstrate capabilities. Variables such as amount of gross sales or costs are also called performance measures.

Personality Measure: An instrument which purports to measure affective characteristics of individuals such as introversion or dominance.

PERT Chart: A flow chart which indicates the planned sequencing, scheduling and estimated times of activities of a project or program. PERT is an acronym for Program Evaluation and Review Technique.

Pilot Study: A preliminary micro-research study which uses the same research procedures as the major study and Ss drawn from the same population but who will not be used in the major study. The purpose of this trial run is to assess the various research procedures prior to the major study so that modifications or estimations can be made, if necessary.

Placebo Group: A group of subjects who are given the same type of attention as the experimental group but who do not receive the experimental treatment. For example, showing a birth control film (the treatment) to the experimental group and a nature film to the placebo group. Also called a "sugar pill" group because, in medical research, sugar/water pills are often given to placebo groups.

Point Estimate: A sample statistic such as a mean or proportion used to estimate the corresponding population parameter. Point estimates estimate a single population value.

Population: All members of a defined category of elements such as people, events or objects. All Walmart stores in the United States could comprise a population while selected Walmart stores might be a sample from that population.

Power: The probability, expressed in a percentage, of rejecting the null hypothesis when it is false and should have been rejected; a correct decision.

Predictive Validity: The degree to which a measure predicts a second future measure.

Predictor Variable: The variable used to predict.

Primary Sources: Sources of information who made direct firsthand recording or reporting of events or which are the physical artifacts themselves. Primary sources were present during the event, experience or time.

Probability: The relative frequency of an event occurring, usually reported as a percentage or fraction.

Probability Sampling: Sampling in which the probability of each element in the population being selected is known and can be specified, and each element has a chance of being selected.

Purposive Sampling: A nonrandom sampling method in which the sample is arbitrarily selected because characteristics which they possess are deemed important for the research. For example, purposely selecting certain Ford managers because they have 10 years of managerial experience. In contrast, in simple random sampling the population would be defined as "Ford managers with 10 years of managerial experience" and the managers would be randomly selected from the defined population. Judgment (expert choice) sampling, when Ss are judged by experts to be appropriate for a study, is also usually considered purposive sampling.

Quasi-experimental Design: A research design which lacks the full control of a true experimental design. The treatment variable often occurs naturally but sometimes the researcher may be able to manipulate it. Observations take place but random assignment of Ss to treatments is usually not feasible. As much control as possible is attempted.

Quota Sampling: A nonrandom sampling method in which elements of the sample are selected until the same proportion of selected characteristics which exists in the population is reached. For example, a population of clients includes 65% females, 35% males; 30% over 65 years old and 70% 65 and younger; and the sample would include these same proportions. While this appears similar to proportional stratified random sampling they are NOT the same because the Ss are not randomly selected from each stratum in quota sampling. Quota sampling is also usually considered purposive sampling.

R

Random Assignment: The assignment of subjects to different experimental or control groups, using random procedures, for the purpose of equating groups prior to conducting the experiment.

Random Events: Events whose individual outcomes cannot be predicted because they occur by chance. However, given a sufficiently large number of these events, the outcomes for a random sample can be predicted for the aggregate with a high degree of accuracy because they tend to occur with the same probability as they do in the population.

Range: A measure of variability which is usually computed by subtracting the smallest score from the largest score. The range is sometimes defined as the largest minus the smallest score plus one, but this should be used "for a discrete distribution in which scores must take on whole-number values" [33, p. 96].

Ranking Responses: Response categories (or materials) which the respondent is asked to place in order according to some variable such as degree of preference.

Rating: Estimation of the degree of a characteristic possessed by some phenomenon such as an object or a person.

Rating Scale: An instrument on which the rater (observer) assigns the factor to be rated to one of two or more categories.

Ratio Level of Measurement: Numbers assigned to objects or events which can be categorized, ordered, assumed to have equal intervals between scale points and have a real (nonarbitrary) zero point.

Ratio Scale: See: Ratio Level of Measurement.

Real Zero: See: Nonarbitrary Zero Point.

Related Observations: Observations which are NOT independent but related in some way and thus one observation might affect another. For example, parents and their children are selected for a study of consumer food preferences. It is highly likely that food preferences of children are related to their parents' food preferences. A commonly used set of related data occurs when people are studied before and after some experiment or event.

Relationship Design: See: Nonexperimental Design.

Reliability: Consistency of measurement. The degree to which an instrument measures the same way each time it is used under the same conditions with the same subjects.

Reliability Coefficient: An estimate of the reliability of a measure usually in the form of a correlation coefficient.

Research Controls: Procedures which rule out potential extraneous causes of research results by defining and restricting the research conditions.

Research Design: A plan for conducting research which usually includes specification of the elements to be examined and the procedures to be used.

Research Hypothesis: A declarative sentence indicating a conjectured relationship between variables which can be tested and which the researcher believes will be demonstrated after hypothesis testing.

Research Process: Specific planned and controlled steps for empirically investigating a problem.

Research Problem: An inquiry which asks to what degree or how two or more phenomena are related, usually stated in question form.

Research Proposal: A plan stating the problem which prompted the research and the research objectives, procedures and budget proposed to answer the questions or solve the problem.

Research Question: An interrogative statement asking about a conjectured relationship between two or more variables.

Research Report: A report, usually submitted to the sponsor(s) of the project or professional journals, which includes concise but inclusive descriptions of the research objectives, methodology and findings. Research reports vary considerably because of the variety of purposes for which they are prepared.

Response Bias: The tendency of a subject to consistently select or demonstrate one type of response from a series of responses.

Review of Related Information: Systematic examination of general information, research studies, data and theories which have been discovered over the years related to the variables of interest and the relationships among them.

Review of the Literature: See Review of Related Information.

Right to Anonymity: The research participant has the right to expect the researcher not to identify specific data with a specific individual.

Right to Confidentiality: The research participant has the right to expect the researcher to limit access to and maintain the security of information obtained from or about the participant.

Right to Free Consent: The potential research participant has the right not to be pressured in any way to participate in the research project.

Right to Informed Consent: The potential research participants must be given sufficient information to make knowledgeable decisions about participation or nonparticipation.

Right to Privacy: Research participants have the right to withhold information about which they feel uncomfortable.

S

Sample: A portion of a larger category of elements called the population.

Sampling: The process of selecting subgroups from a population of elements such as people, objects or events.

Sampling Error: The difference between the parameter value and the sample estimate of the parameter value which occurs when sampling from a population.

Sampling Frame: A list or other representation of the elements in a population from which the sample is selected.

Sampling Unit: The element or object to be sampled or a larger unit containing the objects.

Scaled Responses: Response categories which indicate gradations or a continuum of the variable being measured.

Scheffé Test: A test for post hoc multiple comparisons which uses the F distribution and allows all possible comparisons between means to be tested.

Secondary Sources: Sources of information who were not present at the time of the event and whose information about events or physical artifacts was gathered from other sources.

Significance Level: The probability, expressed in a percentage, of rejecting the null hypothesis when it is true and should not have been rejected.

Significance Testing: See: Hypothesis Testing.

Simple Random Sampling: A probability sampling method in which each element in the population has an EQUAL, known and nonzero chance of being selected.

Split-Half Reliability: A reliability estimate indicated by a correlation of scores from one half of an instrument with scores from the second half of the instrument.

Standard Deviation: A measure of variability which is the square root of the variance. It indicates the average of the scores' deviations from the mean of a distribution of scores which are at the interval or ratio level of measurement.

Standard Error: The standard deviation of a sampling distribution which is computed for sample statistics such as a mean or proportion. It is based on the concept that the sampling errors of a series of samples from the same population will form a normal distribution. A standard deviation of this distribution of errors (standard error) could then be computed. However, instead of using many samples, this standard deviation of errors (or standard error) is usually estimated by using data from a single sample with the appropriate formula.

Statistic: A numerical index of a characteristic (e.g., mean, variance, etc.) computed from sample data, usually to estimate the corresponding population characteristic. For example, average gross sales of the population might be estimated by using gross sales figures from a sample of Walmart stores. Also used to indicate results of a statistical test (e.g., a t test, chi square test, etc.) with phrases such as the "test statistic" or the "chi square statistic."

Statistical Estimation: Estimation of an unknown population value (point estimate) or range of values (interval estimate) from a known sample value.

Stratified Random Sampling: A probability sampling method in which elements are randomly selected from EACH designated subpopulation (stratum) of a population. The strata are determined according to differing types or amounts of a variable which the researcher decides may be associated with the major variable. For example, a population of food stores may be divided into strata on the basis of size: large, medium and small, and a sample randomly selected from each of these strata.

Structured Questionnaire: A questionnaire which includes fixed items, fixed response categories and fixed sequencing of items.

Survey Design: See: Nonexperimental Design.

Systematic Research: Research which uses specific pre-planned procedures in the research process.

Systematic Sampling: A nonrandom sampling method in which every nth element is chosen from a list of numbered elements. Thus, every element does NOT have a chance of being drawn once the starting point is selected. The start is often chosen randomly and sometimes changed several times during the selection process to improve the chances of representativeness, especially in ordered lists. In practice a systematic sample is often treated like a simple random sample and is usually referenced as a probability sampling method if there is a random start.

T-U

t-test: One of several statistical tests used with interval or ratio level data when the hypothesis concerns comparison of means, the scores are normally distributed and the population variances are unknown.

Test-Retest Reliability: A reliability estimate, usually indicated by a correlation coefficient, computed from scores on an instrument administered at one time and scores on the same instrument administered at a later time to the same sample.

Time Sampling: The process of selecting specific time periods for observing phenomena. Time periods can be selected randomly or systematically. For example, in observing T.V. commercials the researcher might select systematic time samples of 3 minutes, beginning at one minute before the hour to two minutes after the hour, between the time periods of 6:59 and 11:02 p.m. For sampling of continuous behavior, such as observation of the interaction of a group of robotics technicians, the researcher might designate five samples of ten minutes each, selected randomly from a specified population of ten minute periods.

Transitivity: A greater than or less than relationship assigned to objects or events representing variables.

Treatment: One type or amount of the independent variable. For example, 3 groups of managers receive either 1, 2 or 3 days of training. Each of these training periods is a treatment.

Treatment Variable: The independent variable which is manipulated by the researcher so that different groups of subjects receive different kinds or amounts. For example, each of 3 groups of managers receives a different number of days of training.

True Zero: See: Nonarbitrary Zero Point.

Two-factor Analysis of Variance: See: Two-way Analysis of Variance.

Two-way Analysis of Variance: An analysis of variance with one dependent and two independent variables.

Type I Error: See: Significance Level.

Type II Error: The probability, expressed in a percentage, of NOT rejecting the null hypothesis when it is false and should have been rejected.

Univariate Techniques: Statistical techniques involving one dependent variable.

Unobtrusive Measure: A measure of a variable which is collected in such a way that subjects are usually unaware that they are being measured. This is also called a nonreactive measure because if Ss are not aware they are being measured they cannot react to the measurement.

V-W

Validity: Accuracy of measurement. The degree to which an instrument measures that which is supposed to be measured.

Validity Coefficient: An estimate of the validity of a measure in the form of a correlation coefficient.

Values Measure: An instrument which purports to measure a person's preference for someone or something.

Variability: The degree to which scores within a distribution of scores differ from each other. The most frequently used measures of variability are the standard deviation and its square, the variance. Both require at least interval level of measurement.

Variable: A factor, phenomenon or characteristic which has more than one value or category, either quantitative or qualitative. (If a characteristic has only one value, it is a constant, not a variable).

Variance: A measure of variability which is the mean of the squared deviations from the mean in a distribution of scores which are at the interval or ratio level of measurement. The variance is the standard deviation squared.

Working Hypothesis: See: Research Hypothesis.

APPENDIX B

GLOSSARY OF ABBREVIATIONS AND SYMBOLS

α	Alpha, the level of significance or probability of Type I error.
ANOVA	Analysis of Variance.
β	Beta, probability of Type II error.
$1-\beta$	Power of a statistical test.
CPM	Critical Path Method.
CROSSTABS	Cross tabulation of observations.
CV	Critical value.
df	Degrees of freedom.
df_B	Degrees of freedom between groups.
df_T	Total degrees of freedom.
df_W	Degrees of freedom within groups.
e	Error (most common meaning).
E	Expected frequency, in the Chi-square formula.
f	Frequency.
F	Statistic resulting from computation of the Analysis of Variance formulas.
Ha	Research or alternative hypothesis. May be H with any alphabetical or numerical subscript except 0.
Ho	Null hypothesis.
k	(1) Number of items, in the Kuder-Richardson formula KR_{20}. (2) Number of groups, in Analysis of Variance.
Mdn	Median.

MDS	Multidimensional scaling.
MED	Median.
MIS	Management Information System.
MS	Mean square, in Analysis of Variance.
MS_B	Mean square between groups, in Analysis of Variance.
MS_W	Mean square within groups, in Analysis of Variance.
μ	Mean of population scores.
n	Number of subjects or observations, usually referring to a sample.
N	Number of subjects or observations, usually referring to a population.
$N(\bar{X},S)$	N indicates that a set of scores is approximately normally distributed, with a given sample mean ($\bar{X}$) and a given sample S (standard deviation). The numerical values of the mean and standard deviation of that particular set of scores are substituted for $\bar{X}$ and S, e.g., $N(20,3)$. Also noted as $ND(\bar{X},S)$.
$N(\mu,\sigma)$	Same meaning as $N(\bar{X},S)$ except the μ refers to the population mean and the σ refers to the population standard deviation; also noted as $ND(\mu,\sigma)$.
$ND(\bar{X},S)$	See $N(\bar{X},S)$.
$ND(\mu,\sigma)$	See $N(\mu,\sigma)$.
O	(1) Observed frequency, in the chi-square formula. (2) Observation (measurement), in the symbolic designations for experimental designs.
ρ	(1) Proportion of correct responses, in the Kuder-Richardson formula KR_{20}. (2) Probability.
PERT	Program Evaluation and Review Technique.
q	Proportion of wrong responses, or $1-\rho$, in the Kuder-Richardson formula KR_{20}.
r	Correlation coefficient, of sample values.
r_{KR20}	Kuder-Richardson reliability coefficient.
r_{xx}	Reliability coefficient.

r_{xy}	(1) Validity coefficient. (2) Correlation between x and y.
R	Random assignment to experimental and control groups, in the symbolic designations for experimental designs.
RFB	Request for Bid.
RFP	Request for Proposal.
RFQ	Request for Quote.
ρ_{xy}	Correlation coefficient, of population scores.
s	Standard deviation, of sample scores.
$s_{\bar{x}}$	Standard error of a mean, when σ is unknown.
s^2	Variance, of sample scores.
SD	(1) Standard deviation. (2) Semantic Differential.
SE	Standard error.
SRS	Simple random sampling.
Ss	Subjects of the Research.
SS	Sum of squares, in Analysis of Variance.
SS_B	Sum of squares between groups.
SS_W	Sum of squares within groups.
SS_T	Total sum of squares.
Σ	(1) Sum of. (2) Add.
σ	Standard deviation, of population scores.
σ_ρ	Standard error of a proportion.
$\sigma_{\bar{x}}$	Standard error of a mean, when σ is known.
σ^2	Variance, of population scores.
t	Statistic resulting from computation of a t-test.
x	Deviation score or x-x̄.

X	(1) Raw score. (2) Experimental treatment, in the symbolic designations for experimental designs.
$\bar{X}$	Mean, of sample scores.
X^2	Statistic resulting from computation of a chi-square test.
$\hat{Y}$	Predicted score, in regression formulas.
z	(1) Standard score, resulting from transforming a raw score with the formula $z = (x-\bar{x})/s$. A set of z scores will always have a mean of zero (0) and a standard deviation of one (1). (2) Statistic resulting from computation of a z test.
3x2 Design	In factorial design, two independent variables, one with 3 levels (types) of the treatment and the other with 2 levels of the treatment. There can be differing numbers of both independent variables and levels of the treatments, e.g., a 2x4 design or a 2x2x2 design.
||	Absolute value.
$<$	Less than.
$>$	Greater than.
$\neq$	Unequal to.
$\leq$	Less than or equal to.
$\geq$	Greater than or equal to.

APPENDIX C

THE GREEK ALPHABET

A	α	alpha
B	β	beta
Γ	γ	gamma
Δ	δ	delta
E	ε	epsilon
Z	ζ	zeta
H	η	eta
Θ	θ	theta
I	i	iota
K	κ	kappa
Λ	λ	lambda
M	μ	mu
N	ν	nu
Ξ	ξ	xi
O	o	omicron
Π	π	pi
P	ρ	rho
Σ	σ	sigma
T	τ	tau
Y	υ	upsilon
Φ	φ	phi

X	x	chi
Ψ	ψ	psi
Ω	ω	omega

APPENDIX D

APPENDIX D.1

RANDOM NUMBERS

Col. 1	Col. 2	Col. 3	Col. 4	Col. 5	Col. 6	Col. 7	Col. 8
3831	7167	1540	1532	6617	1845	3162	0210
6019	4242	1818	4978	8200	7326	5442	7766
6653	7210	0718	2183	0737	4603	2094	1964
8861	5020	6590	5990	3425	9208	5973	9614
9221	6305	6091	8875	6693	8017	8953	5477
2809	9700	8832	0248	3593	4686	9645	3899
1207	0100	3553	8260	7332	7402	9152	5419
6012	3752	2074	7321	5964	7095	2855	6123
0300	0773	5128	0694	3572	5517	3689	7220
1382	2179	5685	9705	9919	1739	0356	7173
0678	7668	4425	6205	4158	6769	7253	8106
8966	0561	9341	8986	8866	2168	7951	9721
6293	3420	9752	9956	7191	1127	7783	2596
9097	7558	1814	0782	0310	7310	5951	8147
3362	3045	6361	4024	1875	4124	7396	3985
5594	1248	2685	1039	0129	5047	6267	0440
6495	8204	9251	1947	9485	3027	9946	7792
9378	0804	7233	2355	1278	8667	5810	8869
2932	4490	0680	8024	4378	9543	4594	8392
2868	7746	1213	0396	9902	4953	2261	8117
3047	6737	5434	9719	8026	9283	6952	1883
3673	2265	5271	4542	2646	1744	2684	4956
0731	8278	9597	0745	9682	8007	7836	2771
2666	3174	0706	6224	4595	2273	0802	9402
5879	3349	9239	2808	8626	8569	6660	9683
7228	8029	3633	6194	9030	1279	2611	3805
4367	2881	3996	8336	7933	6385	5902	1664
1014	9964	1346	4850	1524	1919	7355	4737
6316	4356	7927	6709	1375	0375	8855	3632
2302	6392	5023	8515	1197	9182	4952	1897
7439	5567	1156	9241	0438	0607	1962	0717
1930	7128	6098	6033	5132	5350	1216	0518
4598	6415	1523	4012	8179	9934	8863	8375
2835	5888	8616	7542	5875	2859	6805	4079
4377	5153	9930	0902	8208	6501	9593	1397
3725	7202	6551	7458	4740	8234	4914	0878

Reprinted by permission of John Wiley & Sons, Inc. from *Experimental Psychology* by Burton G. Andreas. Copyright ©1972 by John Wiley & Sons, Inc.

APPENDIX D.2

TABLE OF PROBABILITIES ASSOCIATED WITH VALUES AS EXTREME AS OBSERVED VALUES OF z IN THE NORMAL DISTRIBUTION

The body of the table gives one-tailed probabilities under H_0 of z. The left-hand marginal column gives various values of z to one decimal place. The top row gives various values to the second decimal place. Thus, for example, the one-tailed p of $z \geq .11$ or $z \leq -.11$ is $p = .4562$.

z	.00	.01	.02	.03	.04	.05	.06	.07	.08	.09
.0	.5000	.4960	.4920	.4880	.4840	.4801	.4761	.4721	.4681	.4641
.1	.4602	.4562	.4522	.4483	.4443	.4404	.4364	.4325	.4286	.4247
.2	.4207	.4168	.4129	.4090	.4052	.4013	.3974	.3936	.3897	.3859
.3	.3821	.3783	.3745	.3707	.3669	.3632	.3594	.3557	.3520	.3483
.4	.3446	.3409	.3372	.3336	.3300	.3264	.3228	.3192	.3156	.3121
.5	.3085	.3050	.3015	.2981	.2946	.2912	.2877	.2843	.2810	.2776
.6	.2743	.2709	.2676	.2643	.2611	.2578	.2546	.2514	.2483	.2451
.7	.2420	.2389	.2358	.2327	.2296	.2266	.2236	.2206	.2177	.2148
.8	.2119	.2090	.2061	.2033	.2005	.1977	.1949	.1922	.1894	.1867
.9	.1841	.1814	.1788	.1762	.1736	.1711	.1685	.1660	.1635	.1611
1.0	.1587	.1562	.1539	.1515	.1492	.1469	.1446	.1423	.1401	.1379
1.1	.1357	.1335	.1314	.1292	.1271	.1251	.1230	.1210	.1190	.1170
1.2	.1151	.1131	.1112	.1093	.1075	.1056	.1038	.1020	.1003	.0985
1.3	.0968	.0951	.0934	.0918	.0901	.0885	.0869	.0853	.0838	.0823
1.4	.0808	.0793	.0778	.0764	.0749	.0735	.0721	.0708	.0694	.0681
1.5	.0668	.0655	.0643	.0630	.0618	.0606	.0594	.0582	.0571	.0559
1.6	.0548	.0537	.0526	.0516	.0505	.0495	.0485	.0475	.0465	.0455
1.7	.0446	.0436	.0427	.0418	.0409	.0401	.0392	.0384	.0375	.0367
1.8	.0359	.0351	.0344	.0336	.0329	.0322	.0314	.0307	.0301	.0294
1.9	.0287	.0281	.0274	.0268	.0262	.0256	.0250	.0244	.0239	.0233
2.0	.0228	.0222	.0217	.0212	.0207	.0202	.0197	.0192	.0188	.0183
2.1	.0179	.0174	.0170	.0166	.0162	.0158	.0154	.0150	.0146	.0143
2.2	.0139	.0136	.0132	.0129	.0125	.0122	.0119	.0116	.0113	.0110
2.3	.0107	.0104	.0102	.0099	.0096	.0094	.0091	.0089	.0087	.0084
2.4	.0082	.0080	.0078	.0075	.0073	.0071	.0069	.0068	.0066	.0064
2.5	.0062	.0060	.0059	.0057	.0055	.0054	.0052	.0051	.0049	.0048
2.6	.0047	.0045	.0044	.0043	.0041	.0040	.0039	.0038	.0037	.0036
2.7	.0035	.0034	.0033	.0032	.0031	.0030	.0029	.0028	.0027	.0026
2.8	.0026	.0025	.0024	.0023	.0023	.0022	.0021	.0021	.0020	.0019
2.9	.0019	.0018	.0018	.0017	.0016	.0016	.0015	.0015	.0014	.0014
3.0	.0013	.0013	.0013	.0012	.0012	.0011	.0011	.0011	.0010	.0010
3.1	.0010	.0009	.0009	.0009	.0008	.0008	.0008	.0008	.0007	.0007
3.2	.0007									
3.3	.0005									
3.4	.0003									
3.5	.00023									
3.6	.00016									
3.7	.00011									
3.8	.00007									
3.9	.00005									
4.0	.00003									

Reproduced with permission from *Nonparametric Statistics for the Behavioral Sciences* by Sidney Siegel. Copyright © 1956 by McGraw-Hill Book Company.

APPENDIX D.3
CRITICAL VALUES OF CHI-SQUARE

df	.99	.98	.95	.90	.80	.70	.50	.30	.20	.10	.05	.02	.01
1	.000157	.000628	.00393	.0158	.0642	.148	.455	1.074	1.642	2.706	3.841	5.412	6.635
2	.0201	.0404	.103	.211	.446	.713	1.386	2.408	3.219	4.605	5.991	7.824	9.210
3	.115	.185	.352	.584	1.005	1.424	2.366	3.665	4.642	6.251	7.815	9.837	11.345
4	.297	.429	.711	1.064	1.649	2.195	3.357	4.878	5.989	7.779	9.488	11.668	13.277
5	.554	.752	1.145	1.610	2.343	3.000	4.351	6.064	7.289	9.236	11.070	13.388	15.086
6	.872	1.134	1.635	2.204	3.070	3.828	5.348	7.231	8.558	10.645	12.592	15.033	16.812
7	1.239	1.564	2.167	2.833	3.822	4.671	6.346	8.383	9.803	12.017	14.067	16.622	18.475
8	1.646	2.032	2.733	3.490	4.594	5.527	7.344	9.524	11.030	13.362	15.507	18.168	20.090
9	2.088	2.532	3.325	4.168	5.380	6.393	8.343	10.656	12.242	14.684	16.919	19.679	21.666
10	2.558	3.059	3.940	4.865	6.179	7.267	9.342	11.781	13.442	15.987	18.307	21.161	23.209
11	3.053	3.609	4.575	5.578	6.989	8.148	10.341	12.899	14.631	17.275	19.675	22.618	24.725
12	3.571	4.178	5.226	6.304	7.807	9.034	11.340	14.011	15.812	18.549	21.026	24.054	26.217
13	4.107	4.765	5.892	7.042	8.634	9.926	12.340	15.119	16.985	19.812	22.362	25.472	27.688
14	4.660	5.368	6.571	7.790	9.467	10.821	13.339	16.222	18.151	21.064	23.685	26.873	29.141
15	5.229	5.985	7.261	8.547	10.307	11.721	14.339	17.322	19.311	22.307	24.996	28.259	30.578
16	5.812	6.614	7.962	9.312	11.152	12.624	15.338	18.418	20.465	23.542	26.296	29.633	32.000
17	6.408	7.255	8.672	10.085	12.002	13.531	16.338	19.511	21.615	24.769	27.587	30.995	33.409
18	7.015	7.906	9.390	10.865	12.857	14.440	17.338	20.601	22.760	25.989	28.869	32.346	34.805
19	7.633	8.567	10.117	11.651	13.716	15.352	18.338	21.689	23.900	27.204	30.144	33.687	36.191
20	8.260	9.237	10.851	12.443	14.578	16.266	19.337	22.775	25.038	28.412	31.410	35.020	37.566
21	8.897	9.915	11.591	13.240	15.445	17.182	20.337	23.858	26.171	29.615	32.671	36.343	38.932
22	9.542	10.600	12.338	14.041	16.314	18.101	21.337	24.939	27.301	30.813	33.924	37.659	40.289
23	10.196	11.293	13.091	14.848	17.187	19.021	22.337	26.018	28.429	32.007	35.172	38.968	41.638
24	10.856	11.992	13.848	15.659	18.062	19.943	23.337	27.096	29.553	33.196	36.415	40.270	42.980
25	11.524	12.697	14.611	16.473	18.940	20.867	24.337	28.172	30.675	34.382	37.652	41.566	44.314
26	12.198	13.409	15.379	17.292	19.820	21.792	25.336	29.246	31.795	35.563	38.885	42.856	45.642
27	12.879	14.125	16.151	18.114	20.703	22.710	26.336	30.319	32.912	36.741	40.113	44.140	46.963
28	13.565	14.847	16.928	18.939	21.588	23.647	27.336	31.391	34.027	37.916	41.337	45.419	48.278
29	14.256	15.574	17.708	19.768	22.475	24.577	28.336	32.461	35.139	39.087	42.557	46.693	49.588
30	14.953	16.306	18.493	20.599	23.364	25.508	29.336	33.530	36.250	40.256	43.773	47.962	50.892

For larger values of n, the expression $\sqrt{2x^2} - \sqrt{2n-1}$ may be used as a normal deviate with unit variance.
Reprinted with permission of Macmillan Publishing Company from *Statistical Methods for Research Workers*, 14th ed., pp. 112-113 by Sir Ronald A. Fisher. Copyright © 1970 by University of Adelaide.

APPENDIX D.4

CRITICAL VALUES OF t

Significance level for one-tailed test -- directional alternative hypothesis

	.050	.025	.010	.005

Significance level for two-tailed test --nondirectional alternative hypothesis

df	.10	.05	.02	.01
1	6.314	12.706	31.821	63.657
2	2.920	4.303	6.965	9.925
3	2.353	3.182	4.541	5.841
4	2.132	2.776	3.747	4.604
5	2.015	2.571	3.365	4.032
6	1.943	2.447	3.143	3.707
7	1.895	2.365	2.998	3.499
8	1.860	2.306	2.896	3.355
9	1.833	2.262	2.821	3.250
10	1.812	2.228	2.764	3.169
11	1.796	2.201	2.718	3.106
12	1.782	2.179	2.681	3.055
13	1.771	2.160	2.650	3.012
14	1.761	2.145	2.624	2.977
15	1.753	2.131	2.602	2.947
16	1.746	2.120	2.583	2.921
17	1.740	2.110	2.567	2.898
18	1.734	2.101	2.552	2.878
19	1.729	2.093	2.539	2.861
20	1.725	2.086	2.528	2.845
21	1.721	2.080	2.518	2.831
22	1.717	2.074	2.508	2.819
23	1.714	2.069	2.500	2.807
24	1.711	2.064	2.492	2.797
25	1.708	2.060	2.485	2.787
26	1.706	2.056	2.479	2.779
27	1.703	2.052	2.473	2.771
28	1.701	2.048	2.467	2.763
29	1.699	2.045	2.462	2.756
30	1.697	2.042	2.457	2.750
∞	1.645	1.960	2.326	2.576

APPENDIX D.5

CRITICAL VALUES OF F AT THE .05 (LIGHTFACE TYPE) AND .01 (BOLDFACE TYPE) SIGNIFICANCE LEVELS.

NUMERATOR DEGREES OF FREEDOM ARE ACROSS THE TOP, AND DENOMINATOR DEGREES OF FREEDOM ARE ON THE SIDE.

df	1	2	3	4	5	6	7	8	9	10	11	12	14	16	20	24	30	40	50	75	100	200	500	∞
1	161	200	216	225	230	234	237	239	241	242	243	244	245	246	248	249	250	251	252	253	253	254	254	254
	4,052	**4,999**	**5,403**	**5,625**	**5,764**	**5,859**	**5,928**	**5,981**	**6,022**	**6,056**	**6,082**	**6,106**	**6,142**	**6,169**	**6,208**	**6,234**	**6,261**	**6,286**	**6,302**	**6,323**	**6,334**	**6,352**	**6,361**	**6,366**
2	18.51	19.00	19.16	19.25	19.30	19.33	19.36	19.37	19.38	19.39	19.40	19.41	19.42	19.43	19.44	19.45	19.46	19.47	19.47	19.48	19.49	19.49	19.50	19.50
	98.49	**99.00**	**99.17**	**99.25**	**99.30**	**99.33**	**99.36**	**99.37**	**99.39**	**99.40**	**99.41**	**99.42**	**99.43**	**99.44**	**99.45**	**99.46**	**99.47**	**99.48**	**99.48**	**99.49**	**99.49**	**99.49**	**99.50**	**99.50**
3	10.13	9.55	9.28	9.12	9.01	8.94	8.88	8.84	8.81	8.78	8.76	8.74	8.71	8.69	8.66	8.64	8.62	8.60	8.58	8.57	8.56	8.54	8.54	8.53
	34.12	**30.82**	**29.46**	**28.71**	**28.24**	**27.91**	**27.67**	**27.49**	**27.34**	**27.23**	**27.13**	**27.05**	**26.92**	**26.83**	**26.69**	**26.60**	**26.50**	**26.41**	**26.35**	**26.27**	**26.23**	**26.18**	**26.14**	**26.12**
4	7.71	6.94	6.59	6.39	6.26	6.16	6.09	6.04	6.00	5.96	5.93	5.91	5.87	5.84	5.80	5.77	5.74	5.71	5.70	5.68	5.66	5.65	5.64	5.63
	21.20	**18.00**	**16.69**	**15.98**	**15.52**	**15.21**	**14.98**	**14.80**	**14.66**	**14.54**	**14.45**	**14.37**	**14.24**	**14.15**	**14.02**	**13.93**	**13.83**	**13.74**	**13.69**	**13.61**	**13.57**	**13.52**	**13.48**	**13.46**
5	6.61	5.79	5.41	5.19	5.05	4.95	4.88	4.82	4.78	4.74	4.70	4.68	4.64	4.60	4.56	4.53	4.50	4.46	4.44	4.42	4.40	4.38	4.37	4.36
	16.26	**13.27**	**12.06**	**11.39**	**10.97**	**10.67**	**10.45**	**10.29**	**10.15**	**10.05**	**9.96**	**9.89**	**9.77**	**9.68**	**9.55**	**9.47**	**9.38**	**9.29**	**9.24**	**9.17**	**9.13**	**9.07**	**9.04**	**9.02**
6	5.99	5.14	4.76	4.53	4.39	4.28	4.21	4.15	4.10	4.06	4.03	4.00	3.96	3.92	3.87	3.84	3.81	3.77	3.75	3.72	3.71	3.69	3.68	3.67
	13.74	**10.92**	**9.78**	**9.15**	**8.75**	**8.47**	**8.26**	**8.10**	**7.98**	**7.87**	**7.79**	**7.72**	**7.60**	**7.52**	**7.39**	**7.31**	**7.23**	**7.14**	**7.09**	**7.02**	**6.99**	**6.94**	**6.90**	**6.88**
7	5.59	4.74	4.35	4.12	3.97	3.87	3.79	3.73	3.68	3.63	3.60	3.57	3.52	3.49	3.44	3.41	3.38	3.34	3.32	3.29	3.28	3.25	3.24	3.23
	12.25	**9.55**	**8.45**	**7.85**	**7.46**	**7.19**	**7.00**	**6.84**	**6.71**	**6.62**	**6.54**	**6.47**	**6.35**	**6.27**	**6.15**	**6.07**	**5.98**	**5.90**	**5.85**	**5.78**	**5.75**	**5.70**	**5.67**	**5.65**
8	5.32	4.46	4.07	3.84	3.69	3.58	3.50	3.44	3.39	3.34	3.31	3.28	3.23	3.20	3.15	3.12	3.08	3.05	3.03	3.00	2.98	2.96	2.94	2.93
	11.26	**8.65**	**7.59**	**7.01**	**6.63**	**6.37**	**6.19**	**6.03**	**5.91**	**5.82**	**5.74**	**5.67**	**5.56**	**5.48**	**5.36**	**5.28**	**5.20**	**5.11**	**5.06**	**5.00**	**4.96**	**4.91**	**4.88**	**4.86**
9	5.12	4.26	3.86	3.63	3.48	3.37	3.29	3.23	3.18	3.13	3.10	3.07	3.02	2.98	2.93	2.90	2.86	2.82	2.80	2.77	2.76	2.73	2.72	2.71
	10.56	**8.02**	**6.99**	**6.42**	**6.06**	**5.80**	**5.62**	**5.47**	**5.35**	**5.26**	**5.18**	**5.11**	**5.00**	**4.92**	**4.80**	**4.73**	**4.64**	**4.56**	**4.51**	**4.45**	**4.41**	**4.36**	**4.33**	**4.31**
10	4.96	4.10	3.71	3.48	3.33	3.22	3.14	3.07	3.02	2.97	2.94	2.91	2.86	2.82	2.77	2.74	2.70	2.67	2.64	2.61	2.59	2.56	2.55	2.54
	10.04	**7.56**	**6.55**	**5.99**	**5.64**	**5.39**	**5.21**	**5.06**	**4.95**	**4.85**	**4.78**	**4.71**	**4.60**	**4.52**	**4.41**	**4.33**	**4.25**	**4.17**	**4.12**	**4.05**	**4.01**	**3.96**	**3.93**	**3.91**

Reprinted by permission from Statistical Methods, Seventh edition by George W. Snedecor and William G. Cochran © 1980 by Iowa State University Press, 2121 South State Avenue, Ames, Iowa, 50010.

APPENDIX D.5 (cont.)   CRITICAL VALUES OF F AT THE .05 (LIGHTFACE TYPE) AND .01 (BOLDFACE TYPE) SIGNIFICANCE LEVELS.

df	1	2	3	4	5	6	7	8	9	10	11	12	14	16	20	24	30	40	50	75	100	200	500	∞
11	4.84	3.98	3.59	3.36	3.20	3.09	3.01	2.95	2.90	2.86	2.82	2.79	2.74	2.70	2.65	2.61	2.57	2.53	2.50	2.47	2.45	2.42	2.41	2.40
	9.65	**7.20**	**6.22**	**5.67**	**5.32**	**5.07**	**4.88**	**4.74**	**4.63**	**4.54**	**4.46**	**4.40**	**4.29**	**4.21**	**4.10**	**4.02**	**3.94**	**3.86**	**3.80**	**3.74**	**3.70**	**3.66**	**3.62**	**3.60**
12	4.75	3.88	3.49	3.26	3.11	3.00	2.92	2.85	2.80	2.76	2.72	2.69	2.64	2.60	2.54	2.50	2.46	2.42	2.40	2.36	2.35	2.32	2.31	2.30
	9.33	**6.93**	**5.95**	**5.41**	**5.06**	**4.82**	**4.65**	**4.50**	**4.39**	**4.30**	**4.22**	**4.16**	**4.05**	**3.98**	**3.86**	**3.78**	**3.70**	**3.61**	**3.56**	**3.49**	**3.46**	**3.41**	**3.38**	**3.36**
13	4.67	3.80	3.41	3.18	3.02	2.92	2.84	2.77	2.72	2.67	2.63	2.60	2.55	2.51	2.46	2.42	2.38	2.34	2.32	2.28	2.26	2.24	2.22	2.21
	9.07	**6.70**	**5.74**	**5.20**	**4.86**	**4.62**	**4.44**	**4.30**	**4.19**	**4.10**	**4.02**	**3.96**	**3.85**	**3.78**	**3.67**	**3.59**	**3.51**	**3.42**	**3.37**	**3.30**	**3.27**	**3.21**	**3.18**	**3.16**
14	4.60	3.74	3.34	3.11	2.96	2.85	2.77	2.70	2.65	2.60	2.56	2.53	2.48	2.44	2.39	2.35	2.31	2.27	2.24	2.21	2.19	2.16	2.14	2.13
	8.86	**6.51**	**5.56**	**5.03**	**4.69**	**4.46**	**4.28**	**4.14**	**4.03**	**3.94**	**3.86**	**3.80**	**3.70**	**3.62**	**3.51**	**3.43**	**3.34**	**3.26**	**3.21**	**3.14**	**3.11**	**3.06**	**3.02**	**3.00**
15	4.54	3.68	3.29	3.06	2.90	2.79	2.70	2.64	2.59	2.55	2.51	2.48	2.43	2.39	2.33	2.29	2.25	2.21	2.18	2.15	2.12	2.10	2.08	2.07
	8.68	**6.36**	**5.42**	**4.89**	**4.56**	**4.32**	**4.14**	**4.00**	**3.89**	**3.80**	**3.73**	**3.67**	**3.56**	**3.48**	**3.36**	**3.29**	**3.20**	**3.12**	**3.07**	**3.00**	**2.97**	**2.92**	**2.89**	**2.87**
16	4.49	3.63	3.24	3.01	2.85	2.74	2.66	2.59	2.54	2.49	2.45	2.42	2.37	2.33	2.28	2.24	2.20	2.16	2.13	2.09	2.07	2.04	2.02	2.01
	8.53	**6.23**	**5.29**	**4.77**	**4.44**	**4.20**	**4.03**	**3.89**	**3.78**	**3.69**	**3.61**	**3.55**	**3.45**	**3.37**	**3.25**	**3.18**	**3.10**	**3.01**	**2.96**	**2.89**	**2.86**	**2.80**	**2.77**	**2.75**
17	4.45	3.59	3.20	2.96	2.81	2.70	2.62	2.55	2.50	2.45	2.41	2.38	2.33	2.29	2.23	2.19	2.15	2.11	2.08	2.04	2.02	1.99	1.97	1.96
	8.40	**6.11**	**5.18**	**4.67**	**4.34**	**4.10**	**3.93**	**3.79**	**3.68**	**3.59**	**3.52**	**3.45**	**3.35**	**3.27**	**3.16**	**3.08**	**3.00**	**2.92**	**2.86**	**2.79**	**2.76**	**2.70**	**2.67**	**2.65**
18	4.41	3.55	3.16	2.93	2.77	2.66	2.58	2.51	2.46	2.41	2.37	2.34	2.29	2.25	2.19	2.15	2.11	2.07	2.04	2.00	1.98	1.95	1.93	1.92
	8.28	**6.01**	**5.09**	**4.58**	**4.25**	**4.01**	**3.85**	**3.71**	**3.60**	**3.51**	**3.44**	**3.37**	**3.27**	**3.19**	**3.07**	**3.00**	**2.91**	**2.83**	**2.78**	**2.71**	**2.68**	**2.62**	**2.59**	**2.57**
19	4.38	3.52	3.13	2.90	2.74	2.63	2.55	2.48	2.43	2.38	2.34	2.31	2.26	2.21	2.15	2.11	2.07	2.02	2.00	1.96	1.94	1.91	1.90	1.88
	8.18	**5.93**	**5.01**	**4.50**	**4.17**	**3.94**	**3.77**	**3.63**	**3.52**	**3.43**	**3.36**	**3.30**	**3.19**	**3.12**	**3.00**	**2.92**	**2.84**	**2.76**	**2.70**	**2.63**	**2.60**	**2.54**	**2.51**	**2.49**
20	4.35	3.49	3.10	2.87	2.71	2.60	2.52	2.45	2.40	2.35	2.31	2.28	2.23	2.18	2.12	2.08	2.04	1.99	1.96	1.92	1.90	1.87	1.85	1.84
	8.10	**5.85**	**4.94**	**4.43**	**4.10**	**3.87**	**3.71**	**3.56**	**3.45**	**3.37**	**3.30**	**3.23**	**3.13**	**3.05**	**2.94**	**2.86**	**2.77**	**2.69**	**2.63**	**2.56**	**2.53**	**2.47**	**2.44**	**2.42**
21	4.32	3.47	3.07	2.84	2.68	2.57	2.49	2.42	2.37	2.32	2.28	2.25	2.20	2.15	2.09	2.05	2.00	1.96	1.93	1.89	1.87	1.84	1.82	1.81
	8.02	**5.78**	**4.87**	**4.37**	**4.04**	**3.81**	**3.65**	**3.51**	**3.40**	**3.31**	**3.24**	**3.17**	**3.07**	**2.99**	**2.88**	**2.80**	**2.72**	**2.63**	**2.58**	**2.51**	**2.47**	**2.42**	**2.38**	**2.36**

APPENDIX D.5 (cont.) CRITICAL VALUES OF F AT THE .05 (LIGHTFACE TYPE) AND .01 (BOLDFACE TYPE) SIGNIFICANCE LEVELS.

df	1	2	3	4	5	6	7	8	9	10	11	12	14	16	20	24	30	40	50	75	100	200	500	∞
22	4.30	3.44	3.05	2.82	2.66	2.55	2.47	2.40	2.35	2.30	2.26	2.23	2.18	2.13	2.07	2.03	1.98	1.93	1.91	1.87	1.84	1.81	1.80	1.78
	7.94	**5.72**	**4.82**	**4.31**	**3.99**	**3.76**	**3.59**	**3.45**	**3.35**	**3.26**	**3.18**	**3.12**	**3.02**	**2.94**	**2.83**	**2.75**	**2.67**	**2.58**	**2.53**	**2.46**	**2.42**	**2.37**	**2.33**	**2.31**
23	4.28	3.42	3.03	2.80	2.64	2.53	2.45	2.38	2.32	2.28	2.24	2.20	2.14	2.10	2.04	2.00	1.96	1.91	1.88	1.84	1.82	1.79	1.77	1.76
	7.88	**5.66**	**4.76**	**4.26**	**3.94**	**3.71**	**3.54**	**3.41**	**3.30**	**3.21**	**3.14**	**3.07**	**2.97**	**2.89**	**2.78**	**2.70**	**2.62**	**2.53**	**2.48**	**2.41**	**2.37**	**2.32**	**2.28**	**2.26**
24	4.26	3.40	3.01	2.78	2.62	2.51	2.43	2.36	2.30	2.26	2.22	2.18	2.13	2.09	2.02	1.98	1.94	1.89	1.86	1.82	1.80	1.76	1.74	1.73
	7.82	**5.61**	**4.72**	**4.22**	**3.90**	**3.67**	**3.50**	**3.36**	**3.25**	**3.17**	**3.09**	**3.03**	**2.93**	**2.85**	**2.74**	**2.66**	**2.58**	**2.49**	**2.44**	**2.36**	**2.33**	**2.27**	**2.23**	**2.21**
25	4.24	3.38	2.99	2.76	2.60	2.49	2.41	2.34	2.28	2.24	2.20	2.16	2.11	2.06	2.00	1.96	1.92	1.87	1.84	1.80	1.77	1.74	1.72	1.71
	7.77	**5.57**	**4.68**	**4.18**	**3.86**	**3.63**	**3.46**	**3.32**	**3.21**	**3.13**	**3.05**	**2.99**	**2.89**	**2.81**	**2.70**	**2.62**	**2.54**	**2.45**	**2.40**	**2.32**	**2.29**	**2.23**	**2.19**	**2.17**
26	4.22	3.37	2.98	2.74	2.59	2.47	2.39	2.32	2.27	2.22	2.18	2.15	2.10	2.05	1.99	1.95	1.90	1.85	1.82	1.78	1.76	1.72	1.70	1.69
	7.72	**5.53**	**4.64**	**4.14**	**3.82**	**3.59**	**3.42**	**3.29**	**3.17**	**3.09**	**3.02**	**2.96**	**2.86**	**2.77**	**2.66**	**2.58**	**2.50**	**2.41**	**2.36**	**2.28**	**2.25**	**2.19**	**2.15**	**2.13**
27	4.21	3.35	2.96	2.73	2.57	2.46	2.37	2.30	2.25	2.20	2.16	2.13	2.08	2.03	1.97	1.93	1.88	1.84	1.80	1.76	1.74	1.71	1.68	1.67
	7.68	**5.49**	**4.60**	**4.11**	**3.79**	**3.56**	**3.39**	**3.26**	**3.14**	**3.06**	**2.98**	**2.93**	**2.83**	**2.74**	**2.63**	**2.55**	**2.47**	**2.38**	**2.33**	**2.25**	**2.21**	**2.16**	**2.12**	**2.10**
28	4.20	3.34	2.95	2.71	2.56	2.44	2.36	2.29	2.24	2.19	2.15	2.12	2.06	2.02	1.96	1.91	1.87	1.81	1.78	1.75	1.72	1.69	1.67	1.65
	7.64	**5.45**	**4.57**	**4.07**	**3.76**	**3.53**	**3.36**	**3.23**	**3.11**	**3.03**	**2.95**	**2.90**	**2.80**	**2.71**	**2.60**	**2.52**	**2.44**	**2.35**	**2.30**	**2.22**	**2.18**	**2.13**	**2.09**	**2.06**
29	4.18	3.33	2.93	2.70	2.54	2.43	2.35	2.28	2.22	2.18	2.14	2.10	2.05	2.00	1.94	1.90	1.85	1.80	1.77	1.73	1.71	1.68	1.65	1.64
	7.60	**5.42**	**4.54**	**4.04**	**3.73**	**3.50**	**3.33**	**3.20**	**3.08**	**3.00**	**2.92**	**2.87**	**2.77**	**2.68**	**2.57**	**2.49**	**2.41**	**2.32**	**2.27**	**2.19**	**2.15**	**2.10**	**2.06**	**2.03**
30	4.17	3.32	2.92	2.69	2.53	2.42	2.34	2.27	2.21	2.16	2.12	2.09	2.04	1.99	1.93	1.89	1.84	1.79	1.76	1.72	1.69	1.66	1.64	1.62
	7.56	**5.39**	**4.51**	**4.02**	**3.70**	**3.47**	**3.30**	**3.17**	**3.06**	**2.98**	**2.90**	**2.84**	**2.74**	**2.66**	**2.55**	**2.47**	**2.38**	**2.29**	**2.24**	**2.16**	**2.13**	**2.07**	**2.03**	**2.01**
32	4.15	3.30	2.90	2.67	2.51	2.40	2.32	2.25	2.19	2.14	2.10	2.07	2.02	1.97	1.91	1.86	1.82	1.76	1.74	1.69	1.67	1.64	1.61	1.59
	7.50	**5.34**	**4.46**	**3.97**	**3.66**	**3.42**	**3.25**	**3.12**	**3.01**	**2.94**	**2.86**	**2.80**	**2.70**	**2.62**	**2.51**	**2.42**	**2.34**	**2.25**	**2.20**	**2.12**	**2.08**	**2.02**	**1.98**	**1.96**
34	4.13	3.28	2.88	2.65	2.49	2.38	2.30	2.23	2.17	2.12	2.08	2.05	2.00	1.95	1.89	1.84	1.80	1.74	1.71	1.67	1.64	1.61	1.59	1.57
	7.44	**5.29**	**4.42**	**3.93**	**3.61**	**3.38**	**3.21**	**3.08**	**2.97**	**2.89**	**2.82**	**2.76**	**2.66**	**2.58**	**2.47**	**2.38**	**2.30**	**2.21**	**2.15**	**2.08**	**2.04**	**1.98**	**1.94**	**1.91**

APPENDIX D.5 (cont.)　CRITICAL VALUES OF F AT THE .05 (LIGHTFACE TYPE) AND .01 (BOLDFACE TYPE) SIGNIFICANCE LEVELS.

df	1	2	3	4	5	6	7	8	9	10	11	12	14	16	20	24	30	40	50	75	100	200	500	∞
36	4.11	3.26	2.86	2.63	2.48	2.36	2.28	2.21	2.15	2.10	2.06	2.03	1.98	1.93	1.87	1.82	1.78	1.72	1.69	1.65	1.62	1.59	1.56	1.55
	7.39	**5.25**	**4.38**	**3.89**	**3.58**	**3.35**	**3.18**	**3.04**	**2.94**	**2.86**	**2.78**	**2.72**	**2.62**	**2.54**	**2.43**	**2.35**	**2.26**	**2.17**	**2.12**	**2.04**	**2.00**	**1.94**	**1.90**	**1.87**
38	4.10	3.25	2.85	2.62	2.46	2.35	2.26	2.19	2.14	2.09	2.05	2.02	1.96	1.92	1.85	1.80	1.76	1.71	1.67	1.63	1.60	1.57	1.54	1.53
	7.35	**5.21**	**4.34**	**3.86**	**3.54**	**3.32**	**3.15**	**3.02**	**2.91**	**2.82**	**2.75**	**2.69**	**2.59**	**2.51**	**2.40**	**2.32**	**2.22**	**2.14**	**2.08**	**2.00**	**1.97**	**1.90**	**1.86**	**1.84**
40	4.08	3.23	2.84	2.61	2.45	2.34	2.25	2.18	2.12	2.07	2.04	2.00	1.95	1.90	1.84	1.79	1.74	1.69	1.66	1.61	1.59	1.55	1.53	1.51
	7.31	**5.18**	**4.31**	**3.83**	**3.51**	**3.29**	**3.12**	**2.99**	**2.88**	**2.80**	**2.73**	**2.66**	**2.56**	**2.49**	**2.37**	**2.29**	**2.20**	**2.11**	**2.05**	**1.97**	**1.94**	**1.88**	**1.84**	**1.81**
42	4.07	3.22	2.83	2.59	2.44	2.32	2.24	2.17	2.11	2.06	2.02	1.99	1.94	1.89	1.82	1.78	1.73	1.68	1.64	1.60	1.57	1.54	1.51	1.49
	7.27	**5.15**	**4.29**	**3.80**	**3.49**	**3.26**	**3.10**	**2.96**	**2.86**	**2.77**	**2.70**	**2.64**	**2.54**	**2.46**	**2.35**	**2.26**	**2.17**	**2.08**	**2.02**	**1.94**	**1.91**	**1.85**	**1.80**	**1.78**
44	4.06	3.21	2.82	2.58	2.43	2.31	2.23	2.16	2.10	2.05	2.01	1.98	1.92	1.88	1.81	1.76	1.72	1.66	1.63	1.58	1.56	1.52	1.50	1.48
	7.24	**5.12**	**4.26**	**3.78**	**3.46**	**3.24**	**3.07**	**2.94**	**2.84**	**2.75**	**2.68**	**2.62**	**2.52**	**2.44**	**2.32**	**2.24**	**2.15**	**2.06**	**2.00**	**1.92**	**1.88**	**1.82**	**1.78**	**1.75**
46	4.05	3.20	2.81	2.57	2.42	2.30	2.22	2.14	2.09	2.04	2.00	1.97	1.91	1.87	1.80	1.75	1.71	1.65	1.62	1.57	1.54	1.51	1.48	1.46
	7.21	**5.10**	**4.24**	**3.76**	**3.44**	**3.22**	**3.05**	**2.92**	**2.82**	**2.73**	**2.66**	**2.60**	**2.50**	**2.42**	**2.30**	**2.22**	**2.13**	**2.04**	**1.98**	**1.90**	**1.86**	**1.80**	**1.76**	**1.72**
48	4.04	3.19	2.80	2.56	2.41	2.30	2.21	2.14	2.08	2.03	1.99	1.96	1.90	1.86	1.79	1.74	1.70	1.64	1.61	1.56	1.53	1.50	1.47	1.45
	7.19	**5.08**	**4.22**	**3.74**	**3.42**	**3.20**	**3.04**	**2.90**	**2.80**	**2.71**	**2.64**	**2.58**	**2.48**	**2.40**	**2.28**	**2.20**	**2.11**	**2.02**	**1.96**	**1.88**	**1.84**	**1.78**	**1.73**	**1.70**
50	4.03	3.18	2.79	2.56	2.40	2.29	2.20	2.13	2.07	2.02	1.98	1.95	1.90	1.85	1.78	1.74	1.69	1.63	1.60	1.55	1.52	1.48	1.46	1.44
	7.17	**5.06**	**4.20**	**3.72**	**3.41**	**3.18**	**3.02**	**2.88**	**2.78**	**2.70**	**2.62**	**2.56**	**2.46**	**2.39**	**2.26**	**2.18**	**2.10**	**2.00**	**1.94**	**1.86**	**1.82**	**1.76**	**1.71**	**1.68**
55	4.02	3.17	2.78	2.54	2.38	2.27	2.18	2.11	2.05	2.00	1.97	1.93	1.88	1.83	1.76	1.72	1.67	1.61	1.58	1.52	1.50	1.46	1.43	1.41
	7.12	**5.01**	**4.16**	**3.68**	**3.37**	**3.15**	**2.98**	**2.85**	**2.75**	**2.66**	**2.59**	**2.53**	**2.43**	**2.35**	**2.23**	**2.15**	**2.06**	**1.96**	**1.90**	**1.82**	**1.78**	**1.71**	**1.66**	**1.64**
60	4.00	3.15	2.76	2.52	2.37	2.25	2.17	2.10	2.04	1.99	1.95	1.92	1.86	1.81	1.75	1.70	1.65	1.59	1.56	1.50	1.48	1.44	1.41	1.39
	7.08	**4.98**	**4.13**	**3.65**	**3.34**	**3.12**	**2.95**	**2.82**	**2.72**	**2.63**	**2.56**	**2.50**	**2.40**	**2.32**	**2.20**	**2.12**	**2.03**	**1.93**	**1.87**	**1.79**	**1.74**	**1.68**	**1.63**	**1.60**
65	3.99	3.14	2.75	2.51	2.36	2.24	2.15	2.08	2.02	1.98	1.94	1.90	1.85	1.80	1.73	1.68	1.63	1.57	1.54	1.49	1.46	1.42	1.39	1.37
	7.04	**4.95**	**4.10**	**3.62**	**3.31**	**3.09**	**2.93**	**2.79**	**2.70**	**2.61**	**2.54**	**2.47**	**2.37**	**2.30**	**2.18**	**2.09**	**2.00**	**1.90**	**1.84**	**1.76**	**1.71**	**1.64**	**1.60**	**1.56**

APPENDIX D.5 (cont.)   CRITICAL VALUES OF F AT THE .05 (LIGHTFACE TYPE) AND .01 (BOLDFACE TYPE) SIGNIFICANCE LEVELS

df	1	2	3	4	5	6	7	8	9	10	11	12	14	16	20	24	30	40	50	75	100	200	500	∞
70	3.98	3.13	2.74	2.50	2.35	2.23	2.14	2.07	2.01	1.97	1.93	1.89	1.84	1.79	1.72	1.67	1.62	1.56	1.53	1.47	1.45	1.40	1.37	1.35
	7.01	**4.92**	**4.08**	**3.60**	**3.29**	**3.07**	**2.91**	**2.77**	**2.67**	**2.59**	**2.51**	**2.45**	**2.35**	**2.28**	**2.15**	**2.07**	**1.98**	**1.88**	**1.82**	**1.74**	**1.69**	**1.62**	**1.56**	**1.53**
80	3.96	3.11	2.72	2.48	2.33	2.21	2.12	2.05	1.99	1.95	1.91	1.88	1.82	1.77	1.70	1.65	1.60	1.54	1.51	1.45	1.42	1.38	1.35	1.32
	6.96	**4.88**	**4.04**	**3.56**	**3.25**	**3.04**	**2.87**	**2.74**	**2.64**	**2.55**	**2.48**	**2.41**	**2.32**	**2.24**	**2.11**	**2.03**	**1.94**	**1.84**	**1.78**	**1.70**	**1.65**	**1.57**	**1.52**	**1.49**
100	3.94	3.09	2.70	2.46	2.30	2.19	2.10	2.03	1.97	1.92	1.88	1.85	1.79	1.75	1.68	1.63	1.57	1.51	1.48	1.42	1.39	1.34	1.30	1.28
	6.90	**4.82**	**3.98**	**3.51**	**3.20**	**2.99**	**2.82**	**2.69**	**2.59**	**2.51**	**2.43**	**2.36**	**2.26**	**2.19**	**2.06**	**1.98**	**1.89**	**1.79**	**1.73**	**1.64**	**1.59**	**1.51**	**1.46**	**1.43**
125	3.92	3.07	2.68	2.44	2.29	2.17	2.08	2.01	1.95	1.90	1.86	1.83	1.77	1.72	1.65	1.60	1.55	1.49	1.45	1.39	1.36	1.31	1.27	1.25
	6.84	**4.78**	**3.94**	**3.47**	**3.17**	**2.95**	**2.79**	**2.65**	**2.56**	**2.47**	**2.40**	**2.33**	**2.23**	**2.15**	**2.03**	**1.94**	**1.85**	**1.75**	**1.68**	**1.59**	**1.54**	**1.46**	**1.40**	**1.37**
150	3.91	3.06	2.67	2.43	2.27	2.16	2.07	2.00	1.94	1.89	1.85	1.82	1.76	1.71	1.64	1.59	1.54	1.47	1.44	1.37	1.34	1.29	1.25	1.22
	6.81	**4.75**	**3.91**	**3.44**	**3.14**	**2.92**	**2.76**	**2.62**	**2.53**	**2.44**	**2.37**	**2.30**	**2.20**	**2.12**	**2.00**	**1.91**	**1.83**	**1.72**	**1.66**	**1.56**	**1.51**	**1.43**	**1.37**	**1.33**
200	3.89	3.04	2.65	2.41	2.26	2.14	2.05	1.98	1.92	1.87	1.83	1.80	1.74	1.69	1.62	1.57	1.52	1.45	1.42	1.35	1.32	1.26	1.22	1.19
	6.76	**4.71**	**3.88**	**3.41**	**3.11**	**2.90**	**2.73**	**2.60**	**2.50**	**2.41**	**2.34**	**2.28**	**2.17**	**2.09**	**1.97**	**1.88**	**1.79**	**1.69**	**1.62**	**1.53**	**1.48**	**1.39**	**1.33**	**1.28**
400	3.86	3.02	2.62	2.39	2.23	2.12	2.03	1.96	1.90	1.85	1.81	1.78	1.72	1.67	1.60	1.54	1.49	1.42	1.38	1.32	1.28	1.22	1.16	1.13
	6.70	**4.66**	**3.83**	**3.36**	**3.06**	**2.85**	**2.69**	**2.55**	**2.46**	**2.37**	**2.29**	**2.23**	**2.12**	**2.04**	**1.92**	**1.84**	**1.74**	**1.64**	**1.57**	**1.47**	**1.42**	**1.32**	**1.24**	**1.19**
1000	3.85	3.00	2.61	2.38	2.22	2.10	2.02	1.95	1.89	1.84	1.80	1.76	1.70	1.65	1.58	1.53	1.47	1.41	1.36	1.30	1.26	1.19	1.13	1.08
	6.66	**4.62**	**3.80**	**3.34**	**3.04**	**2.82**	**2.66**	**2.53**	**2.43**	**2.34**	**2.26**	**2.20**	**2.09**	**2.01**	**1.89**	**1.81**	**1.71**	**1.61**	**1.54**	**1.44**	**1.38**	**1.28**	**1.19**	**1.11**
∞	3.84	2.99	2.60	2.37	2.21	2.09	2.01	1.94	1.88	1.83	1.79	1.75	1.69	1.64	1.57	1.52	1.46	1.40	1.35	1.28	1.24	1.17	1.11	1.00
	6.63	**4.60**	**3.78**	**3.32**	**3.02**	**2.80**	**2.64**	**2.51**	**2.41**	**2.32**	**2.24**	**2.18**	**2.07**	**1.99**	**1.87**	**1.79**	**1.69**	**1.59**	**1.52**	**1.41**	**1.36**	**1.25**	**1.15**	**1.00**

APPENDIX D.6

CRITICAL VALUES OF THE CORRELATION COEFFICIENT, r, FOR DIFFERENT LEVELS OF SIGNIFICANCE (TWO-TAILED TEST)

df	.10	.05	.02	.01.
1	.98769	.996917	.9995066	.9998766
2	.90000	.95000	.98000	.990000
3	.8054	.8783	.93433	.95873
4	.7293	.8114	.8822	.91720
5	.6694	.7545	.8329	.8745
6	.6215	.7067	.7887	.8343
7	.5822	.6664	.7498	.7977
8	.5494	.6319	.7155	.7646
9	.5214	.6021	.6851	.7348
10	.4973	.5760	.6581	.7079
11	.4762	.5529	.6339	.6835
12	.4575	.5324	.6120	.6614
13	.4409	.5139	.5923	.6411
14	.4259	.4973	.5742	.6226
15	.4124	.4821	.5577	.6055
16	.4000	.4683	.5425	.5897
17	.3887	.4555	.5285	.5751
18	.3783	.4438	.5155	.5614
19	.3687	.4329	.5034	.5487
20	.3598	.4227	.4921	.5368
25	.3233	.3809	.4451	.4869
30	.2960	.3494	.4093	.4487
35	.2746	.3246	.3810	.4182
40	.2573	.3044	.3578	.3932
45	.2428	.2875	.3384	.3721
50	.2306	.2732	.3218	.3541
60	.2108	.2500	.2948	.3248
70	.1954	.2319	.2737	.3017
80	.1829	.2172	.2565	.2830
90	.1726	.2050	.2422	.2673
100	.1638	.1946	.2301	.2540

For a total correlation, n is 2 less than the number of pairs in the sample; for a partial correlation, the number of eliminated variates also should be subtracted.

Reprinted with permission of Macmillan Publishing Company from *Statistical Methods for Research Workers*, 14th ed., p. 211, by Sir Ronald A. Fisher. Copyright © 1970 by University of Adelaide.

REFERENCES: INDEX OF RECOMMENDED AND CITED SOURCES

		Recommended on pages	Cited in this book on pages
1.	American Psychological Association. *Publication Manual* (3rd ed.). Washington, D.C.: American Psychological Association, 1983.		339
2.	American Psychological Association. *Ethical Principles in the Conduct of Research with Human Participants.* Washington, D.C.: American Psychological Association, 1973.	10	10
3.	American Psychological Association, American Educational Research Association & National Council on Measurement in Education, Joint Committee.* *Standards for Educational and Psychological Tests* (Rev. ed.). Washington, D.C.: American Psychological Association, 1974.	76	75
4.	Anastasi, A. *Psychological Testing* (4th ed.). New York: Macmillan, 1976.		183, 183
5.	Baker, R.L., & Schutz, R.E. (eds.). *Instructional Product Research.* New York: Van Nostrand, 1972.		8
6.	Bales, R. *Interaction Process Analysis.* Cambridge, Mass.: Addison-Wesley, 1951.		245
7.	Berelson, B. *Content Analysis in Communication Research.* New York: The Free Press of Glencoe, 1952.	245	
8.	Blalock, H.M. "Theory Building and Causal Inferences." In Blalock, H.M. & Blalock, A.B. (eds.), *Methodology in Social Research.* New York: McGraw-Hill, 1968.	142	

		Recom- mended on pages	Cited in this book on pages
9.	Budd, R.W., Thorp, R.K. & Donohew, L. *Content Analysis of Communications.* New York: Macmillan, 1967.	245	
10.	Buros, O.K. (ed.).* *Eighth Mental Measurements Yearbook.* Highland Park, N.J.: Gryphon Press, 1978.	179	183
11.	Buros, O.K. (ed.).* *Tests In Print II.* Highland Park, N.J.: Gryphon Press, 1974.	179	
12.	Campbell, D.T. & Stanley, J.C. *Experimental and Quasi-Experimental Designs for Research.* Chicago: Rand McNally, 1963.	142, 149	135, 136, 138, 139, 142, 146, 148, 152
13.	Chein, I. "An Introduction to Sampling." In Selltiz, C., Jahoda, M., Deutsch, M. & Cook, S.W. (eds.). *Research Methods in Social Relations* (Rev. ed.). New York: Holt, Rinehart & Winston, 1959.	116, 126	
14.	Churchman, C.W. *Theory of Experimental Inference.* New York: Macmillan, 1948.	142	
15.	Cochran, W.G. "Some Methods for Strengthening the Common X^2 Tests." *Biometrics*, 1954, 10, 417-451.	273	
16.	Cochran, W.G. *Sampling Techniques* (2nd ed.). New York: Wiley, 1963.	116, 126	
17.	Cook, T.D. & Campbell, D.T. *Quasi-Experimentation: Design and Analysis Issues for Field Settings.* Boston: Houghton Mifflin, 1979.	149	
18.	Cook, T.D. & Campbell, D.T. "Four Kinds of Validity." In Monday, R.T. & Steers, R.M. (eds.). *Research in Organizations: Issues and Controversies.* Santa Monica, Ca.: Goodyear, 1979.	76	
19.	Coombs, C.H. "Theory and Methods of Social Measurement." In Festinger, L. & Katz, D. (eds.). *Research Methods in the Behavioral Sciences.* New York: Holt, Rinehart & Winston, 1966.	73	

	Recommended on pages	Cited in this book on pages
20. Cronbach, L.J. "Coefficient Alpha and the Internal Structure of Tests." *Psychometrika*, 1951, 16, 297-334.		86
21. Cronbach, L.J. *Essentials of Psychological Testing* (3rd ed.). New York: Harper & Row, 1970.	76	75
22. Davis, D. & Cosenza, R.M. *Business Research for Decision Making*. Boston: Kent, 1985.	25	25, 255
23. Dialog Information Services, Inc. *Dialog Data Base Catalog*. Palo Alto, Ca.: Dialog Information Services, Inc., 1985.		96, 98
24. Dyer, J.R. *Understanding and Evaluating Educational Research*. Reading, Mass.: Addison-Wesley, 1979.		102, 119
25. Edwards, A.L. *Experimental Design in Psychological Research* (4th ed.). New York: Holt, Rinehart & Winston, 1972.	289	
26. Edwards, A.L. *Techniques of Attitude Scale Construction*. New York: Appleton-Century-Crofts, 1957.	227, 233, 239	
27. Emory, C.W. *Business Research Methods* (Rev. ed.). Homewood, Il.: Irwin, 1980.		8
28. Festinger, L. "Laboratory Experiments." In Festinger, L. & Katz, D. (eds.). *Research Methods in the Behavioral Sciences*. New York: Holt, Rinehart & Winston, 1966.	142	
29. Fisher, R. *The Design of Experiments* (6th ed.). New York: Hafner, 1951.		135
30. Green, P.E. & Carmone, F.J. *Multidimensional Scaling*. Boston: Allyn & Bacon, 1970.	233	
31. Greene, P.E. & Tull, D.S. *Research for Marketing Decisions* (3rd ed.). Englewood Cliffs, N.J.: Prentice-Hall, 1975.		8

		Recommended on pages	Cited in this book on pages
32.	Guilford, J.P. *Psychometric Methods.* New York: McGraw-Hill, 1954.	225, 235	
33.	Harshbarger, T.R. *Introductory Statistics: A Decision Map* (2nd ed.). New York: Macmillan, 1977.	257	254, 256, 312
34.	Hays, W.L. *Statistics for the Social Sciences* (2nd ed.). New York: Holt, Rinehart & Winston, 1973.	257	
35.	Kelly, F.J., Beggs, D.L., McNeil, K.A., Eichelberger, T. & Lyon, J. *Research Design in the Behavioral Sciences: Multiple Regression Approach.* Carbondale, Il.: Southern Illinois University Press, 1969.	257	
36.	Kerlinger, F.N. *Foundations of Behavioral Research* (2nd ed.). New York: Holt, Rinehart & Winston, 1973.	238, 289	167, 215, 222, 255
37.	Kerlinger, F.N. *Behavioral Research: A Conceptual Approach.* New York: Holt, Rinehart & Winston, 1979	6, 94	30, 44, 109, 110, 150, 255
38.	Kim, J. & Mueller, C.W. *Introduction to Factor Analysis: What It Is and How To Do It.* Beverly Hills, Ca.: Sage, 1978 (a).	151	
39.	Kim, J. & Mueller, C.W. *Factor Analysis: Statistical Methods and Practical Issues.* Beverly Hills, Ca.: Sage, 1978 (b).	151	
40.	Kish, L. *Survey Sampling.* New York: Wiley, 1965.	116, 126	117
41.	Kornhauser, A. & Sheatsley, P.B. "Questionnaire Construction and Interview Procedures." In Selltiz et al. *Research Methods in Social Relations.* New York: Holt, Rinehart & Winston, 1959.	203	

	Recom-mended on pages	Cited in this book on pages
42. Krathwohl, D.R. *How to Prepare a Research Proposal* (2nd ed.). Syracuse: Syracuse University Bookstore, 1976.	16	
43. Kuder, G.F. & Richardson, M.W. "The Theory of Estimation of Test Reliability." *Psychometrika*, 1937, 2, 151-160.		86
44. Leedy, P.D. *Practical Research: Planning and Design*. New York: Macmillan, 1974.		8
45. Lindzey, G. "On the Classification of Projective Techniques." *Psychological Bulletin*. 1959, LVI, 158-168.	243	242
46. Linstone, H.A. & Turoff, M. (eds.). *The Delphi Method: Techniques and Applications*. Reading, Mass.: Addison Wesley, 1975.	241	
47. Marascuilo, L.A. & McSweeney, M. *Nonparametric and Distribution-Free Methods for the Social Sciences*. Monterey, Ca.: Brooks/Cole, 1977.	257	
48. McNemar, Q. *Psychological Statistics* (2nd ed.). New York: Wiley, 1955.	273	254
49. Mosteller, F. & Tukey, J.W. "Data Analysis Including Statistics." In Lindzey, G. & Aronson, E. (eds.). *The Handbook of Social Psychology*. Vol. II. Reading, Mass.: Addison-Wesley, 1968, 80-200.	257	
50. Nie, N.H., Hull, C.H., Jenkins, J.G., Steinbrenner, K. & Bent, D.H. *Statistical Package for the Social Sciences* (2nd ed.). New York: McGraw-Hill, 1975.		315
51. Osgood, C., Suci, G. & Tannenbaum, P. *The Measurement of Meaning*. Urbana: University of Illinois Press, 1957.	230	229

		Recom- mended on pages	Cited in this book on pages
52.	Payne, S.L. *The Art of Asking Questions.* Princeton, N.J.: Princeton University Press, 1951.	203	
53.	Pool, I. de Sola. *Trends in Content Analysis.* Urbana: University of Illinois Press, 1957.	245	
54.	Rosenthal, R. *Experimenter Effects in Behavioral Research.* New York: Appleton-Century-Crofts, 1966.	142	
55	Selltiz, C., Jahoda, M., Deutsch, M. & Cook, S.W. *Research Methods in Social Relations* (Rev. ed.). New York: Holt, Rinehart & Winston, 1959.		8
56.	Selltiz, C., Wrightsman, L.S. & Cook, S.W. *Research Methods in Social Relations* (3rd ed.). New York: Holt, Rinehart & Winston, 1976.	94	
57.	Sharp, V.F. *Statistics for the Social Sciences.* Boston: Little, Brown & Co., 1979.	257	254
58.	Siegel, S. *Nonparametric Statistics for the Behavioral Sciences.* New York: McGraw-Hill, 1956.	59, 273	57, 58, 254, 260
59.	Stephenson, W. *The Study of Behavior.* Chicago: University of Chicago Press, 1953.	238	
60.	Stevens, S.S. "On the Theory of Scales of Measurement." *Science.* 1946, 103, 677-680.	73	67
61.	Stone, E. *Research Methods in Organizational Behavior.* Santa Monica, Ca.: Goodyear, 1978.		8
62.	Stone, P.J., Dunphy, D.C., Smith, M.S. & Olgilvie, D.M. *The General Inquirer: A Computer Approach to Content Analysis.* Cambridge, Mass.: The M.I.T. Press, 1966.		244

		Recom- mended on pages	Cited in this book on pages

63. Tatsuoka, M.M. *Discriminant Analysis.*   151
No. 6 in a series, *Selected Topics in*
Advanced Statistics. Champaign, Il.:
Institute for Personality Ability Testing,
1970.

64. Thorndike, R.L. & Hagen, E.   74, 82
Measurement and Evaluation in
Psychology and Education (3rd ed.).
New York: Wiley, 1969.

65. Thurstone, L.L. *The Measurement of*   228
Values. Chicago: University of Chicago
Press, 1959.

66. Thurstone, L.L. & Chave, E.J. *The*   183
Measurement of Attitude. Chicago:
University of Chicago Press, 1929.

67. Torgenson, W.S. *Theory and Methods*   69
of Scaling. New York: Wiley, 1958.

68. Tull, D.S. & Hawkins, D.I. *Marketing*   25   16, 25,
Research: Meaning, Measurement, and   151, 256
Method. New York: Macmillan, 1976.

69. U.S. Department of Health and Human   10   10
Services. *Code of Federal Regulations.*
Part 46 -- Protection of Human Subjects.
Washington, D.C.: U.S. Government
Printing Office, March 8, 1983.

70. Webb, E.J., Campbell, D.T., Schwartz,   170   170
R.D. & Sechrest, L. *Unobtrusive Measures:*
Nonreactive Research in the Social Sciences.
Chicago: Rand McNally, 1966.

71. Yaremko, R.M., Harari, H., Harrison, R.C.   87, 255,
& Lynn, E. *Reference Handbook of*   256, 260
Research and Statistical Methods in
Psychology. New York: Harper and Row,
1982.

*There are updated editions of the starred references, but the novice researcher will find it useful to examine these particular editions also in order to better understand changes in the field.

INDEX

A

Abbreviations and symbols, glossary of, 373-376
Absolute zero, definition,72
Accidental sampling, definition,117
Alpha
    error, definition, 57
    level, definition, 57
Alternate forms reliability, definition, 83
Alternate hypotheses, 51
Analysis of covariance, definition, 353
Analysis of variance, 277-289
    definition, 277, 353
    F table of values, 383-387
    one-way analysis of variance, 278-283
    Scheffé test, 284-286
    two-way analysis of variance, 287-289
ANOVA, see analysis of variance
Applied research, 7, 8
    definition, 7, 353
Arbitrary zero point, definition,71, 353
Association design, definition, 150
Attitudes, measures of, definition, 182, 353

B

Bar graphs, 341
    example of, 343
Basic research, 7, 8
    definition, 7, 353
Beliefs, measures of, definition, 183, 354
Beta
    error, definition, 57
    level, definition, 57
Bias, definition, 354
Bivariate
    plots, 342, 348, example of, 346
    regression, 289-293
    techniques, definition, 264-354
Blind studies, definition, 354
Blocking, definition, 354

C

Categorical responses, definition, 195, 354

example of, 196
Category rating scale, definition, 222, 354
    example of, 223
Central limit theorem, definition, 354
Central tendency, 306-309
    comparative summary of, 310
    definition, 306, 361
    mean, 306-308
    median, 308
    mode, 309
Checklists, 239-240
Chi-square Test of Independence, 268-273
    computation of, 272
    definition, 268, 354
    formula for, 269
    requirements for use, 269
    table of values, 381
Chunk sampling, definition, 117
Cluster sampling, 118, 119
    definition, 118, 354
Coefficient Alpha, 86-87
    definition, 86, 355
Computer, use for analysis, 314-317
Concurrent validity, 80
    definition, 80, 355
Condition, definition, 134
Confidence
    interval, definition, 120, 355
        for means, computation, 122
    level, definition, 120, 355
        frequently used levels, 120
    limits, definition, 120, 355
Confounding, definition, 355
Constant sum method, 235, 236
Construct validity, 80-82
    definition, 80, 355
Content analysis, 243-245
Content validity, 76-79
    definition, 76, 355
Contingency table, 312-314
    definition, 312, 355
Control group, definition, 134, 355
Control mechanisms, 134, 135
Control variables, 31, 32
    definition, 31, 355
Convenience sampling, 117
    definition, 117, 355

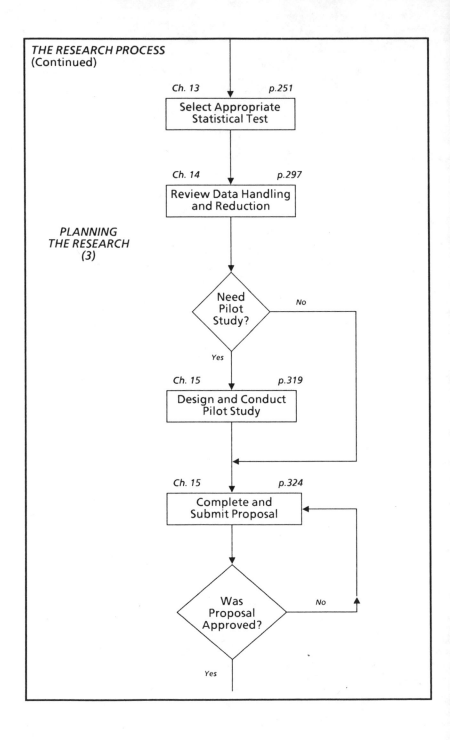

THE RESEARCH PROCESS
(Continued)

Ch. 13   p.251
Select Appropriate
Statistical Test

Ch. 14   p.297
Review Data Handling
and Reduction

PLANNING
THE RESEARCH
(3)

Need
Pilot
Study?   No

Yes

Ch. 15   p.319
Design and Conduct
Pilot Study

Ch. 15   p.324
Complete and
Submit Proposal

Was
Proposal
Approved?   No

Yes

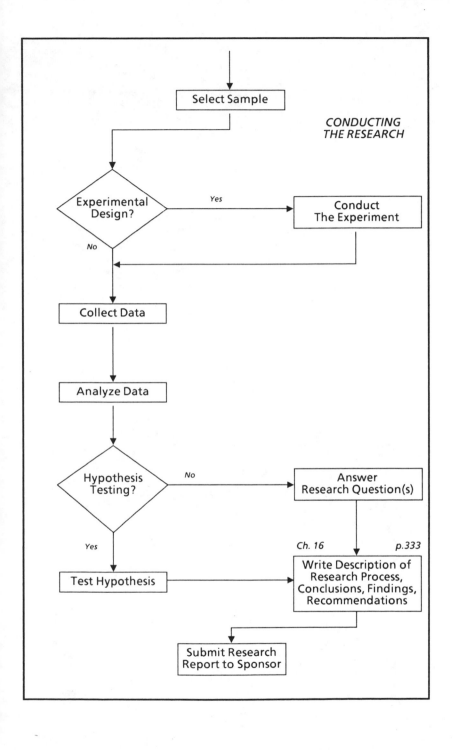